ART and the CREATIVE CONSCIOUSNESS

Graham Collier

*Introduction by René Huyghe
de l'Académie française*

PRENTICE-HALL, INC., ENGLEWOOD CLIFFS, NEW JERSEY

Library of Congress Cataloging in Publication Data

COLLIER, GRAHAM.
    Art and the creative consciousness.

    Includes bibliographical references.
    1. Art — Philosophy.   2. Art — Psychology.
    I. Title.
N70.C597   701'.15   72-5634
ISBN 0-13-046755-3
ISBN 0-13-046706-5(Pbk)

Front cover: Egyptian Figurine (Pre-dynastic). Courtesy of the
              British Museum, London
Back cover: Photograph by Robert Smeltzer

10   9   8   7   6   5   4   3   2   1

PRINTED IN THE UNITED STATES OF AMERICA

Prentice-Hall International, Inc., London
Prentice-Hall of Australia Pty. Ltd., Sydney
Prentice-Hall of Canada, Ltd., Toronto
Prentice-Hall of India Private Limited, New Delhi
Prentice-Hall of Japan, Inc., Tokyo

To Helena

Man can embody truth but he cannot know it. — W. B. Yeats

CONTENTS

v

PREFACE

The difficult thing in writing a preface is not in deciding whom to include in the acknowledgments, but whom to leave out. This becomes a matter of concern, for without the support of the many individuals and institutions who are always so willing to help, it would not be possible to produce a book of this sort. The presence of a credit line beneath an illustration does not reveal the efficiency of a museum's "permissions" department; or, in the case of the private galleries, the willingness to search out and loan rather rare photographs. I am most grateful to those curators whom I visited personally in Europe, and to those with whom I have been in correspondence. And I would like to add a particular note of thanks to Mr. Henry Moore for both his hospitality and the fine photographs he lent to me.

But, nearer home, I must mention some of those who were more directly concerned with the writing itself. Lamar Dodd kept nudging my elbow to keep the work going and saw to it that departmental, professional distractions did not get in the way. Boyd McWhorter put me on to several sources in literature which enabled me to discuss more fully the issue of time in art and life; and Erwin Gerschefski was always happy to be consulted about the accuracy of musical analogies.

In the early stages of writing Yancey Robertson was a constant tower of strength. It was largely his faith in the manuscript that persuaded me to continue, and thus to ultimately discover the "shape" of the book. Over the last three years my colleague Edmund Feldman has pondered many questions for me, and his objectivity has helped me resolve some awkward intellectual and semantic problems. When we come to the chores of typing and re-typing, in order that the author may edit and compose, I have to thank my wife Helena. She has worked hard without complaint, despite lack of recompense. And I must thank Barbara Christenberry, my most efficient and understanding editor.

Finally, I am honored that René Huyghe, the distinguished French scholar, art historian, and man of letters should write an introduction to this work. And I thank Madame France Bernard Boney for undertaking the translation of René Huyghe's introduction.

Athens, Georgia   *Graham Collier*
May 1972

INTRODUCTION

Everything moves quickly in the world today, especially ideas. The study of art has not escaped this process; it has been undergoing transformation for a number of years. Formal university teaching must surely be prepared to keep this in mind more and more. A book such as the one which Graham Collier has just written will contribute powerfully to this evolution, for it presents a complete and global picture of the phenomenon of art.

In the past there was the History of Art and there was Aesthetics, two clearly separate domains between which there was no bridge. On one side the works of art; on the other the search for their raison d'etre. Up to the Renaissance works of art were usually dedicated to God and followed the rules laid down by the Church. It is only with the Renaissance that they ceased to be strictly devotional objects and were appreciated for their own sake. The development of art history at this time began through using anecdotes which recounted the sometimes legendary life of the artist. *Delle Vite de' piu eccelenti pittori, scultori, ed architectori* of good old Giorgio Vasari, himself a painter and architect, was, in the middle of the sixteenth century, the model book of stories circulating in the studios. On the other hand, Aesthetics, making the most of the resurrection of the antique philosophers, particularly Plato, started to debate and dogmatize on the goals which the artist should pursue — to attempt to define the essence of art, namely beauty. By the first half of the fifteenth century Leon Battiste Alberti had established the permanent model for such Treatises.

From then on History and Aesthetics went their own way. History acquired more and more rigorous methods and proceeded to classify works, to date them and to assign them in time and space. In the nineteenth century an increasing effort was made to relate works of art to general history, to the surroundings and events attending their birth. The *Philosophy of Art,* published by Taine in 1882, pushed art and its evolution into the general scheme of determinism ruling the life of societies. Art was no more than a part of general history and subject to the same laws.

ix

Meanwhile, Aesthetics was coming down from the clouds of general theory. The work of art was seen as the product of a specifically human activity whose mode of functioning it should be possible to discover; it should also be possible to discover the laws which this activity obeyed. The Germans, particularly Dessoir and Utitz, were founding the Science of Art, the *Kunstwissenschaft*. The result was principally a study of "styles," characterizing the evolution of form according to centuries and countries; and it was then that the general theories of classicism, the baroque, and mannerism preoccupied intellects eager to discover the alternating rhythms of art.

Thus, on all levels, the "how" of the work of art was becoming more precise; either trying to find it springing from the external pressures of the social context, or to distinguish it in the *Life of Forms,* to use the title of Henri Focillon's great book — forms which evolve rhythmically according to their own laws. All these findings were becoming clearer and more precise, but they did not yet constitute a full explanation.

To grasp the full implications of the problem we had to come to a Psychology of Art. Henceforth, the "why" of the work was to take first place. Founded by Fechner in 1860, the psycho-physiology of the nineteenth century confined itself somewhat shyly to the study of peripheral sensations. But the *gestalt theory* at the beginning of the twentieth century represented a step forward and showed how forms were conceived by the mind — a mind whose capacity to structure an ensemble furnished from random sensations was suddenly revealed and analyzed. Certainly we were penetrating the inner life, but we were still dealing with mental faculties of organized representations of perceptual experience; that is, with the most obvious and intellectual aspects of the mind.

There remained the immense shadow of the psychological depth of man, where obviously the genesis of the work of art was taking place in the ardent forge of the personality. German thought, again, brought a major contribution with *Einfühlung,* which, in touching on sensibility as the source of creation, was inquiring how this aspect of the psyche came into direct communication with nature and universal life through the work of art.

And then, although only a first approach, the claiming and the exploration of the unconscious initiated by Freud in the first years of the twentieth century, was going to allow the further probing of these unknown areas which lie beyond the grasp of rationality — areas where the work of art germinates. By 1929, the Swiss writer Baudouin had published a *Psychoanalysis of Art.*

But, as the Gestalt theory had shown that form cannot be broken down without changing its essential significance, psychology was to realize that the many activities of the psyche cannot be separated without annihilating their essential meaning. The need therefore, for a general psychology of art was deeply felt; one that would restore to the sensations, to the feelings, and to the unconscious depths, their complex unity as manifested in the structure of the image — a unity which makes the human soul indivisible and to always function globally in its living truth. Only then could the "how" and the "why" of the work of art be revealed. Andre

Malraux became the intuitive prophet of this new quest with the three volumes of his *Psychology of Art* which appeared between 1947 and 1950. This same year the Collège de France created the first chair dedicated to the *Psychology of the Plastic Arts,* of which I have the honor to be the first holder.

In a masterly book, *Form, Space, and Vision,* Graham Collier, enriched by the double experience of being both painter and teacher, has already studied the formal elements which, when compositionally organized, constitute the work of art. This time, he proceeds to a progressive and total examination of artistic creation, and in his search he brings together both the nature of art and of man.

We know only two realities: the one around us and the one within us. The first reality is the Universe; the second is the life of the psyche. Communication from the first to the second is effected through the senses in the messages which they register; while communication from the second to the first is made through action — action which enables us to project our forces into the outside world and to observe the consequences. But even if the two realities are thus brought together, there remains an irreducible disparity between them: that which is around us appears to be disposed in space, but that which is within us unfolds and is felt in time. There lies, perhaps, the main mystery of the world: the impossible abyss which separates the two sides — the side where the Self lives, and opposite, the side where the Other extends. Yet man has discovered the means by which the two sides may merge together in a most subtle way, and this is in the work of art: for he projects and inserts into it the very substance of his inner life which thus becomes inscribed in space as both image and object . . . perceptible to others. And although this work of art is made up of materials and dimensions borrowed from the outside world, it reflects images born of sight and memory that show the world transformed.

Thus the work of art, far from being an ornament, a fanciful addition to reality, lies at the heart of the mystery of Being.

In his first great work, as in the first panel of a diptych, Graham Collier examined the elements brought in from the outside world: form and space. In this book, the second panel of the same diptych, he ventures up the steeper slope, that which rises from the depths of the self, always unconscious and thus unknown to one, and, as a stream may fill up with floating substances, so he encounters the fluid and solid zones of sensibility. It is then the job of the intellect to canalize the current, take it in hand and organize its shape as a theme. It is from such an encounter between the internal forces and the body of knowledge provided by the world, that a work of art is born; and thus represents a double and total reality — one which only man knows how to conceive and accomplish as the fulfillment of his capacities.

Having reached this point, the psychology of art rises above the history of art and the geographical and chronological divisions where it is parcelled out and dispersed. As a summit from where the totality of the landscape can be realized — the landscape in which one used to get lost while wandering through twisty paths and detours — the psychology of art pronounces the unity of the artistic phenomenon. Now the continuity of past and present art can be seen, and the difficulties of making connections disappear. Everything is related. There are only the many iridescent facets of a single block for which we have found the center of gravity.

It is thus that Graham Collier, overcoming the dissimilarities and the conflicts which cause so many of our contemporaries to lose their way, can pass objectively from ancient art to modern art, finding the same principles of explanation in each one, and allowing them to fuse into a profound continuity — a continuity which ordinarily escapes attention. And not the least merit of his work is to allow our comprehension of the light of the past and of the masters of other days to benefit from the knowledge gained in today's research.

In passing across the superposed levels of the psyche, as in passing across the apparent contradictions in art history, Graham Collier has been able to find and free the unity of art and the unity of man.

Paris, May 1972

Réne Huyghe
de l'Académie française:

Professeur au Collegè de France:

Vice-Président du Conseil des
Musées de France

I
FIRST, WHY BOTHER?

Public interest in the visual arts has been booming since the end of World War II. This is evidenced by art's high place in contemporary university education, by today's large museum-going crowds, by the omnipresent art book on the coffee table, and the reproduction on the wall. We should examine this cultural prosperity carefully and try to distinguish the real values from the pseudo values. For there are already too many books on art, and there is no point in adding one more to the list unless it can cut through to something integral in the popular experience of art. Hence the rather cynical title to this chapter.

Why all this attention?

In the beginning, art was a kind of magic — a conjuring up of invisible powers and presences. It was a ritual performance and the first artists were often the priests, the shamans, the witch doctors, or other persons initiated into the mysteries. Similarly, the early poets were esteemed as prophets, as men possessing the gift of seeing beyond the immediate present, able to reveal truths that satisfied the spirit and the imagination. Sculpture, painting, and poetry were ways to express certain secrets present in the imagination of man.

Since those first days, both art and poetry have evolved through many stages. At times in their history they have lost touch with the imaginative realities which first inspired them and, instead of revealing special insights about the nature of things, have been content to merely describe things as they seem to be, physically speaking. It was to protest the art of description that William Blake wrote:

> He who does not imagine in stronger and better lineaments,
> and in stronger and better light, than his perishing mortal
> eye can see, does not imagine at all.

As a painter, I have been fortunate in knowing many artists — some great. Most would agree that when we talk about art, we talk about images and imagining.

We do not talk about techniques or style, for these are taken for granted as the means to an end, as aspects of the process unselfconsciously used by the artist. We agree that the roots of art are to be found deep in the soil of the imagination. If and when all is ever known to man, and his rational intellect grasps and controls the vital principles of spirit, matter, and energy, there will be no need of the imagination, no secrets in the irrational subsoil of our consciousness and, therefore, no art. Would it be reasonable to suggest that the reason for the strong position of the visual arts today is that they cater to a deficiency in our life — an imaginative deficiency? Poetry also is in great demand. Talking to the Oxford University Poetry Society, Robert Graves, one of the great poets of our time, said:

> The present remarkable public demand for poetry keeps pace with the growing affluence of life throughout the Western world and the gradual shrinking of the work week. Never before have such efforts been made to satisfy the demand, yet never have there been fewer original poets. "This is a critical, not a poetic age," I am told. "Inspiration is out. Contemporary poems must reflect the prevailing analytic spirit." But I am old-fashioned enough to demand *báraka*, an inspirational gift not yet extinct, which defies critical analysis.[1]

I have quoted this statement of Robert Graves because it underlines my own reasons for writing this book. In art, as in poetry, there are few original artists. Also the public demand for and approbation of art is strong. The professional critic of art has much power and his analysis of an image is often regarded as more important than the image itself. And the word "inspiration" (*báraka*) is very suspect for many a critic, many a teacher, many a historian. But not for many an artist.

Therefore I feel that if a painter is to write a book (and so lay himself open to those who would echo Paul Valéry's remark "Don't talk, painter, paint"), he should attempt to expose some of the things that go on in the imaginative life, insofar as words will serve to discuss them. For I believe that it is a genuine hunger for imaginative experience of a timeless nature, which drives a bored but affluent public to support museums and buy paintings and books. Man has still a need for the magic of art. I believe also that a major justification for the inclusion of introductory art courses in universities is to treat the phenomenon of the human imagination. And I believe that students are hungrier than any other group of persons in our society for this exposure.

There are many good books which introduce the visual arts by presenting a historical survey of man's artistic achievements. They deal comprehensively with architecture, sculpture, and painting and discuss the sociological, technical, and aesthetic implications of the objects produced in their changing historical contexts.

---

[1] Robert Graves, *Oxford Addresses on Poetry* (London: Cassell, 1961), p. 105.

It is customary for this stream of art images[2] to be presented as seen through the eyes of the scholar and historian. Although we recognize the value and importance of art history as a discipline, it is not always effective in imparting the sensual and psychological flavor of art forms. For this, one must be sufficiently free and permissive to know a personal response — to harken to the bleeps of the internal radar system, which tells us, by flickering across hidden mental and emotional conductors, that we are in the presence of an image. Such a private reaction is natural and instinctual and indicates that there are some sensitive spots in consciousness which are stimulated specifically by man-made shapes. To cultivate this way of gaining access to art's secrets, it is not necessary to depend upon "learning" in the academic sense — that is, to assimilate history-associated facts about style and period.

Some artists talk constantly about the *plastic problem.* It is a term which must be explained, for it is central to this discussion. They are referring to two aspects of the creative act:

1. the plastic aspect, the *shaping* in two or three dimensions of some malleable material, be it paint which is brushed or marble which is carved, to create the necessary form.
2. the expressive aspect, the *discovery* in and through the shaping process of the forms which embody the ideas and feelings present in a state of heightened consciousness.[3]

For the man working on a plastic problem there is no separating these two aspects of the act. They seem to operate simultaneously yet unilaterally. Shaping and discovery — discovery and shaping; order and priority are lost and become fused in action. This is a paradox, but paradoxes abound as language and logic attempt to describe the processes of art and the imagination.

It is thus possible to think of the sculptor or painter as a transmitter and the rest of us as receivers. But we must remember that the medium for this communication is some physical material, shaped in a significant way, under a special set of conscious circumstances. The crux of the matter and the prime answer to the question "why bother about art?" is:

that the created image is a statement — a statement embodying the artist's comprehension of reality as he experiences
events of the world in his own consciousness. It represents
a plastic mode of conceiving life and the world as significant

---

[2] I shall use the word "image" generally throughout the book to denote the work of art. To distinguish between images held in the mind — in the mind's eye, as we say — and the work of art in its physical reality, I will refer to the *mental* image and the *concrete* image.

[3] I use the term "heightened consciousness" to signify the unusually intense states of sensory perception, ideational activity, and emotional charge experienced by the creative person. Inasmuch as this condition would seem to be a primary phase of cogent imaginative sensibility, the term will be cropping up constantly throughout the book in differing contexts.

3   FIRST, WHY BOTHER?

as the linguistic mode (by means of words) or the mathematical mode (by means of measurement and number). The
visual arts involve the full imaginative life of the man
himself as he confronts the external realities of the world
itself. If the resulting image is a good one, it acts as a bridge
between the heart and mind of the artist and the heart and
mind of the viewer, who gains new insights into the nature
of things.

In such a visual dialogue there is none of the directness and precision which can
distinguish linguistic communication. Nothing is "said." And because we are such a
verbal culture nowadays, it is necessary to relearn the language of plastic statements
if images are to possess their ancient credibility and power to move us. The fact
remains that a sculptor can transmit experiences and attitudes through a carved
stone, a painter through a colored configuration, and an architect through the
design of spatial environments. I consider these three examples to represent the
most significant kinds of image making.

Let an artist himself speak about the true imaginative values of art.

Reality is more than the thing itself. I look always for the
super-reality. Reality lies in how you see things. A green
parrot is also a green salad *and* a green parrot. He who
makes it only a parrot diminishes its reality. A painter who
copies a tree blinds himself to the real tree. I see things
otherwise. A palm tree can become a horse.[4]

Look for a moment at Figure 1-1, Picasso's drawing of a toad. If a palm tree can
become a horse, we see here that a rock, a leaf, or a piece of seaweed can become
a toad. This drawing does not imitate nature's toad. Instead, it reveals how Picasso
sees the toad for himself; how nature's shape is transformed to serve all the
imagined associations and feeling-attitudes triggered by the thing called a toad. The
super-reality of which Picasso speaks is thus a double reality — the physical fact of
the object discerned by the eye of the senses plus its secret significance for the
artist beyond the truth of appearances.

This is a strange kind of relationship to have with an object and one which I
think only artists and poets experience at the highest level, as we shall see in
Chapter 10. Yet most of us experience it to a lesser degree when we find our eye
caught by something — a flower, a tree, a piece of driftwood, a stone. Therefore we
see that the artist involved in the act of fashioning his image (drawing, carving,
modeling, etc.) is attempting two things. First, to realize his perceptions of the
object by analyzing the characteristics of its overall form in order that he may
arrive at its essential structure and shape. Second, to modify these basic characteristics of structure and shape in whatever way is necessary to convey the flavor of his

---

[4] Pablo Picasso, "A Palm Tree Can Become a Horse," *Sunday Observer* (London), July 10, 1950,
Sec. 2, p. 1.

FIG. 1-1   Pablo Picasso (b. 1881–   ). *The Toad* **1949. Lithograph.** Permission French Reproduction Rights Inc.

imaginative involvement. The great artist seems to accomplish both of these things knowingly and unknowingly as he works. As he perceives and analyzes, "feeling out" the emerging forms, he is also imparting his own creative attitude to the developing image, transforming an objective statement into one that is also very personally his own. Working in this way the artist is able to use and exploit all the plastic possibilities of his chosen medium, so that the formal characteristics of the image possess the sensuous qualities that will best convey the imaginative content. And we who view the finished work respond through the sensuous quality of its form to the imaginative nature of its content. As we view a work of art, we are aware of the proportionate shapes of both physical surfaces and spaces and of their curvilinear or angular peculiarities, and we respond to the way they "rhyme" with each other. Many varieties of line contribute to the sensuous form of the image, not to mention the contrasts between plane and curved surfaces and changes in texture from rough to smooth, hard to soft, opaque to transparent. There are numerous ways in which all these sensuous possibilities can be combined, and any one way possesses its own kind of visual melody or counterpoint. Therefore we can respond to Picasso's toad purely as a visual melody, appreciating its sensuous qualities for their own sake and not asking what it is meant to represent. The eye can skate over the lines of the drawing, finding some to be fast moving, others slow; as on a roller-coaster ride, a sudden sweep downhill is counteracted by an uphill surge and the pace changes. The expansive sweeps of surfaces, spaces, and lines, which may be likened to the flow of legato sound in music, slow up, and we sense the tenseness which results. We may react positively or negatively to these formal relationships, whether they be over the two-dimensional surface of a drawing or painting, making up the three-dimensional form of sculpture, or comprising the spaces and physical surfaces of architecture.

Consequently, we might say that an image always presents some degree of *formal eloquence* in its plastic aspect, and we should therefore realize that form alone can affect us. Yet I find it almost impossible to separate the formal or plastic eloquence of a work from the nature of its imaginative content. For what is form save the shape taken by content as it is tangibly embodied in the image? It is the shape by which we recognize the man, the artist, who is in the work; it is the shape of his mood, his prophetic vision, his intuitive insights, his hopes, anxieties, and joys. It is as Émile Zola wrote in his novel *Mes Haines,* ". . . in the picture (the work of art), I seek, I love the man, the artist." Therefore, although we can respond to form purely at the level of its plastic eloquence, the *psychological eloquence* it displays in revealing the life and consciousness of the man who brought it into being is inextricably linked to its plastic rhythms.

Hence, a work of art transmits on two wave bands — the sensuous and formal, and the imaginative and psychological. We can tune in to one or the other, but it is very difficult to tune in to one without the other. As we shall see in Chapter 2, these wave bands are not mutually independent and do not seem to operate sequentially for the observer. It is as if the image transmits on both bands simultaneously, although one signal may be stronger than the other. In viewing Picasso's toad I find that both plastic and psychological signals are equally strong. The sensuous rhythms and textures are a new visual experience, holding the eye as the musical rhythms and textures of Stravinsky hold the ear; and I find myself tactilely involved, feeling this toad under my hand. At the same time one is aware that this form possesses an elemental grandeur, as if Picasso has discovered the one essential toad shape from which all other toads are descended. The plastic configuration of this image is so biomorphically credible that it seems as if Picasso has discovered a shape whose rhythms can only echo a fundamental plastic truth of nature. Psychologically, I share some of the artist's fascination for the creature. I move in Picasso's imagination, in the avenues of fantasy and dream, hypnotized out of the twentieth century. For this bejeweled yet slime-textured image recalls some slow-breathing, inscrutable, prehistoric amphibian; it is an eerie witness testifying to the mutability of life and the enormity of time's span.

Was all this going through Picasso's mind? I really cannot say. The psychological eloquence of the work for me is as I have described it, and to me it is the man Picasso who invested this image with such content. Because the toad of the image comes to life in the imagination I find it more credible than any toad

6

discovered in the garden. The toad in the garden is quickly forgotten. The toad in the drawing I cannot forget. Although I first saw it several years ago it still haunts the memory.

> If you bring a mirror near to a real picture, it ought to become covered with steam, with living breath, because it is alive. . . .[5]

Does this toad's damp breath steam the mirror you hold before it?

---

[5] Picasso, "A Palm Tree Can Become a Horse."

II
BEAUTY AND
THE BEAST

In this chapter we will compare two pieces of sculpture. Although they are quite different in size and are separated in time by approximately 4,000 years, they treat the same idea and use the same object in nature as their model. In setting one image against the other it will be possible to indicate the range of imaginative response to a common theme. Also, I wish to provoke the reader to discover his own bias and form his own point of view; to realize where his sympathies lie when faced with the two plastic extremes. But first, a few theories should be explained in order to prepare the ground and to consolidate the discussion of the first chapter.

THE CREATIVE POSITION

An important proposition established in Chapter I is that a work of art manifests a double reality; that art shapes man's visual perceptions of things outside himself while embodying also the workings of his inner mental life. Theoretically, such a correspondence between objective and subjective realities presents an ideally balanced creative position. For it means that the artist is a participating intelligence in the life of nature, yet is led back into himself as the reverberations cause him to experience new levels of thinking and feeling. As I have said previously, an image that results from such a confrontation relates to the life of the world (nature) and to the life of man (psychological attitude). The Swiss artist Paul Klee (1879-1940) puts it simply:

> By contemplating the optical-physical appearance, the ego
> arrives at intuitive conclusions about the inner substance.[1]

However, one purpose of this chapter is to show that in such a confrontation the image may *emphasize* either the visual, material truth of nature, or the psychological

---

[1] Sybil Moholy-Nagy, *Paul Klee Pedagogical Sketchbook* (New York: Praeger, 1953), p. 9.

state of man the artist. For it will become obvious as we proceed that a nicely balanced, fifty-fifty relationship between man and object is not supported by many images. In the past, many artists have been concerned with exploring the world of visual appearances, but any extreme preoccupation with objective reality has tended to inhibit a personal and imaginative response. In such cases the objects emerge supreme, and it is hard to find the men who made them — although one may recognize their technical virtuosity. (Remember William Blake's censure of such art quoted in Chapter 1.) Conversely, there have been many instances when an artist's inner life of mood and dream has been so powerful that his chosen models become vehicles to carry his visions. In this event they lose their natural appearance, for the artist is not concerned with visual truth. In such images it is man who emerges supreme, and it is hard to find the object. (The argument here is based on the assumption that we are discussing a nature-oriented art. But as the art of this century moved to a state of total abstraction, it became obvious that sculptors and painters were inventing their own forms without any perceptual recourse to nature's models — even though we must allow that some residual visual memory remained. This nonobjective art, or non-nature oriented art, must be treated separately. In Chapter 11 we will discuss its imaginative significance vis-à-vis the images which are based on a subject-object relationship. For in theory at least, nonobjective imagery represents man's final alienation from the thrall of nature and the beginning of imagistic odysseys on the sea of his own psyche.)

The problem of emphasis in a nature-oriented art revolves around the confrontation of the two entities involved — the object which attracts and is thus an event in its own right and the man who is to use it for his own ends. In the ritual of image making this becomes a tug of war between the two. A diagram (Figure 2-1) may serve to illustrate the possibilities more efficiently. In each of the four sketches in this diagram, the seesaw on its fulcrum represents the visual-mental balancing board comprising man's optical sensations of the outside world (left of the fulcrum) and the interior mental world of his consciousness (the shaded area to the right of center). The black circle is the object of attraction present in the physical world; the gray circle represents man the artist. Let us assume that in sketch 1 there is no strong visual attraction between object and man — both exist independently on their own side of the fulcrum. This is the situation for many people who have neither the eye nor the mind for a life of participation, discovery, or creativity. The seesaw remains in a passive and static equilibrium. In sketch 2 this equilibrium has disappeared. The artist is attracted to the form of the object because it in some way corresponds to, or triggers, curiosity, mood, or concept. The hitherto neutral object thus becomes the chosen motif. At this point the process offers two extreme possibilities. The man who is drawing, painting, or carving may experience a compulsion to comprehend the structural characteristics of the model, and his visual perceptions become highly efficient as he explores and analyzes its form. If things stop here, the seesaw is heavily tilted into the world of appearances and the resultant image testifies only to the presence of a specific object in the world, however acutely the artist's sensations are realized in the work. But if objective perception is

9

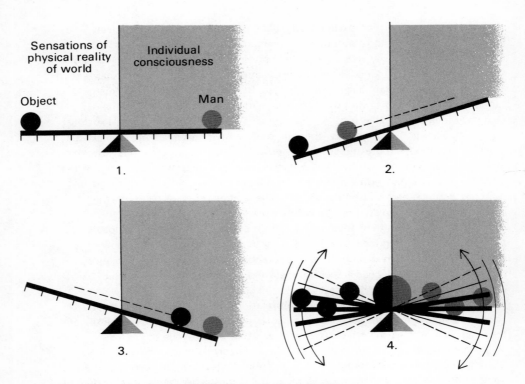

FIG. 2-1   Diagram of subject-object "seesaw" relationship

not an end in itself and does not proceed to such a scientific extreme, the motif
produces psychological reverberations in the artist which go beyond a desire to
clarify visual sensations. In this event, whatever degree of perceptual knowledge he
has gained is at the service of deeper imaginative experiences. The object of attraction acts as a catalyst, and man moves from the material reality of the model to
the intense psychological reality of himself. When this happens, the seesaw tilts in
the opposite direction (sketch 3). Yet once again, if the process stops in that
extreme position, the drawing, painting, or sculpture shapes the event as realized in
the esoteric consciousness of the self, and the perceptual reality of the object may
be lost. Sketch 4 represents a situation in which neither of the two extreme positions just described have won the tug of war. It suggests a hypothetical equilibrium
achieved in the confrontation of artist and object. But this is not meant to indicate
a passive and static balance. As the artist allows both objective sensations and
subjective attitudes their say, they move back and forth on the seesaw, causing it to
fluctuate up and down without striking ground at either end. This motion produces
a tension between the worlds on either side of the fulcrum, and the degree to
which this tension can be fused into an artistic whole as image depends upon the
artistic personality and vision of the man. The diagram indicates that there are

BEAUTY AND THE BEAST

degrees of emphasis as either man or model moves towards the middle position. Consequently, works of art that result from such a balance may emphasize the concrete appearance of things or the imaginative life of the artist. But the object-subject duality and tension will be present in some degree. The complete fusing of the two at the center, as shown in sketch 4, is a didactic hypothesis. For it represents too perfect a solution — one that neutralizes both elements. We have seen how Picasso's toad compels because it maintains the tension between perceptual (objective) and imaginative (subjective) knowledge.

A statement concerning the function of art by the German philosopher Max Scheler refers to the three sorts of image an artist can produce. It is not difficult to relate the three postulates to sketches 2, 3, and 4; and I quote his remarks because they affirm in powerful language the thesis of this chapter:

> The purpose of art is not to reproduce what is *already* given (which would be superfluous), nor to create something in the pure play of *subjective fancy* (which can only be transitory and must necessarily be a matter of complete indifference to other people), but to press forward into the whole of the *external world and the soul*, to see and communicate those objective realities within it which rule and convention have hitherto concealed.[2]

In comparing the two sculptures which I have called, half-seriously, "Beauty and the Beast," it will help to keep the theory of the seesaw in mind. The two works are material examples of the opposing emphases we have discussed.

THE PRIMITIVE "BEAST" AND THE CLASSICAL "BEAUTY"

Figure 2-2 is a predynastic Egyptian clay figurine, modeled from Nile mud sometime between 6,500 and 3,500 B.C. It is not quite 12 inches high. Figure 2-3 is a life-size marble work of the fourth century B.C. It was made by the Greek sculptor Praxiteles and even in its own time was famed throughout the Eastern Mediterranean. Both pieces are fashioned in the shape of a woman, but the early Egyptian figurine is less like the real thing. We know that the Greek sculpture represents Aphrodite, goddess of love and beauty. We do not know exactly what the figurine represents, save that it is feminine. Thus, we have two images of "the feminine"; two forms shaped in the round, serving two imaginative attitudes toward a basic theme. In discussing their differences we may discover more about the relationship of form to idea and feeling and see how the broad spectrum of imaginative possibilities can move from rational to nonrational extremes. Both works have

---

[2] Max Scheler, *The Nature of Sympathy,* trans. P. Heath (London: Routledge & Kegan Paul, 1954), p. 253. Courtesy reprint edition by Archon Books, Hamden, Connecticut. (Italics added.)

been photographed from more than one position, and the differing views reproduced
throughout this chapter will help the pieces speak directly to us.[3]

The theme of the feminine goddess is very old; it is found in the concept of
the Earth Mother which has been present in man's imagination since earliest times.
She is the personification of Nature, containing the mystery of the birth-to-death
cycle and the life force of the world. Numerous goddesses spring from her and
appear in countless mythologies and religions. They symbolize many aspects of the
Earth Mother, from the sexual-fertile-maternal side to the funereal and spiritual. The

---

[3] The scale of these pieces — one 11 inches high and the other life size — would render their
juxtaposition in a museum ineffective if not ludicrous. But I feel it is valid to juxtapose
photographs and play one off against the other. This may both stimulate the viewer and
reveal characteristics of each that will help determine their individual effectiveness.

model for the graphic and sculptural images of the goddesses has constantly been, understandably enough, woman. Bearing these things in mind, I suspect that a majority of readers will find the Greek Aphrodite more to their immediate taste. After all, it is Greek, skillfully fashioned, and traditionally excellent. In contrast, the goddess from Egypt appears crude and primitive, more an archaeological specimen than a work of art. Yet before we account for the differences by simply granting the Greeks the benefits of a civilized and sophisticated culture, we must

FIG. 2–3a **Praxiteles.** *Aphrodite of Knidos.* **c. 350 B.C.** Roman copy, Vatican Museum

remember Aphrodite's role in Greek mythology. For despite all intellectual and spiritual refinements of her function, she remained the goddess of the *act* of love. Indeed, she inspired some of the most orgiastic festivals of the Greek world. At one level, therefore, she represents as basic an instinctual (or primitive) response to the sexual-fertile ground of the feminine as that suggested by the much earthier figurine. It seems that we must find other reasons to account for Aphrodite's rational elegance and apparently faithful likeness to the model, when contrasted with the bizarre appearance of the clay figure.

It is not known how the Egyptian figure was used or for what specific purpose it was intended. We can just point generally to a long line of such small female images from paleolithic times. Many have been found in the greater Mediterranean area, and all are distorted from the natural. The British Museum has a large collection of predynastic Egyptian figurines similar to the one illustrated here. Our example may have been used (perhaps at a local level) as a fetish object in the performance of some fertility ritual, for her form and attitude suggest the sexual and fertile aspects of the Earth Mother goddess rather than the maternal or spiritual sides. Her magical ability to promote and protect life may have been invoked merely by the act of making her in clay or simply by possessing her as an amulet. But however she was used, it is likely that the figurine goddess magically involved man as a participant in the otherwise frighteningly impersonal cycle of birth and death.

It is obviously impossible for us to comprehend the significance this figurine would have for an Egyptian living at the time. We are 5,000 years on, conditioned by Western culture in our way of seeing, thinking, and feeling, and able to only partially respond to the image. Our appraisal can be severely limited by the confines of our culture pattern. It is, of course, possible to talk about its plastic qualities; the pleasing or not so pleasing rhymes and rhythms of lines, surfaces, and volumes. But in considering this aspect, we should remember that we know only as much about pleasing plastic harmonies as our innate or acquired aesthetic sensitivity allows. We are not justified, for example, in saying that Aphrodite is beautiful and the Egyptian goddess is not, despite the title to this chapter! For our present understanding of the lives of primitive societies reveals the existence of an indigenous aesthetic awareness. Primitive men believe that objects which are to be used in a ritual will be religiously or magically powerful only if they are well made — if they conform to a standard of craftsmanship and are shaped and decorated to satisfy a sense of what is fine and right. Having said this, we must remember that the prime motive for making the fertility goddess in the first place was surely to *embody the idea of the goddess.* It was not to self-consciously create purely plastic relationships, to produce art for art's sake, which is often the aim of sophisticated societies. In primitive cultures art is created for life's sake. Therefore we should not value this figurine by reference to the popular view of what is the "artistic" image of female beauty. Instead, we can let it silently penetrate our consciousness and trigger some unfamiliar nerve of response. It may affirm the fact that the mythology of the Earth Mother still retains much of its poetic grandeur and power.

A story told by Dr. F. Sierksma about a child's response to an ancient work of art illustrates the timeless potency of such encounters. He writes:

> More than a half-truth was spoken by a small boy of nine or ten who was wandering through a museum with a few friends one rainy afternoon. With a glance that expressed fierce disapproval and a gesture that gave his pointing finger inquisitorial dimensions he said: "That is an idol." Silence followed this devastating judgment. But then the balance of justice was restored, then the *full* truth was spoken. Half surprised, half indignant, one of his companions reported: "That's not an idol. That is the Buddha." To the adult who stood by, the Buddha was never so real as in that moment, and also so far beyond all thought of beauty or ugliness. The quiet bronze statue before him was not an idol, condemned by a child spokesman of orthodox Christianity together with all other idols of the world, nor a wonderful work of art, nor a fine piece, as they call it in a museum, but the Buddha, expressing a unique conception of the life of man, giving a profound meaning to the reality of human existence. *The statue embodied this reality by implying it. . . .*[4]

The italics in the foregoing quotation are mine, for I want to emphasize that we also can respond in one of two ways to the little Egyptian goddess. Like the first small boy, we may see her with an eye conditioned by the intellectual judgments and associations of our own culture; hence, visual prejudice may inhibit response to the plastic eloquence of the image — and intellectual rationalization may preclude the response of our more intuitive feelings and understandings in communing with the work. Or, like his indignant companion, we may see the goddess with a fresh, permissive eye and an open, receptive mind; then we respond instinctively, cutting through the centuries to sense her plastic poetry and to experience certain mental and emotional reactions. In this case, we accept her as an image of erotic power, as the embodiment of an attitude to the feminine transcending time and place.

The anonymous Egyptian who modeled the clay prototype of a series created a hybrid goddess. He did not stick to his visual perceptions of how a woman is, but borrowed freely from the animal world and invented a creature-woman. Only the shoulders, breasts, and hips show the artist shaping the figure naturalistically, according to his visual knowledge of the human model. And it is the distinct emphasis he gives to the curvature and swelling volumes of these areas that give the form a powerful and earthy sensuality. In contrast, the limbs, hands, and head are treated irrationally. The upraised arms with their clenched, claw-like hands, and the loosely shaped reptilian head, suggest some primordial beast tensely declaiming its animal passion. (Figure 2-4 shows a spiny-tailed agama from Saudi Arabia. This is a two-foot long, plant-eating lizard that lives in gravel plains and sandy flats. The

---

[4] F. Sierksma, *The Gods As We Shape Them* (London: Routledge & Kegan Paul, 1960), p. 12. (Italics added.)

FIG. 2–2b   Egyptian Figurine (Pre-dynastic) 12"
high. Courtesy of the Trustees of the British Museum,
London

general shape and posture of the head and neck remind one of the figurine. I am
not attempting to draw any specific conclusions from this association; the resem-
blance is interesting in itself. But the later, dynastic Egyptians frequently used
animal forms as symbols of abstract, religious concepts. The lizard is a reptile, and
the head of the figurine-goddess has always struck me as being reptile inspired. . . .)

There will be those who dismiss this image unreservedly. It will appear crudely
fashioned, lacking objective reality as an image of woman, and meaningless as an
embodiment of the myth-dream of the feminine goddess. Yet there will be others
who do not have these problems. The work will affect them strongly, triggering
unusual thoughts and feelings. They will find themselves still sensitive to the
primitive and ubiquitous sway of the feminine; to two levels of response — the
mystical feminine and the sexual feminine.

FIG. 2–4   Spiny-tailed Lizard. Courtesy Arabian American Oil Company, Aramco
World Magazine

I have already mentioned that Aphrodite represented many aspects of the feminine in Greek mythology. As the goddess of love, she apparently worked on two levels, that of the spiritual and mystical and that of the erotic and physical. I suppose most of us would agree that male-female love is a combination of physical and spiritual attractions — a state which affects the body sexually and the psyche or spirit devotionally. And, when the Greeks created a goddess of love in sculpture, they humanized the elemental and generalized idea of the feminine by making Aphrodite an individual — a particular person with whom one might identify. Because of this I would suggest that the Greeks recognized love as a compound of sexual and mental attractions between individual men and women. In contrast, the early Egyptian figurine has no individualized characteristics. Instead, the image seems to symbolize a more general or collective attitude toward some erotic mystique of the feminine, representing a universal principle of female procreative power rather than a personal involvement with it. We do not know whether this figurine is related to male-female love at a personal level; and we do not even know whether individual men and women at this time experienced the combination of devotional (spiritual-mental) and physical attraction in their relationships. It seems safe to suggest, therefore, that the figure of Aphrodite represents a more humanized and intelligible concept of the feminine theme we call love than does the figurine of predynastic Egypt. For Aphrodite may signify not only the general and impersonal principle of fertility in nature, but also, and perhaps to a greater degree, the compulsive attraction of a particular woman in the life of a particular man. She is able to preside over a more personal ritual of male-female attraction, as well as embodying a collective and generalized idea of the feminine. Consequently, the

FIG. 2–3b   Praxiteles. *Aphrodite of Knidos.* c. 350 B.C. Roman copy, Vatican Museum

sculptural image of the Greek goddess takes the human figure as its motif; whereas the clay goddess of Egypt is a hybrid creature, part beast and part woman. But we should also recognize that it is through such ambiguity that the figurine gains her strange power, for she relates less to particular human experience than to an idea, less to what we individually know than to what lies beyond human experience. And we see that when the mythic theme of the feminine becomes specifically human, as it does in the Greek work, much of the mystery and power is lost.

It was central to Greek mythology to imagine that man was cast in the same shape as the gods; and, possessing this belief, it was logical to consider man to be the highest of nature's creatures. The human figure, therefore, became the model in nature considered most worthy of treatment by art. As early as the seventh century B.C., we can see, in the large sculptures of the archaic period, that the Greeks have differentiated the human from other living things in nature. Yet, as we stare at Aphrodite, we wonder if she isn't too good to be true, and the suspicion grows that Praxiteles has taken certain liberties with his model. Do women exist who stand so lightly and gracefully poised? Whose delicate oval heads crown such firm yet fluid, monumental bodies? The sculptor has made Aphrodite's legs long; they flow high into the pelvis, supporting it and the trunk in much the same way an architect will support horizontal masses with powerful up-thrusting vertical columns. He has

emphasized the breadth of her shoulders in order to create satisfactory horizontal-vertical proportions; and he has compacted the torso so that the thoracic and lumbar regions assume the right proportionate volume — a mass supported by the legs. The surfaces of the various parts of the body flow smoothly, ironing out awkward transitions and eliminating wrinkles and folds in the flesh. These are just a few of the more obvious modifications imposed on the natural figure in the name of art.

The overall result is a carved marble figure in which lines and volumes flow in a system of rhythmic and proportionate harmonies. Yet, as anyone familiar with drawing from the nude model knows, nature has not made woman so formally perfect. In life she does possess wrinkles and pouches, imperfect proportions, and awkward transitions between part and part. It seems that Praxiteles was not content with woman as she is but sought to perfect her through art in the shape of the goddess. He was not alone in this — Greek sculpture was moving to this end from the early seventh century B.C. — and the sculpture of the Classical period from Polycleitus to Praxiteles (c. 450 to 350 B.C.) sees this idea of fineness or beauty fully realized. This is not the place to discuss the theory of classical Greek art, but the idea that art should perfect the human model and create its *ideal* form becomes the central issue in debating the imaginative processes of the Greeks and those of the more primitive early Egyptians.

TWO BASIC CREATIVE POSSIBILITIES

Greek sculptors spent two or three hundred years looking hard at the body's structure, observing how it worked in its movements and generally accumulating a store of anatomical knowledge. But they seemed to ignore the fact that there are long and short, fat and thin men in the world, not to mention all the in-between sizes. And in the Classical period we see no short and stout Apollos, no humpbacked youths or squat maidens.[5] Therefore, as Greek artists searched out the naturalistic form of the figure, they also imposed an ideal regularity on the wide variety of human physical types. This was achieved by formulating certain canons or rules of visual harmony to be applied in art and architecture. These rules were based on mathematical and geometrical principles; for, to the Greek mind, the most pleasing proportionate relationships between part and part were those which followed harmonious numerical ratios. For example, Euclidean geometry, by its formula for cutting "a given finite line in extreme and mean ratio," gives a proportion or ratio of roughly 8:5 in order to allow the maximum harmonious "play" between the longer and shorter parts. Thus, satisfying visual rhythms were created by using numerical relationships in sculptural images of the figure. The canon of sculpture formulated by Polycleitus has not come down to us, but he is supposed to have suggested that "the success of a work of art . . . comes about through many

---

[5] Verism, or realism, the artistic faithfulness to life does not appear until the Hellenistic period, in the late third and second centuries B.C. after the disintegration of Classical Greece.

numerical relationships, in the process of which a trifle tilts the balance." Clearly, it was not a static harmony that was desired — not a fifty-fifty balance — but a ratio that allowed just enough variability between the parts to tilt the balance and so achieve a dynamic relationship. ("Since the early days of Greek philosophy men have tried to find in art a geometrical law, for if art — which they identify with beauty — is harmony, and harmony is the due observance of proportions, it seems reasonable to assume that these proportions are fixed. The geometrical proportion known as the Golden Section has for centuries been regarded as such a key to the mysteries of art. . . . It is formulated in two propositions of Euclid: Book II, proposition II; . . . and Book VI, proposition 30, 'to cut a given finite line in extreme and mean ration.' The usual formula is: to cut a finite line so that the shorter part is to the longer part as the longer part is to the whole. . . .")[6]

Seen in this light the sculpture of Aphrodite becomes an aesthetic object; that is, she satisfies the demand of Greek sense perceptions that the volumes, surfaces, and lines of a work of art should be dynamically proportionate to each other and to the whole. Yet she is still the goddess of the act of love, embodying all of the strong instinctual drives towards the feminine which this idea arouses. Or is she? Is this aspect of her function lost in the sculpture as the artist strives to apply a geometrical law commensurate with the concept of beauty? Kenneth Clark writes: "One of the few classical canons of proportion of which we can be certain is that which, in a female nude, took the same unit of measurement for the distance between the breasts, the distance from the lower breast to the navel, and again from the navel to the division of the legs."[7] It is difficult to imagine aesthetic considerations such as this influencing the man who made the Egyptian goddess.

The Greek imagination which thus formed its gods and goddesses, and its sculptured youths and maidens, was complex. It embraced the idea of men cast in the image of the gods; the idea that man holds the dominant and supreme position in nature; and the belief that artistic and philosophical truth is to be found in the laws of mathematics. The type of idealized human beauty which Classical sculpture reveals is the plastic result of this composite imaginative experience. As William Blake put it in his *Descriptive Catalogue,* "Greek statues are all of them representations of spiritual existences, of gods immortal to the mortal perishing organs of sight; and yet they are embodied and organized in solid marble." Blake's suggestion that art may reveal spiritual truths through such idealization of the human form contrasts strongly with what we see in the figurine. While we have no historical records to tell us what was going on in the Egyptian mind, the clay goddess herself gives us some clues. It is immediately obvious that the more primitive imagination does not focus on man as the model *par excellence* — that the gods are not humanized — and that mathematical and geometrical canons are not used to impart a physical regularity or perceptual logic to the image. Instead, it

---

[6] Sir Herbert Read, *The Meaning of Art* (London: Faber and Faber Ltd., 1964), p. 21, and Praeger Publishers, Inc., New York.

[7] Sir Kenneth Clark, *The Nude* (Princeton: Princeton University Press, 1956), p. 42.

FIG. 2–3c Praxiteles. *Aphrodite of Knidos.* c. 350 B.C. Roman copy, Vatican Museum. Photograph by Helena Wessler

stands for the reverse side of the coin. The figurine springs from an imaginative attitude which does not separate man from the rest of nature; which is not humanistic in the Greek sense. Rather, there is an instinct to take nature as a whole, to combine in the one image varied manifestations of life, and to leave the mythological or spiritual issue as dark, mysterious, and unresolved, so far as man, *sui generis*, is concerned. For me, she is analogous to the Valkyrie of Wagner — a magnificent hysteria of sound. Her roughly modeled and organically-free volumes bypass rational understanding and evoke the elemental dream-mystery of the myth of the fertile-mother goddess. In contrast, Aphrodite is akin to a Bach fugue — a contrapuntal organization of theme and counter-theme, in which, despite the presence of a major motive, a classical balance is maintained. Her carefully formed volumes flow rhythmically, and eye and intellect respond with pleasure to the order and cohesion presented. But our emotions are soothed rather than stirred; we feel secure with Aphrodite for her form suggests little mystery or ambiguity.

It was said in Chapter 1 (page 6) that a work of art transmits a signal on two wave bands — that it is eloquent plastically as an organization of form-to-space rhymes and rhythms, and psychologically as a manifestation of human subjective consciousness. In the preceding paragraph I have suggested that the Greek work speaks strongly as form to the rational intellect, while the figurine goddess speaks a more emotional and intuitive psychological language. But now we realize that the situation is not as simple as this. It is not a question of an image appealing just in one way or the other. The work of art sends both signals simultaneously, even though one signal, depending upon the artist's motivation and intention, might be more distinct than the other. For behind the form and plastic eloquence of Aphrodite lies the Greek imagination in all of its psychological significance. And carrying the psychological eloquence of the Egyptian figurine is shaped clay in all of its formal significance. The two signals are really mutually dependent.

The key issue thus becomes the question of the artist's intention and motivation. Granting the presence of a common object to serve as motif, we see from our two images of the feminine that the imaginative operations of the psyche can pull the artist in two ways. And the purpose of this chapter is to suggest that the two most fundamental imaginative forces experienced by the artist spring from the rational and nonrational aspects of his consciousness respectively. Aphrodite represents the firmness of Greek perceptions and the lucidity of the Greek intellect. The predynastic goddess embodies the mystery of the mythological drama of the feminine, intuitively and emotionally conceived.

We have seen that the rational imagination tends to follow the way of deductive reasoning, of moving from objective fact or a-priori hypothesis. It seeks to impose an intellectual order and clarification on the confusion of multi-sense impressions from outside and on the thoughts and feelings that spring from inside, and to understand the relationship between these external and internal realities. The nonrational imagination, on the other hand, is just sheer imagination; it comes spontaneously in strong feelings, mental images, and ideas that seem to spring forth fully formed into consciousness; it does not necessarily keep faith with objective fact or the reasonable assumptions of the intellect and tends to use the model as only an initial "given" shape from which to create new forms. The rational imagination, however, tends to stay closer to the perceptual reality of the model, or to the canons of reason that govern and define the aesthetic principles of formal harmony and beauty.

These two aspects of the imaginative consciousness introduce a complication into the simple diagram of the seesaw. Now we see that it is necessary to incorporate both imaginative possibilities on the right-hand side of the fulcrum. This area, signifying consciousness, would have to show, diagrammatically, the potential operation of an intuitive and feeling source of imagery, as well as that of a more rational and intellectual one. Such a differentiation would also help to clarify my references, made on page 10, to "perceptual knowledge" (which springs from the rational area) and to "deeper imaginative experiences" (which belong to the intuitive, nonrational area).

We have seen that the main intention of Praxiteles was to create a sculpture in which carefully considered plastic relationships were sought, rather than allowing the form to materialize through a spontaneous overflow of sheer imagination. He

BEAUTY AND THE BEAST

was not concerned with expressing a unique vision of the goddess of love and beauty. His motivation came from the Greek will to perfect the human figure through sculpture — to make abstract concepts of truth and beauty available to our sense perceptions — and he was preoccupied with the problem of formal plastic harmonies. Consequently, Aphrodite speaks loudly of aesthetic issues invented by the reasoning mind and not of the day-to-day drama of powerful surges of interior feeling and mythological idea. But the beauty of her form leads us to consider yet another aspect of the Greek imagination. For Greek sculpture reveals how well their art rationalized the many tragic factors affecting human life: the mystery and fear of death, suffering and tragedy, the purpose of human existence, and so on. The serene perfection we see in the anthropomorphized gods and in the idealized athletes and maidens presents a most optimistic view of man's destiny and importance. In one sense we may regard Greek art as an escape from the insecurity, fear, and dread of real life.

If Praxiteles acted calculatingly, inspired by both the perceptual reality of the model and Greek aesthetic theory, the Egyptian artist apparently worked freely and spontaneously.[8] The figurine suggests a form springing to life, as if it were

[8] Of course, the fact that Aphrodite is life-size and carved in marble imposes a prolonged and deliberate operation on the sculptor, whereas a clay piece only 11 inches high may be quickly modeled. However, I am not referring to mechanical actions dictated by medium or scale but to the constant mental discipline experienced by Greek sculptors in working to fine limits of aesthetic tolerance, as opposed to the intuitive freedom of primitive artists who create prototypes.

BEAUTY AND THE BEAST

already formed in the artist before delivery to the clay. One feels that the intention of the Egyptian artist was to translate into clay a combination of deep feeling and fantasy picture-idea, both pushed spontaneously into his consciousness. And for this to happen, he must participate totally with all his being in the myth of the fertile goddess. The human figure serves only as an initial, given shape, and perceptual analysis or aesthetic calculation has no place in an impassioned act which discovers the goddess only as she is being shaped. So it is the power of an intuitive vision that signals first here, for the image conveys in a way no written description could the potency of the fertile goddess and her presence in the elemental dream-ideas of man. She shrieks the mythological drama of life, mediating between man and the unknown. It is almost impossible to see this clay shape as form — in the Greek sense — and separate it from the psychological drama. It is difficult to appreciate plastic rhymes and rhythms in their own right when they result from such ecstatic, numinous states of being.

We have seen that these sculptural images of the feminine represent the two basic creative attitudes in the history of art. I believe it is more important to understand what these attitudes are and how they work and manifest themselves than it is to merely know the labels which apply to them. But let us close the chapter by saying that the image of Aphrodite may be described in art terminology as *classical*, while that of the figurine would be considered *romantic*.

III

THE COMPASS POINTS
OF CONSCIOUSNESS

It is time to be more specific about the nature of the artistic consciousness.
We have already talked in general terms of perception and heightened perception,
rational and nonrational mental activity, and intuitive feelings and ideas — all of
which describe certain operative aspects of consciousness. But in order to
comprehend the range and intensity of awareness that distinguishes the artist, it is
necessary to try to see the creative consciousness as a whole. The analogy of
consciousness to a compass, with its four major points of orientation, provides a
useful mental image. This chapter is organized around a diagrammatic representation
of consciousness which, like a compass, indicates the four main points of awareness
by which an artist navigates.[1]

It could be argued that this discussion of consciousness should initiate the
book, but I feel that it is more meaningful if introduced now, after the reader has
struggled with some propositions and related them to particular images. This
chapter does not represent a presumptuous attempt to systematize the creative
consciousness by means of analogy and diagram. After all, we know little enough
about the connection between the neurophysiology of the brain and the psychology
of the mind. A major difficulty is that a subject can never entirely know the nature
of its own self, even though aspects may be isolated and examined more objectively.
If we admit this limitation in "consciously" trying to know consciousness
absolutely, we may still attempt to piece together some of the parts to help us
understand why men make art. In my view, this entails investigating how we
become aware of both the world's existence and our own, and why there is the urge
to translate these conscious events into images.

---

[1] I am indebted to Fr. Joseph Goldbrunner for providing the idea for a diagram of consciousness.
In his book *Individuation* (Notre Dame, Ind.: University of Notre Dame Press, 1964), he
discusses the role of the senses, intellect, feeling, and intuition, and provides a diagrammatic
representation of the psyche.

And then it was clear to me that whatever secrets there are in Nature, I can unravel and understand them only through the images which my consciousness forms of my experiences. The images of our life, as well as of Nature, can only be understood when we take them for what they are in our experience, namely as works of art created by our consciousness.[2]

So writes Naum Gabo, painter and sculptor. He goes on to say:

The artist's mind is a turbulent sea full of all kinds of impressions, responses and experiences as well as feelings and emotions. Some experts on art assert that the artist does not really have more of these emotions and feelings and impressions than the ordinary man who is not an artist. This may be true or false, but what they apparently fail to see and to assert is that in the artist these feelings and responses are in a more agitated state. He is more concerned with them, and the urge to express these experiences is more intense in him than it is in the ordinary man. And that, I suppose, is the reason why the artist's mind is not only turbulent but sometimes, alas, troublesome also. . . .[3]

Thus we must confront the artist on his own ground — the battlefield of his consciousness. I have heard artists assert that without an act of consciousness nothing exists; that the palm tree does not exist until it becomes an event in a man's consciousness. This emphasis on the importance of subjective experience is characteristic of the artist. It is well expressed in Gabo's statements. Put another way, the assertion is that we can never be completely sure that things exist in their own autonomous domain because if man's consciousness of them ceases to exist, so, to all intents and purposes, do they. For example, can we be sure that the mental experience of a tree in consciousness represents the tree as it is for itself? Or is there something illusory and limited about this experience — about all conscious experience of the world — because we realize that what we call reality is always based on our own presence and participation as observers. We realize today that there can be no such thing as an ideal objectivity toward the natural order — that man is not a godlike spectator of a mechanical universe but only a participating observer in an ongoing process. The enlightened scientist is as much aware of this as is the artist. But the scientist will strive to neutralize himself as subject and produce hypotheses about the natural order which are acceptable if they are shown to work in the maximum number of possible cases. For him, patterns in external events come first. Naum Gabo's belief that "in the artist . . . feelings and responses are in a more agitated state . . . and the urge to express these experiences is more intense in

---

[2] Naum Gabo, *Of Divers Arts,* Bollingen Foundation Series XXXV. 8 in the A. W. Mellon Lectures in the Fine Arts (© 1962 by the Trustees of the National Gallery of Art, Washington, D.C.), reprinted by permission of Princeton University Press: quote from p. 23.

[3] *Ibid.,* p. 6.

him than it is in the ordinary man" tells us that for the painter, sculptor, or poet, mental images and events in his own consciousness come first. To a much greater degree than the scientist, the artist must chisel out the image of his own existence as he confronts the world.

The evolution of consciousness in man places him in what we believe to be a unique position vis-à-vis nature. While we do not know the range of awareness possessed by animals, it seems to differ from man's in one important respect. As far as we know, an animal is not conscious of itself as a distinct and individual entity which must ultimately suffer death. It is not so positively aware of its own existence as one phenomenon and the forms of nature as something else. Therefore, when we say that man's evolved consciousness (or self-consciousness) has alienated him from nature and the world, we mean that he is not blindly a part of nature — that he distinguishes himself as a separate being. This sense of his separateness leads him to experience his consciousness as constituting a world of its own, and so each individual becomes, for himself, a unique subject. But although this is generally true, it is obvious that some men are more aware of and more involved with the nature of their own consciousness than are others. These men are the thinkers, the artists, the poets, the idealists. It is true that the more finely developed a man's consciousness, the more intensely he comprehends and uses the outside world. Yet it is also true that the more he ventures outside himself in this way, the more he is subjected to powerful *reactions* in his own consciousness. He experiences mental and emotional states which expose particular sensibilities and thus intensify his realization of himself and his distinctiveness. For example, a man who is drawn to mountains will live among them, come to know them, climb them, and thus satisfy this demand of his consciousness. But as he climbs he faces his own responses to fear and danger; he must test his own resources of perseverance and discover in himself all the moods and attitudes occasioned by the confrontation. In the end, he may know more about himself than he does about the mountain. In persons of duller consciousness, this process apparently goes on at a less intensive level. Neither the outward movement to satisfy the involvement demanded by consciousness, nor the reactions then experienced in the self, constitute the kind of discovery that produces an agitated mind and spirit. Certainly this more average man knows who he is, but he tends to accept the world without much question; his dialogue with it, and with himself, does not result in the inner turbulence which Gabo describes.

For the artist, the dialogue between consciousness and the outer world produces such a quickening of his capacity to feel and to comprehend a new psychic reality that the resulting flash of identity leaves him naked and alone, unrelated to anything save himself. I think most of us would agree that such a revelation may cause the mind to be troubled. This state of mental or emotional restlessness is the mark of the artist. It does not necessarily imply that he is unhappy or pessimistic or depressed. It means that his consciousness is taut; that the forms his restless imagination weaves are poised like the arrows on a tight bowstring, waiting to be projected into the world as the concrete images of art. The artistic consciousness is involved in a circle of perpetual movement. Man projects himself into the world only to be turned back into himself through the intensity of his psychic reaction; this mental and emotional activity is released in the form of an image and so is returned to the world as a work of art. To be thwarted at any point in this round can frustrate some artists to the point where they suffer the extremes of despair.

THE FOUR BASIC MODES OF AWARENESS

Figure 3-1 represents the microcosm of consciousness. It is a diagram which is generally applicable, but we will discuss it specifically as the sensitive instrument of the creative personality. In the diagram the heavy black circle of consciousness fits snugly into a cradle-like support labeled "the ground of consciousness." Thus, consciousness may be visualized as a structure of modes of awareness supported by a dynamic ground directing and shaping mental activity — a ground of which we are not normally aware. It may seem perverse to initiate a discussion of conscious awareness by immediately referring to unconscious processes; but it is just as realistic as surveying an iceberg and taking into account the mass beneath the sea, in addition to the tip that shows above the surface. In fact this is a reasonable analogy to make. Figure 3-1 may be seen as the iceberg of mental activity. This is an important point to make at the outset: that the theory of a constantly active "underground" mental life feeding into consciousness is generally recognized as necessary in order to account for the evolution of human thought and behavior as well as for the persistence of common, collective traits and themes. And many a philosopher-scientist holds the view that such a concept of *the unconscious* is also the only way to explain highly creative or original acts. Lancelot Whyte writes:

> The main purpose of this study . . . is to trace in more detail the progressive recognition in the systematic thought which developed after Galileo, Kepler and Descartes, that it is necessary to infer that *mental factors which are not directly available to our awareness* influence both our behaviour and the conscious aspects of our thought.[4]

The importance of presenting this comprehensive view of human awareness — unconscious and conscious both — will be realized when we develop the discussion in succeeding chapters and suggest the role played by unconscious mental factors in the creation of images.

You will observe in the diagram that the circle of consciousness is open in two places. These openings, at opposite poles, represent the two channels through which consciousness receives its impressions. Streaming in from the outside is the fantastic quantity of information provided by the senses. We see things, hear sounds, smell odors, touch surfaces, and taste food and drink. Without these sensory capabilities we would have no awareness of the world at any level; we would not even know the

---

[4] Lancelot Law Whyte, *The Unconscious Before Freud* (New York: Basic Books, Inc., 1962), p. 16. (Italics added.)

THE COMPASS POINTS OF CONSCIOUSNESS

form of our own bodies. The prime function of the senses is to tell us of the presence of things and provide information about their physical characteristics. (For the artist, it is obviously the visual sense that is all-important, but I have heard painters and sculptors say that sounds and smells stimulate and intensify the production of mental images. Music, for example, is a powerful stimulant. And sculptors are strongly affected by tactile sensations as they work and feel the form.) The senses feed the workings of consciousness which I have labeled *"deductive"* in the diagram; that is, the operation of the rational intellect and the objective feelings.

FIG. 3-1   Diagram of the Compass Points of Consciousness

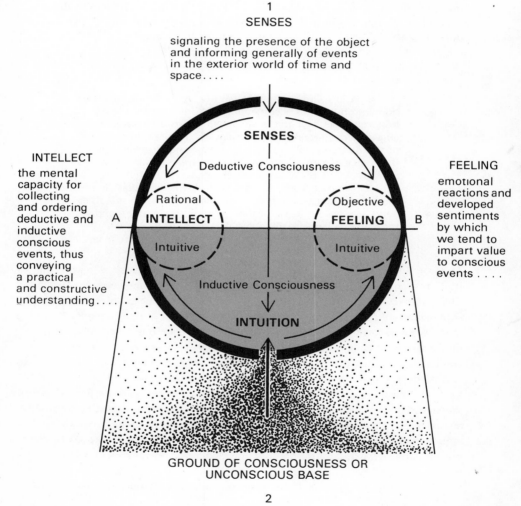

1
SENSES

signaling the presence of the object and informing generally of events in the exterior world of time and space....

SENSES

Deductive Consciousness

INTELLECT
the mental capacity for collecting and ordering deductive and inductive conscious events, thus conveying a practical and constructive understanding....

Rational
A   **INTELLECT**
Intuitive

Objective
FEELING   B
Intuitive

FEELING
emotional reactions and developed sentiments by which we tend to impart value to conscious events ....

Inductive Consciousness

INTUITION

GROUND OF CONSCIOUSNESS OR
UNCONSCIOUS BASE

2
INTUITION
signaling from within. A mode of experiencing thought and feeling independently of the senses... leading to an illumination or apprehension of truth and essential relationships, meaning, etc.

The second channel into consciousness lies at the other pole, and impressions of a different sort come via the intuition. Intuitive impressions reflect attitudes or states of being from within the self and serve the inductive consciousness — the operation of intuitive intellect and feeling. These internally generated currents are of two kinds. There are those which are true intuitive responses to external situations — intuitive attitudes which yield insight into events, independently of the deductive processes of the rational intellect — and those currents from the deep unconscious proper which, as we will see in the next chapter, operate quite arbitrarily and apparently have no relationship with time, place, or event. The intuition has sometimes been described as "instant wisdom," and if the function of the senses is to tell us of the presence of outside things, it seems that the intuition allows us to apprehend a different kind of truth. For it helps us discern why things are the way they are, enabling us to grasp the relationships between events and create associations which are not logically or sensorially apparent. Our intuitive "hunches" allow us to catch a glimpse from time to time of invisible forces and patterns in the overall scheme of things. Herbert Read writes:

> A distinction which runs through the whole development of
> human thought has become blurred during the past two
> hundred years. Implicit in all ancient philosophy, acknowl-
> edged by mediaeval scholastics and the natural philosophers
> of the Renaissance, and even by Locke and Newton, is a
> difference of kind, if not of value, between *wisdom* and
> *understanding*. By wisdom was meant an intuitive
> apprehension of truth, and the attitude involved was
> receptive or contemplative. . . . Understanding, on the other
> hand, was always a practical or constructive activity, and
> *ratio* was its name — the power by means of which we
> perceive, know, remember and judge sensible phenomena....[5]

The words "receptive" and "contemplative" suggest a consciousness waiting on itself, responsive to impressions from within which enjoy some degree of autonomy. These impressions are not necessarily linked chronologically to objective sensory experience, although they may well refer to some aspect of it. The mark of intuitive impressions is that they seem to spring from, and reflect, one's own values and distinctive insights. It is a mark of the artist to possess a powerful intuitive consciousness; it has often been described as spiritual in essence — as leading him to truths beyond the range of material, objective experience.

Our diagram, therefore, shows one arrow breaking through the gate of the senses and one through the gate of the intuition. But whereas we can be specific about the source of sensory information — the world itself — we can only talk vaguely about an inner source of psychic activity for intuitive impressions. In the diagram, the arrow of the intuition is embedded in the unconscious, and I have

---

[5] Sir Herbert Read, *The Forms of Things Unknown* (New York: Horizon Press, 1960), p. 15. Reprinted by permission of the publisher.

shown the contents of the unconscious ground clustering together as they move into consciousness. It may be that our intuition is partly grounded in the unconscious, or it may be that it represents a very deep level of consciousness; in any event, these two areas seem to merge imperceptibly into each other. The distinction between completely unconscious mental activity and more conscious intuitive processes is, as we have already said, that the latter do tend to relate to our awareness of events in time and place — whereas the unconscious proper can throw impressions into consciousness which have nothing to do with our direct experiences of living.

A breakthrough into consciousness at either pole is followed by a circulation of the impressions received. The arrows inside the circle in Figure 3-1 indicate this movement. For example, in watching a sea gull as it hovers and glides in the air currents, events are as follows. First, the physiological processes of sight are involved as light strikes the retina and passes, via the optic nerve, to the screen of the brain to form the mental image of the gull. It is not possible to say where these physiological processes stop and the psychological processes start — as one expert has said, apples and pears are not the same thing — but once the mechanical operation of the sense organs is complete, the subjective consciousness is immediately involved. The mental image of the gull is picked up by the intellect which relates it to past visual experience, allows it a particular degree of significance by comparison and association with prior data, and files the new information in the memory vaults. Thus, the intellect, through these ratiocinative processes, acts like a computer, ordering, associating, analyzing, judging, and remembering, and gives the present experience of the gull its particular significance in our knowledge systems. By these means, sensory experience takes on *meaning*; meaning which undergoes continual modification. But the image of the gull is also absorbed into the intellect's opposite pole, into the deep reservoir of our feelings. For an emotional response accompanies every sensory encounter with the world. And the range of feelings we undergo is considerable. As the sea gull performs so surely and gracefully we may feel pleasure at witnessing such efficient instinctual behavior; we may feel a frustration at not being able to move our own bodies in the air so naturally and beautifully; we may have a desire to understand the aerodynamics involved; or we may simply feel completely relaxed, passive, and emotionally still, at one with nature through a sympathetic response to the bird.

If you think about it, you will realize that an emotional attitude is part of every act of awareness. (Even as you read this book you will be feeling bored, or interested, or even mildly amused. . . .) As we live through the years, random emotional responses become organized into more specific patterns called sentiments, thus allowing an individual to develop a reasonably stable emotional personality. The feeling-sentiments play a dual role in consciousness. They move us to action — as fear will cause us to run and evade danger, or enjoyment of reading will drive us to read — and they cause us to determine the relative *values* of conscious events; how deeply significant they are to us ultra-personally. When we say that a person is "poorly motivated," we are saying that he does not feel strongly enough about the situation to act positively. The need to do something results from an emotional drive. The most rational scientist spending years on research, *likes* what he does. The intellect alone would not sustain the activity.

The orignial light sensations of the sea gull received by the retina have therefore created a complex situation in the viewer's subjective consciousness. Imagine that the brilliant Renaissance artist-scientist Leonardo da Vinci is watching the gull. (Even the mechanics of sight intrigued Leonardo, and the combination of his research into optics plus the natural endowment of an incredibly keen eye made him a formidable observer.) As he watches the bird the reasoning intellect is recording, associating, and analyzing the sense impressions; it is "putting two and two together" to comprehend how the gull performs its flights. Thus, as Leonardo construes the rules of aerodynamics, the bird's performance becomes especially meaningful. Simultaneously, the same sense impressions give rise to certain feelings which, for Leonardo, constitute a *passion* to know how things work. Leonardo's drawings are a result of this drive to understand and aid him in formulating his theories. It is important to keep in mind that without the drive of such strong feelings of curiosity, Leonardo da Vinci would not be the genius we know. Neither should we forget an important third factor — that of the intuition. Although the visual sense has activated intellect and feeling directly, intuitive understanding — if there is any — seems to come in its own time, in its own way. In some people intuitive attitudes seem almost nonexistent; they experience no insights which bypass the deductive processes and inform of hidden truths. We cannot say this about Leonardo. He was able to reach such inventive, original conclusions about the *modus operandi* of things that we must grant him the possession of not only a great rational intellect, but also a powerful intuitive intellect.

So we see in the diagram that the senses make a direct two-pronged attack on the centers of intellect and feeling and may manage a long-range foray to make contact with the intuition. We see also that the intuition bombards intellect and feeling centers from its own position. For we think of the senses as the sensors of external happenings, and of the intuition as the radar for the synthesizing or creative forces contained within the self. Consequently, it is necessary to qualify the titles "intellect" and "feeling" which describe the receiving centers for all these impressions. It is more accurate to talk about the *intuitive intellect* (the structure of knowledge developed by insight) and the *rational intellect* (the structure of knowledge developed by objective and deductive experience). Similarly, we could refer to intuitive feelings and objective feelings.

This presentation of consciousness appears deceptively clinical and tidy, whereas, in fact, the process is enormously complex. The translation of so many differing signals from so many different sources into cognitive and affective (feeling) attitudes is a marvelous physio-psychological operation. The unconscious itself remains a mystery. Earlier in this chapter I suggested how we might distinguish between intuitive responses and true unconscious stirrings, but it can be seen from the diagram how closely they are allied. The intuition may be the spokesman for the unconscious content — in which case it will operate independently of normal conscious experiences of events in time. On the other hand, an intuitive response is more usually part of normal consciousness — albeit at a deep level of awareness. Possibly the visual presentation of the problem in Figure 3-1 may present a clearer picture than any verbal discussion. Certainly we will return to it constantly as we continue to discuss aspects of consciousness in later chapters.

In Chapter 2, the analogy of the seesaw was used to illustrate the interaction between artist and object in the making of a work of art. I suggested that the created image could reflect two extreme possibilities. It could be completely faithful to the natural appearance of the object, thus embodying little of the man, or it could represent the man's attitude more completely and thus embody less of the natural reality of the object. These opposing possibilities produced the two extreme positions for the seesaw. Having briefly suggested how the artist's consciousness works, it can now be seen that the earlier seesaw diagrams were overly simplistic. For if we were to assign seesaw positions for "Beauty" and the "Beast" in the light of this knowledge of consciousness, the diagram would have to show the degree of intellect or feeling behind the image and whether a particular emphasis of one or the other relates to the deductive or inductive modes of consciousness.

Let us look at Aphrodite again and see how she relates to the diagram of consciousness in Figure 3-1. It seems fairly obvious that Praxiteles was navigating primarily by the visual sense and the rational intellect. Yet we must allow that the Greek attitude regarding mathematical harmonies and truths is, in itself, partly

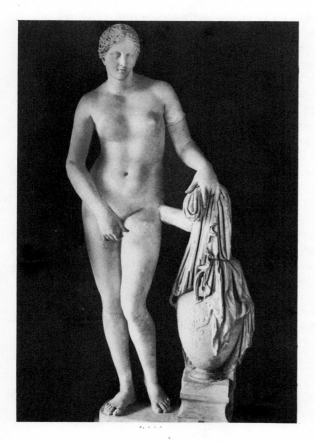

intuitive; therefore, the intuitive intellect and feelings are also playing a part in the creation of this work. But I think most of us would agree that the sculptor's personal feelings toward woman are not revealed. The image of Aphrodite is very impersonal. I find the "pulse" of the work to be concentrated around the left-hand side of the diagrammatic circle of consciousness — embracing both deductive and inductive "halves" with the emphasis on the deductive.

A similar diagrammatic analysis shows a reversal of this situation for the primitive Egyptian figurine. As I see it, the primary trigger for the release of this image is an unconscious force. Gathered in the unconscious ground are powerful dispositions for imagistic experience of the feminine goddess theme which, from time to time, may constellate into consciousness. The clay figurine herself is a concrete example of such an illumination transformed into a work of art. Therefore, I suggest that the pulse of the work may be found around the right-hand side of the circle, embracing both inductive and deductive aspects, but with a strong emphasis on the former. The artist would seem to be navigating primarily by his intuitive feelings, which are activated as unconscious dispositions for the theme of the feminine break through into consciousness. Yet the visual sense is involved deductively at some stage, for visual experience of the object (woman) has obviously played a part in shaping the figurine. But it is my view that this sensory information merely serves to help fashion and validate a mental image which has already been discovered intuitively.

I should say that interpretations such as these are academic; they only serve to aid an understanding of the *process*, not of the image itself. In attempting to discuss the forces that drive men to make art, we are dealing with a most complex weave. There are many levels of "truth" involved and many levels of conscious and unconscious experience. But the image which affects us strongly symbolizes the less tangible, ineffable strands of this weave which we realize cannot be "known" intellectually through verbal exposition; otherwise man would have neither need nor reason to make plastic statements. Consequently, in the final analysis, we must rely on our own inner eye and hope that it reflects some connoisseurship and sensibility.

THE IMAGINATIVE CONSCIOUSNESS

The question now is: "When do we consider the normal processes of consciousness to have become that rarer phenomenon, the imaginative consciousness?" Let me repeat Naum Gabo's thoughts on this:

> The artist's mind is a turbulent sea full of all kinds of impressions, responses and experiences as well as feelings and emotions. Some experts on art assert that the artist does not really have more of these emotions and feelings and impressions than the ordinary man who is not an artist. This may be true or false, but what they apparently fail to see and to assert is that in the artist these feelings and responses are in a more agitated state. He is more concerned with them, and the urge to express these experiences is more intense in him than it is in the ordinary man. And that, I suppose, is the reason why the artist's mind is not only more turbulent but sometimes, alas, troublesome also. . . .[6]

If we substitute the word "consciousness" for "mind" throughout this statement, we realize that Gabo might be describing our diagram of consciousness. But at the same time, he is making an important distinction between the conscious life of the "ordinary man" and that of the artist. The difference, as Gabo describes it, is the difference between the normal every day consciousness and the intensity of awareness that distinguishes the man of vision. The imagination is, in part, dependent upon the capacity of the mental life to proceed beyond the simple recognition of an a-priori objective fact. And the degree to which the subjective consciousness is involved after the first act of recognition determines the level of originality or uniqueness of the imaginative experience. For, after all, to imagine is to do precisely what the word implies — to experience mental images or realizations. These images may be intellectually organized as intuitive or rational ideas, or they may present themselves on the feeling side of consciousness as very positive value judgments, moods or "dream-feelings." If every man possesses some degree of imagination, which we must surely admit, the *creative* man is distinguished by the intense sharpness and quality of his ideas, by the mental and emotional agitation they cause him, by the urge to relieve the internal pressure through some formative

---

[6] Naum Gabo, *Of Divers Arts,* p. 6.

action, and by the ability of the image he creates to illuminate a broader spectrum of consciousness. For those men of powerful imagination, an event which affects the subjective consciousness in this way assumes the quality and nature of the revelation — a disclosure of previously unknown realities.

Earlier I used the phrase, "the ideas and feelings present in a state of heightened consciousness" (page 3), and the full meaning of this remark may now be clearer. It goes without saying that when the creative artist experiences any combination of sensory and intuitive impressions, activating any combination of intellectual or feeling images, he is navigating with a very sensitive compass. Unlike the ordinary man, all four compass points of his consciousness are capable of operating at more than usually intense levels. Throughout this discussion we have talked of the mental life and suggested that every conscious experience becomes ultimately something "known" in the mind. Even physical things such as pain as well as general feelings and moods become mental events in this sense. This chapter may have helped to suggest the range of interaction between the compass points of consciousness which lead to such an omnifarious mental response. But some readers will have been wondering how this terminology embraces those aspects of the process of knowing that we have called unconscious. For to talk about the mental life is to refer to a conscious process. Therefore, it will be better in future to use the term, *the life of the psyche,* which has a much more comprehensive connotation. The psyche connotes the total self; it refers to both conscious and unconscious mental activity. And if we need to distinguish further between the artist and the ordinary man, I would suggest that we look to the potency of the artist's unconscious and intuitive inspiration to help explain and identify the phenomenon of the creative personality.

We conclude this chapter by referring to four illustrations — three drawings and one painting — all images of animals. Allowing that there are many ways of looking at these works, I am using them here to illustrate these theories of consciousness in terms of each artist's discernible attitude to his animal motif; the reader may then try for himself to assess the possible combinations of sense, intuition, intellect, and feeling as suggested by Figure 3-1.

Albrecht Dürer's watercolor drawing of a hare (Figure 3-2), is remarkably naturalistic — the hare itself seems to sit there on the page before you. Dürer has observed with a keen eye and intellectually organized his visual impressions to recreate the animal as his senses perceive it. Although the drawing conveys something of the "sympathy" felt by man for animals, I think it is obvious that the artist displays more rational objectivity than strong feeling. There is great attention to detail, displaying the same kind of scientific accuracy that one finds in the drawings of Leonardo da Vinci. All in all, the compass needle of Dürer's consciousness seems to swing between the senses and the intellect, despite the odd flickerings it may make to the other points on the dial. Contrasted with Dürer's hare, the pen and wash drawing of a tiger by Eugéne Delacroix (Figure 3-3) is more expressive. We can see that the artist was not interested in conveying every detail — in making a highly organized analytical drawing of the animal. The image is

FIG. 3-2　Albrecht Dürer
(1471-1528). *Hare* 1502. Watercolor. Vienna, Albertina Museum

executed with rapid and nervous movements of the brush which capture the slinky
alertness of the tiger's movement. One feels the "tigerness" of the drawing even
though Delacroix does not give us comprehensive information about the visual
appearance of the tiger down to the very last hair. We are affected by the artist's
excitement for his subject, expressed through the vitality of the brush's jabbing
and stroking marks. Our feelings are also stirred by the tigerish menace implied in
the exaggerated, powerful hindquarters of the beast. And although the viewer
might feel that the compass needle flickered all round the compass when Delacroix

FIG. 3-3　Eugéne Delacroix (1779-1863). *Tiger.* Pen and Wash drawing. Bayonne, Museum
Bonnat. Photograph, Archives Photographiques

made this drawing, I would conclude that it eventually moved between the senses and the feelings. Visual experience of the tiger serves to allow this artist to express an emotional response rather than pursue a rational inquiry into the nature of the animal's form.

So what are we to say about Picasso's bull (Figure 3-4)? It is certainly less like the real thing than either of the other two drawings, and we must conclude that visual observation of the object did not play an important part in the experience. The bull in nature hardly seems present at all. Yet the basic shape of the bull is there. We know that Picasso has been involved with bulls much of his life. At this stage he needs no model. His drawing is an intuitive response to the animal. But is is so explicitly organized and the elemental bull-form is so clear that we must assign the drawing to the intuitive intellect. No doubt intuitive feelings are involved also, as are some residual sense impressions, but I see the compass needle hovering in the inductive consciousness between the intuition and the intellect. Like all intuitive images, this drawing makes an ambiguous statement. It relates to something we know called a bull; it also touches on the undefinable reverberations this object produces deep in consciousness. Jean Dubuffet's cow (Figure 3-5), like Picasso's bull, is far removed from nature. But the painting shows none of the elemental simplification which the intuitive geometry of Picasso brings to the bull drawing.

FIG. 3–4   **Pablo Picasso (b. 1881–   ).** *Bull* **1946. Lithograph.** Permission French Reproduction Rights Inc. Photograph Bibliotheque Nationale, Cabinet des Estampes

FIG. 3–5   Jean Dubuffet (b. 1901–   ). *La belle ecornée* **1954. Oil on canvas.** Collection
G. Limbor, Paris. Courtesy of the artist

The cow's form is confused and awkward rather than clear and basic. Still, I
believe that Dubuffet's painting springs from the inductive consciousness no less
than does Picasso's bull. Yet the form of Dubuffet's image lacks the intuitive logic
that makes Picasso's bull so intellectually credible; it seems to be more spontaneously
shaped from an intuitive feeling for the cow theme. Here we have a true dream-cow,
intellectually alogical and unbelievable, yet expressing poetically a convincing
feeling and mood. Allowing the compass needle a few wild gyrations before settling
down, I sense that it finally hovered in the inductive consciousness, between the
gate of the intuition and the receptive intuitive feelings.

IV

THE UNCONSCIOUS AND THE PERSISTENCE OF ELEMENTAL IMAGERY

We have likened consciousness to that part of the iceberg showing above the surface of the water and have suggested that the iceberg's invisible base corresponds to a reservoir of human resources of which we are not aware, known as the unconscious. It therefore becomes a matter of particular interest when artists regard their work as a *fait accompli* and themselves as merely an instrument of the creative process. Speaking from personal experience, I would have to agree that at times an unconscious factor does take over. After completing their best works, many artists have been unable to understand how or why the image has taken on a particular form or quality. On some occasions it seems that from the first, the emerging image has dictated the nature of its own genesis and development. The American painter, Mark Rothko, said:

> The most important tool the artist fashions through
> constant practice is faith in his ability to produce miracles
> when they are needed. Pictures must be miraculous: the
> instant one is completed, the intimacy between the creation
> and the creator is ended. He is an outsider. The picture
> must be for him, as for anyone experiencing it later, a
> revelation, an unexpected and unprecedented resolution of
> an eternally familiar need.[1]

There is often an element of surprise present in the accomplishment of truly creative acts — a standing back by the artist and a silent exclamation: "How on earth did I do that!" To lose one's self-awareness in the making of a work of art is to become tuned in to a guiding and controlling force not present in the routine operations of consciousness. We have no reason for thinking that this unconscious aspect of the creative process is a new development. On the contrary, our knowledge

---

[1] Eric Protter, *Painters on Painting* (New York: Grosset & Dunlap, 1963), p. 238.

of primitive cultures indicates that it has long been a powerful factor stimulating the imagination — an unconscious drive that distinguished artist and shaman from the ordinary man. As we become familiar with more and more objects of art, we discover certain similarities between images which are thousands of years and miles apart. One way to explain these similarities is to take up Rothko's suggestion that the artist is "an outsider" in the creation of his own work — and so surmise that the twentieth-century artist is prey to unconscious forces which are not dissimilar to those affecting his prehistoric colleague. As to the content of these forces, we are led by the visual evidence to suggest that they possess some common elements which manifest themselves the world over. Despite regional and cultural influences, these archetypal similarities appear in the plastic arts irrespective of historical period.

THE CREATIVE UNCONSCIOUS

We are talking now about a source of creative energy that has fed the artist's imaginative visions for perhaps 40,000 years. It is the source which Roger Fry describes as "the substratum of all the emotional colors of life . . . something which underlies all the particular and specialized emotions of actual life."[2] (The reader may recognize this as a description of the unconscious ground supporting the circle in Figure 3-1.) As an underground river in limestone country can burst forth and become a raging surface torrent after heavy rains, so, apparently, can a deep unconscious current thrust images into consciousness and drive the artist to action. This is a hypothetical current about which we can prove nothing, but we can suggest its probability by pointing to certain elemental aspects of imaginative experience and behavior which have persisted throughout man's history. For example, clinical psychiatric experience has shown that despite ethnic origin or cultural conditioning, men dream the same kind of dreams during sleep; the descriptions of men's dreams in history reveal distinct similarities to our own dreams. Also, any comparative study of mythological and religious systems far apart in time and space indicates the presence of common themes. There are virgin births, violent deaths and resurrections, and stories with a common theme explaining the genesis of the world. Even the supposedly sophisticated man living in a contemporary Western city is not immune from the need to live life "mythologically" in terms of escapist rituals and a wide variety of religious theories; neither can he avoid the strange dream images that break forth as he sleeps.

The unconscious may be likened to a ready-made storeroom and powerhouse combined. When the artist is affected by the current from this source, the rational consciousness retreats and has little say in the shaping of the image and little control over the tide of pure feeling. Further, the artist cannot control the mechanism by which these primary deposits of imaginative experience move into consciousness. It is not possible for him to *will* these elemental images to come or to suppress their

---

[2] Sir Herbert Read, *The Meaning of Art* (London: Faber & Faber, 1946), p. 64.

coming. They operate clandestinely across the border separating the unconscious from conscious awareness, and even that alert border guard known as "reason" seems powerless to control the infiltration. For there are times during the creation of a work when the artist finds his mind empty and all objective or externally stimulated feeling suspended. In such a vacuum, the act of drawing, painting, or modeling becomes an ideationless, trance-like activity. Yet it is at a time like this that the content of the substratum breaks through, and the man works under the compelling influence of an image which is slowly developing and making itself known to him. Then, as Rothko says, the finished result is as much a revelation for the artist as it is for anyone else.

In Chapter 3 we made a distinction between two aspects of consciousness — the deductive and the inductive — and discussed the difficulty of distinguishing between intuitive mental activity which is linked to sensory experience and completely autonomous intuition springing from unconscious sources which is completely autonomous in its operation. The distinction should now become clearer as we proceed in this chapter to discuss the elemental ground of the unconscious. Today, we think of ourselves as rational beings, and certainly we have moved far in this direction from our primitive ancestors. But it is important to realize that the unconscious base of an artist's emotional and imagistic life can remain unaffected by the development of objective, sophisticated powers of reasoning. Although our culture's present scientific involvement with natural phenomena results from logical and analytical methods of procedural reasoning, for many an artist today the nonrational, elemental core of the imagination is, internally, as strong as ever.

It is the art of our century which has rediscovered, or re-released, this basic and universal source of imaginative experience. Consequently, an important exhibition of contemporary art seen in London a few years ago was named "40,000 Years of Modern Art." In his book, *The Eternal Present,* Professor Giedion devotes many chapters to this problem. He writes:

> Both above and below the surface of our present age there is a new demand for continuity. It has again become apparent that human life is not limited to a single life-span but goes far beyond. It is as impossible to sever its contacts with the past as to prevent its contacts with the future. Something lives within us which forms part of the very backbone of human dignity. I call this the demand for continuity. . . .
> . . . . Contemporary art was born out of the urge for the elemental. The artist plunged into the depths of human experience. A real inner affinity suddenly appeared between the longings of the man of today and the longings of primæval man, crystallized in signs and symbols on the cavern walls.[3]

---

[3] S. Giedion, *The Eternal Present: The Beginnings of Art,* Bollingen Series XXXV, vol. 1. (© 1962 by the Trustees of the National Gallery of Art, Washington, D.C.), p. xx. Reprinted by permission of Princeton University Press.

When we look at Jean Dubuffet's painting of a bearded head (Figure 4-1) and see that it was made in 1959, any thoughts that art should evolve rationally, parallel with the development of the objective and scientific consciousness, receive a bit of a jolt. For it would seem that this contemporary image should antedate the early Egyptian figurine, rather than appear 6,000 years later. It is roughly fashioned, discounts rational perception, and shows no concern for concepts of human beauty or formal harmonies. Does this painting reflect man's intellectual growth from caveman to astronaut? Obviously not; instead it is an example of the modern elementalism described by Professor Giedion. The image testifies to the persistence in consciousness of irrational dream states in which the natural reality of things is not involved. Whatever image of man is projected by Dubuffet's painting, it embraces feelings of man out of time, of an imaginative continuum or principle which persists in the face of death and history and which, like the sphinx of ancient Egypt, remains inscrutable.

It is not difficult to find visual support for Giedion's suggestion that "contemporary art was born out of the urge for the elemental." Look for a moment at the paleolithic head from the cavern of Les Combarelles in the Dordogne area of France (Figure 4-2). This primitive head is incised in the rock with a deeply cut outline. It shows some similarity to Dubuffet's head, being broad-topped, angular, and roughly polyhedron in shape. Both heads possess wide-open, staring eyes situated in a flat expanse of face, while a simple linear treatment serves to define

FIG. 4–2   Incised Head from Les Combarelles (Dordogne). From *The Eternal Present,* by S. Giedion. Bollingen Foundation, New York. Reproduced by permission of Princeton University Press

the nose and mouth. But it is the eyes that dominate and hold one. The eyes have long been recognized as the dominant feature of the face; as the "windows of the soul," having the power to hypnotize, to command, and to express the intensity of emotion and will. The *eyes that watch* appear constantly in all forms of art. Whether they be the eyes of the political "Big Brother" from the campaign posters, the eyes of a twelfth-century "Christ in Glory" in the tympanum of a Romanesque cathedral, or the eyes of this 25,000-year-old face from Les Combarelles, we feel a little uneasy in their presence. There are other roughly hewn heads of the paleolithic era in the caves of Europe, many with open staring eyes. This characteristic treatment of the face persists in the art of many cultures when it is required that the image possess psychological or mystical authority. It is possible that Jean Dubuffet's painting would have possessed considerable authority for the prehistoric cave dweller had it appeared on the rock wall. For there is a primitive and elemental power to its watching.

The drawing in Figure 4–3 was made by a six-year-old girl. Its similarity to the paleolithic head in Figure 4–2 can be clearly seen. The rough polyhedron shape, the big round eyes, and the lines for nose and mouth are common to both images. The interesting thing is that the child named her drawing "Ghostie." Now the essential meaning of the word "ghost" is breath, spirit, or soul, and I do not know how the child understood the word. But I did watch her make the drawing and could see that making the drawing and *putting the name to it* were one and the same operation. For when the drawing was complete, she did not pause to consider what name she should give it but reached immediately for a pencil and wrote the title spontaneously. Then, and only then, did she relax, lean back in her chair, and contemplate

THE UNCONSCIOUS AND ELEMENTAL IMAGERY

her work with a great deal of satisfaction. Normally the title of a work is irrelevant in terms of appreciating its plastic and psychological eloquence; yet, in this case, word and image were synchronized as one expressive act. If we accept this as signifying some integral relationship between image and title, the word "ghostie" tells us something about the content of the child's imagination as she made the drawing. Possibly she was thinking consciously of the idea of a ghost in the popular sense, yet it is also possible that she was moved by unconscious and elemental attitudes to life and death — by the thought of the spirit as distinct from the body — an idea which, from time to time, haunts us all.

We do not know what compelled the cave artist to carve his image or whether he "named" it with any sounds once it was done. Neither do we know what inner necessity provoked Jean Dubuffet to shape his unreal and enigmatic figure. Still, despite the absence of records or statements, the *visual* similarities are real enough to indicate some common imaginative experience for the three artists concerned. Perhaps we should seek the clues to this problem in the work of gifted child-artists like the little girl who drew *Ghostie*. Up to the age of seven or eight such children are not perceptually involved with the world — they are not visually clarifying the form and scale of objects. Instead, they tend when drawing to project their own private fancies upon natural objects and to treat them very simply as basic shapes capable of being easily felt in the hands. In teaching the highly imaginative child it becomes obvious that drawing represents an invitation to daydream. And many of these daydream drawings reveal a strangely pantheistic world — a world in which trees and flowers and rocks are given a personality which is sometimes human, sometimes nonhuman. Fairies, demons, and kindred spirits animate the still forms of nature. Even if the work does not go this far, the drawings show a graphically vitalistic attitude towards nature. During a discussion of children's art with the

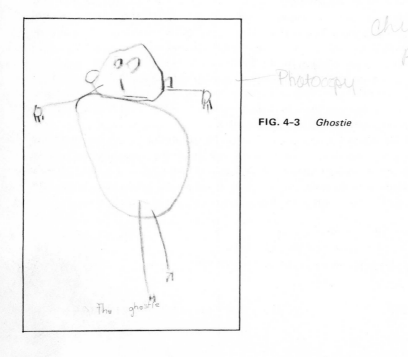

FIG. 4–3 *Ghostie*

English painter, John Piper, he commented: "Yes, I have always thought that child-artists are the natural enemies of adult ones. . . ,"[4] In one very important sense he was right. For these children appear to operate as artists without any act of will — as mediums through which a fantasy imagination flows freely. Adults, on the other hand, are impeded by their selfconsciousness and their acts of rational perception. It is not so easy for the adult artist to tap the rich veins of fantasy. Unfortunately, nonrational dreams and imaginings seem to be self-generating; the artist cannot prepare for work and call them to the surface at will. Some young children, however, can shift into a trance-like communion with themselves remarkably easily, and it is then when they experience the imaginative contents of this inner world.

If these observations present a reasonably accurate description of one aspect of child art, we can use the drawing of "the ghostie" to suggest that the three images of the head (Figures 4-1 and 4-3) spring from a common imaginative root. The thousands of years that separate these works do not seem to have modified either the vitality or the persistence of the theme — the ubiquitous watching eyes of unseen presences and spirit forces. For in a treatise on the evolution of ape and man a well-known physical anthropologist says, almost with surprise, of man: "This creature lives on dreams."[5]

In 1937 Pablo Picasso was working on the now famous painting, *Guernica.*[6] This is an impassioned protest against the indiscriminate bombing of the town of Guernica during the Spanish Civil War, a cry against the viscious and evil forces that cause humanity so much suffering. My intention is not to discuss the complex symbolism of this large and powerful work but to examine the horse's head reproduced here which is similar to that occupying a central position in the painting. It brays a protest no less anguished than that we see in the *Horse Head* image shown in Figure 4-4. Made in May 1937, this study for the horse in the painting proper is a *tour de force* of outrage; its power is compelling. In fable, legend, and myth, the horse symbolizes magical potency, wind, sea, fire, and light — sometimes the cosmos itself. Even today we regard horses as "noble" creatures. In seeing its form so terribly distorted we feel its pain and its violation and are uneasy, not only because of the outrage suffered by the animal, but also because of the wider, symbolic implications. For we are aware of principles involved that transcend particular incidents of suffering; of darkness and evil overcoming virtue and light, or of blind destruction opposed to the vital movements of life. And it is right that we should be awed by the sound issuing from those jaws.

Many aspects of the painting work together to produce these strong effects. There is the painful, upward twisting of the head, with the huge nostrils distended in fear — the three teeth clinging so precariously to the lower jaw, while those above are attached unnaturally alongside the nostrils, suggesting a physical disintegration and ultimate metamorphosis — the fearful pinpoint eyes as consciousness flees — the

---

[4] Conversation, March 17, 1957.

[5] F. Sierksma, *The Gods As We Shape Them*, p. 16.

[6] In the collection of the Museum of Modern Art, New York.

FIG. 4-4   Pablo Picasso (b. 1881-   ). *Horse Head* 1937. **Oil on canvas.** Collection Picasso. Permission French Reproduction Rights, Inc.

rigidly paralyzed ears and straw-like mane. Dominating all is the agonizingly distorted open jaw and the spearing tongue which transfixes it. The horse gives a final cry, and the usually flaccid tongue stiffens to become a sword, thrusting out and forcing open the jaws in the last extremity of pain.

Some eleven hundred years before Picasso chose an animal-head motif to convey his attitude to war and despoilation, Scandinavian artists were placing similar forms on the prows of their Viking ships. The wooden animal head of about 825 A.D. (see Figure 4-5) found in a buried Viking ship at Oseberg in southern Norway, was also used to express the theme of war — but to declare war rather than decry it. Nevertheless, despite the difference of intention, we can see that the common theme of war not only occasioned the choice of similar motifs, but also inspired the imagination to *shape* both animal heads in a similar way. Despite differences of time, place, and intention, these images have much in common. We notice that the Viking animal's nostrils are also flared, that the inside of the wide-open mouth is ridged like that of Picasso's horse, and that the teeth also protruded menacingly. These distortions of the organic parts contrast strongly with the semigeometric patterning of the rest of the head (derived from the linear interlacings of designs in metal), and violate our normal perceptual experience of natural animals. Picasso achieves the same kind of visual shock by imposing a frontal view of the horse's nostrils onto a profile view of the jaw in order to violate natural perception. Again, in turning to the Viking animal, we are struck by the upward

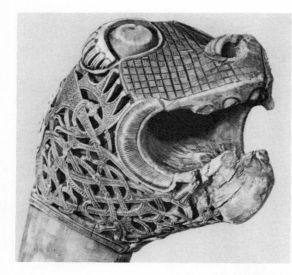

FIG. 4-5   **Animal Head from the Ose-berg Ship-Burial. c. 825 A.D. Wood.** University Museum of Antiquities, Oslo

thrust of the head, the open jaws with the exaggerated semicircular sweep at the corners of the mouth, and the eyes which stare blindly upwards. These characteristics are also to be found in Picasso's image, although in a more distorted form. Now look closely at the Scandinavian animal's open mouth and you will notice that the lines of the upper and lower jaw are not parallel, but spread wider apart towards the far side of the mouth. Although less severely developed, this unnatural twist of the jaw is similar to the twisted distortion Picasso imparts to the horse's mouth. And it produces the same result, imparting a physical tension to the "flesh" of the image, and a psychological tension in the beholder who sees a threat to life in both creatures.

Snarling animals such as these raised themselves from the prows of Viking ships and served a threefold purpose. They provided a figurehead to complete the main post of the prow; they acted symbolically to transform an ordinary ship into a threatening and alien monster which spelled death and unvanquishable power to those who waited on the beaches; and they aided the morale of the Viking by transforming the warrior crew into supermen.

War and aggression, then, are the common themes for both Picasso and his Viking colleagues. Both images are capable of striking fear and foreboding into those who see them. And both artists use an animal-head motif. Yet it is obvious that the Viking beast is the aggressor, while the Picasso creature is the victim. The reasons for this are not difficult to find. First, we are able to identify Picasso's animal head quite positively as that of a horse, and I believe that we still regard the horse in the traditional manner — it still stands for the principles of nobility and gentleness — and as the creature who travels fast over land, or flys supernaturally as the winged horse Pegasus, its vitalistic movement symbolizes the physical and spiritual unity of earth and cosmos. On the other hand, no such easy identification is possible with the Viking animal. Is it serpent, dragon, tiger. . . ? Its very ambiguity evokes the fear of the unknown . . . of the monster coming from the dark waters, suggesting the primordial and blind movements of life rather than sensitive and intelligent consciousness. There is no soaring toward the light of the sun for this creature. Second, there is a considerable difference in the degree of distortion employed by the two artists. Picasso imposes such a violent degree of distortion on the horse's jaw and nostrils and twists the parts so strongly against each other that we cannot help but see the horse as the victim of some deadly outrage and fear. In contrast, the Viking animal is not suffering in this way, for the degree of distortion has not gone far enough. Only if the monster's snarl were to turn into the distressing shriek of the horse, causing the form to be pulled more severely from the natural, would it become a similar victim. Also, it is difficult to avoid the implications of the spearing tongue as it forces open the horse's jaws. Rather than giving a menacing appearance to the head — for it could suggest a spear thrusting towards the enemy — it has the reverse effect. The horse is impaled on its own tongue in the body's final agony. But in the empty, growling throat of the Viking animal, there is no such threat to itself.

Yet, in recognizing these differences that allow one image to represent the victim and the other the aggressor, we cannot overlook the fact that violence and death constitute the common themes with which they are concerned. And the interesting fact remains that a twentieth century artist and one from the ninth century employ an iconography that is similar in so many basic details. We can only speculate about the nature of the psychological energy which delivers the animal-head form to the creative imagination in both ninth and twentieth centuries — delivers it as a motif capable of conveying the violence of being. But poetry, myth, and art seem to be continuously concerned with imagery in which the animal plays an important symbolic and expressive role. Given the two extremes in our thoughts about life, of a purpose, harmony, and serenity in the natural order on the one hand, and a chaotic, meaningless, and violent struggle on the other, it is the animal body which becomes the vehicle to carry the feelings and ideas. Man's long association with animals cannot be denied and we shall see in Chapter 10 how preoccupied with animals was the mind of the palaeolithic cave painter, who was the first significant artist in prehistory. And I believe that in our own time we still preserve an elemental and nonlogical link with the mystery of nature and life through our relationship with animals.

But we should realize how far Picasso has strayed from the sophisticated tradition of Greek and Renaissance art which has supported the Western artist for so many years — how much he has moved to a "naive" or elemental form of expression. To see how far he has strayed from either an aesthetic or a naturalistic concern in rendering his horse, we should study the horse-head illustrated in Figure 4-6. This classical Greek piece by Pheidias and his assistants was positioned on the East pediment of the Parthenon between 438 and 431 B.C. It is the *Horse of Selene*, the Moon, who descended with her horses at one end of the pediment, as Helios, the Sun, ascended at the other. It is, without doubt, a noble marble head. The subtlety of the modeling endows the marble with all the animated and

vibrant life of the horse in nature. At the same time there is an ideal grace given to the form, and, once again, we see Greek aestheticism in action. After Picasso's violent distortion of nature, the Greek horse seems to be almost the real thing even though we are aware of the subtle changes from the natural which produce its ideal elegance. The *Horse of Selene*, as an object of high Greek art, represents a sophisticated concept, namely, the creation of a dynamic grace and beauty in form. In making this comparison we see that, in this instance, Picasso is no Greek. He is more closely related to the Viking artist inasmuch as both horse and sea dragon are *expressive* images. That is to say, they spring from an urge to release and shape strong feelings and elemental attitudes. (Or, to use the terminology established in Chapter 2, art which follows the Greek concepts of formal order and reasonable harmonies and proportions is described as Classical, while art that is expressive is described as Romantic. But as I suggested before, we shoud not place too much reliance on these labels; there is often some overlapping present in any one image.)

THE CONTINUUM OF DISCOVERY

Professor Giedion's statement, "Contemporary art was born out of the urge for the elemental. . . ." is an important comment on the often misunderstood sculptures and paintings of the twentieth century. For it is the art of our own time which has rediscovered some of our deepest, most elemental secrets. Today, a large body of public opinion still errs in the belief that art should idealize nature or be faithful to the natural appearance of things and produce images which are vaguely and sometimes sentimentally regarded as beautiful. Unforfortunately, the word "beautiful" has lost its classical meaning, is frivolously used in commercial jargon, and has become synonymous with that rather derogatory word "nice." This narrow attitude is the somewhat spurious result of a classical tradition which has remained uppermost for many years. Greek art and theory have so strongly influenced the European art scene since the rise of Italian painting in the fourteenth century that they represent the democratic norm for the average layman! Even in the late nineteenth century, after several seventeenth-century resurgences of expressive or romantic imagery, the taste of the general public was still for neoclassical works.

Henry Moore is a contemporary British sculptor of great renown. One of his early works is the alabaster peice entitled *Composition* (Figure 4-7). The similarity of this work to our old friend the predynastic Egyptian figurine (made between 6,000 and 4,000 B.C.) is striking. As a visual reinforcement of our thesis that a strong, elemental link exists between primitive and contemporary art, Moore's sculpture perhaps says more than all the words in this chapter. Therefore I will not dissipate the effect with a prolonged discussion. It is only necessary to point out that much of Henry Moore's work embodies strong feelings and attitudes he holds for the theme of "the feminine." Here in Figure 4-7 is the perennial fertility goddess, revealing herself in the twentieth century as impressively as she did 8,000 years ago in lands far distant from Britain.

The work of many contemporary artists shows that the wheel has come full circle. After serving a number of sophisticated masters, the plastic arts are again involved in expressing the surges of primitive and elemental imaginative experience. There is one particularly important conclusion to draw from this development. Hitherto, we have suggested that because of the intense activity of the life of the psyche (the conscious and unconscious mental life), the artist is a man apart. But we now see that he is moved by themes which have also been part of other artist's lives and is, at times, shaping collective experience rather than specifically private

link between past & present modes of imaginative thought & expression

FIG. 4-7   Henry Moore (b. 1898-   ). *Composition* **1931.** Courtesy of the artist

experience. If we allow him the distinct individuality that comes from the vitality of his consciousness (as discussed in Chapter 3), we realize also that he can be an impersonal medium — a channel through which unconscious, universal life forces are expressed and shaped. The persistence of certain themes in the long history of art and the fact that a man today will respond to an image 20,000 years old suggests that mankind shares certain common experiences of an inner, psychological sort. In Chapter 5, we will delve into the workings of the creative imagination to capture the flavor of the force we call inspiration. There we will see the historical constancy of the relationship existing between the deep unconscious life of the artist and the plastic forms it supports. In his essay, *Concerning the Spiritual in Art*, published in 1912, Wassily Kandinsky wrote:

> When there is, as sometimes happens, a similarity of inner
> direction in an entire moral and spiritual milieu, a
> similarity of ideals, at first closely pursued but later lost
> to sight, a similarity of "inner mood" between one period
> and another, the logical consequence will be a revival of the
> external forms which served to express those insights in the
> earlier age. This may account partially for our sympathy
> and affinity with and our comprehension of the work of
> primitives. [7]

"Pictures," said Mark Rothko, "must be miraculous. . . ." When art can communicate across thousands of years, it is not difficult to agree with him. But we will let a scientist have the last word. René Dubos, a microbiologist, writes:

> The parallelism of the agricultural, social, and artistic
> achievements in prehistoric America with those of Africa,
> Asia, and Europe constitutes perhaps the best evidence for
> the unity of man's nature. It proves that the most
> fundamental and universal characteristics of the human
> mind were fully developed by the time Paleolithic man first
> penetrated to the American continent and did not undergo
> significant changes during the thousands of years of isolation
> that followed. . . . [8]

---

[7] Wassily Kandinsky, "Concerning the Spiritual in Art," from *Documents of Modern Art,* vol. 5. (New York: George Wittenborn, Inc., n.d.).

[8] René Dubos, *So Human an Animal* (New York: Scribner's, 1968), p. 49.

V

INSPIRATION

"This is a critical, not a poetic age," I am told. "Inspiration is out. Contemporary poems must reflect the prevailing analytic spirit." But I am old-fashioned enough to demand *báraka*, an inspirational gift not yet extinct, which defies critical analysis.[1]

So spoke the poet Robert Graves to the Oxford University Poetry Society. I make no apologies for quoting this statement a second time, for it raises the issue of artistic or poetic inspiration, while at the same time stating the contemporary objection to it. It is true that for much of this century the so-called gift of inspiration has been suspect. Even artists and poets have shunned it, believing that twentieth-century rational existentialism, scientific positivism, and egalitarianism have exposed it as a latter-day romantic fallacy. Yet despite the fashionable analytical and critical mood and the proliferation of mediocre paintings, poems, and sculptures, an elite group of artists still produce highly original work which transcends the limitations of established critical standards. I feel sure that none of them would object to Robert Graves being their spokesman. These men who open our eyes to some of the profound and enduring values of human experience are not to be found in large numbers. E. M. Forster, the late British novelist, once remarked that the constant presence throughout history of a small group of men of genius gave him hope for mankind. And Eugéne Delacroix, the nineteenth-century French painter, writes in his *Journal* that "men of genius have a way utterly peculiar to themselves of seeing things."[2] In living amongst writers and painters of merit — and this has been my privilege — one is struck by the prevalence of a constant admission. The talk that goes on until the early hours of the morning discloses that there are moments, sometimes frequent, often infrequent, when one or another has been possessed by a strange state of consciousness. On these occasions the artists have been taken over by a range of feeling and thought so compelling in intensity that the sense of normal reality is completely lost.

In the year 1913, the Russian painter Kasimir Malevich (1878–1935) exhibited a picture which consisted of only a black square on a white ground.

---

[1] Robert Graves, *Oxford Addresses on Poetry,* p. 2.

[2] Eugéne Delacroix, *The Journal* (New York: Grove Press, 1961), p. 46.

It was one of the early showings of nonobjective art and, as we would expect, drew a withering criticism from both public and critics. Malevich's essay *Suprematism,* published in Germany in 1927, reveals the changes which he experienced in consciousness . . . in movement from a "normal" sense of reality that led him to make this painting.

> The ascent to the heights of non-objective art is arduous and painful . . . but it is nevertheless rewarding. The familiar recedes even further and further into the background. . . . The contours of the objective world fade more and more and so it goes, step by step, until finally the world — "everything we loved and by which we have lived" (*the cry of the general public*) — becomes lost to sight. No more "likeness of reality," no idealistic images — nothing but a desert.
> But this desert is filled with the spirit of non-objective sensation which pervades everything. Even I was gripped by a kind of timidity bordering on fear when it came to leaving "the world of will and idea," in which I had lived and worked and in the reality of which I had believed. But a blissful sense of liberating non-objectivity drew me forth into the "desert," where nothing is real except feeling . . . and so feeling became the substance of my life. This was no empty square which I had exhibited but rather the feeling of non-objectivity.[3]

It is important to realize that possession by a changed state of consciousness may lie behind such an apparently simple and totally abstract geometric painting. All too often it is assumed that only romantic figurative images, organic rather than geometric, owe their origin to a take-over of this kind. Piet Mondrian (1872–1944), another artist of this century whose later work was totally abstract and geometric, writes in a similar vein:

> Art shows that . . . intuition becomes more and more conscious and instinct more and more purified. . . . Intuition enlightens and so links up with pure thought. They together become an intelligence which is not simply of the brain, which does not calculate, but which feels and thinks. Which is creative both in art and life.[4]

Mondrian is noted for his compositions of harmonious rectangles and, although such geometric equilibrium may be described as classical in style, we see from his writing that his art is generated by a special kind of "intelligence," made up of "intuition" and "pure thought." His paintings are not merely design productions of a clever,

---

[3] Kasimir Malevich, "The Non-Objective World." (Chicago: Paul Theobald and Company, 1959) Italics added.

[4] Piet Mondrian, "Plastic Art & Pure Plastic Art," in *Documents of Modern Art* (New York: Wittenborn, Schultz, 1945). Introduction by Harry Holtzman.

calculating mind. Therefore we must stress that such meaningful illuminations of consciousness, producing an expanded spectrum of awareness, underlie *all* highly creative acts; they are not the prerogative of artists whose work is overtly romantic or expressive.

These creative occasions may be called periods of vision — using the word "vision" to denote not the physiological act of perceiving concrete objects, but rather the psychological experience of feeling or apprehending a new level of one's being. Thus, we are led back again to the imaginative inner life of the artist, the fecundity of which drove Picasso to say, "Reality is more than the thing itself" (see Chapter 1, p. 4). In this chapter we can only attempt to capture the flavor of such moments, believing with Robert Graves that they defy critical analysis, yet knowing that without vision the greatest achievements of the phenomenon we call art would not exist. To quote again from *The Journal*, Eugéne Delacroix, commenting on what makes a painting a true work of art, refers to a remark made by Correggio, an important sixteenth-century Italian painter:

> When Correggio said his famous *Anch'io son' pittore,* he meant: "There is a fine work, but I should have put into it something which is not there."[5]

Delacroix implies that Correggio was satisfied with the craftsmanship of the work — that it was well done — but that he felt it lacked the vision necessary to make it a great work of art. Writing in his *Journal* on April 21, 1853, the day following the entry quoted above, the artist states:

> . . . . at this exhibition, as at Delsarte's concert in the evening, I felt for the thousandth time that, with the arts, and even with the best works in them, one must content oneself with the few gleams representing the moments when the artist was inspired.[6]

humbled in the vastness of vision.

The second entry reveals that Delacroix's standards for judging a work of art as inspired were extremely high. And, as one reads through the *Journal,* it becomes clear that he judged his own work no less harshly than the work of others. Inspiration, evidently, is not always present. So what is this "something" which Delacroix determined was not there for Correggio and which he says is represented by only a "few gleams" in an artist's life?

A SCALE OF CREATIVE LEVELS

It will be obvious to some readers that we have suggested the answer to the preceding question earlier, when it was stated that a work of art possesses both a

---

[5] *The Journal,* p. 295.

[6] *Ibid.*

formal and psychological eloquence. Presumably, Correggio was satisfied with the formal craftsmanship of his painting but unhappy with its psychological quality. Some readers may also be wondering if this chapter is not redundant, realizing that our previous description of imaginative experience as a "state of heightened consciousness" has already partially defined inspiration. But now it is time to qualify these earlier statements. States of heightened consciousness, for example, vary in their quality and intensity. As we regard a man's artistic production, accomplished over a two- or three-year period, we realize, like Delacroix, that the works differ in quality. We judge some to be much better than others; and if we were to demand as high a standard as Delacroix, we might consider only a dozen paintings or sculptures from a lifetime's output to be truly inspired. Consequently, it is realistic to recognize that a scale of creative levels exists *within* the general imaginative condition of heightened consciousness. And while we should continue to acknowledge that all true art springs from this special state of awareness, we should distinguish the higher levels of eloquence achieved by the more outstanding images. Therefore, let us reserve the word "inspiration" for those occasions when the image reveals that the man was moved by an intense level of vision.

I wonder if Delacroix would mind my juxtaposing two of his drawings — both of a horse and rider — and suggesting that one is more inspired than the other? In the impulsive brush drawing, *The Constable of Bourbon and His Conscience* (Figure 5-1), I recognize the gleam of inspiration of which the artist speaks in his

FIG. 5-1   Eugéne Delacroix (1799–1863). *The Constable of Bourbon and his Conscience* 1835. Wash drawing. Collection G. Aubry, Paris

FIG. 5-2　Eugene Dela-
croix (1799-1863). *Study
for Attila.* **c. 1842. Pen
drawing.** Cabinet des Des-
sins, Louvre, Paris

Journal. Whereas, in his pen drawing, *Study for Attila* (Figure 5-2), I do not find
it. There is an incredible plastic vitality to the first drawing. The volumes of man
and horse push through space; slow, liquid, and sensual lines run with lines which
are broken, brittle, and speedy; strong black lines and the areas of volume they
define stand before softer gray lines and their accompanying areas, creating a
depth to the ground on which the figures move; and this three-dimensional space
itself is not static, but thrusts in and around the forms. Such formal eloquence
carries its own psychological power — a dramatic mood is created by these sensuous
rhymes and rhythms which we sense without having recourse to the horse and rider
subject matter. Then one becomes involved with the detachment and
uncomfortable posture of the man on the horse, with the form that peers over his
shoulder, and with the horse's own anxiety. The drawing now reveals a particular
human situation — a man riding alone but accompanied by the unremitting and
unseen presence of the "other self" — and so the image intensifies its specific
psychological hold over us. In contrast, the *Study for Attila* is more conventional.
While it has a certain plastic and psychological vitality, this appears almost wooden
when seen against the inspired vitality of Figure 5-1. The reader will see for himself
that the statements just made about the drawing of *The Constable* could not be
applied to the drawing of Attila — they would flatter the image. There is no doubt
in my own mind that when Delacroix was drawing *The Constable of Bourbon,* he
was possessed by an intensity of feeling and insight which was not present when he
made the relatively academic study for *Attila.* This higher level of vision springs
from the roots of the psyche; embodied in a work of art, it arouses its own echo
in those viewers who potentially share the artist's sensitivity. Face to face with

a drawing of this power we recognize those formidable twins, genius and inspiration.

There are no formal criteria for assessing creative inspiration that one can take and apply to a work of art. But when many persons respond to the same image and there is a collective realization of its significance — even though this may not happen within the lifetime of the artist — then we know that the artist has touched on some universal quality or truth. Talking about the secret of creativeness, Carl Jung distinguishes the great (or inspired) performances in terms of their universal appeal:

> The essence of a work of art is not to be found in the personal idiosyncrasies that creep into it — indeed, the more there are of them, the less it is a work of art — but in its rising above the personal and speaking from the mind and heart of the artist to the heart and mind of mankind. The personal aspect of art is a limitation and even a vice. Art that is only personal, or predominantly so, truly deserves to be treated as a neurosis.[7]

Inspiration moves the artist away from a sense of normal reality — "the contours of the objective world fade more and more," as Malevich says — into what Mondrian describes as a state of pure feeling—thinking intelligence. This achieved, the creative personality is free to surpass the personal and speak of things that lie hidden in our common humanness. Once again we face an apparent paradox. For we have been constantly stressing the distinctly individual nature of the creative consciousness, only to arrive at a point where we say that the *inspired* artist rises above the personal. Yet we know that extremes can merge into their opposites — that helpless laughter can easily turn into tears, or an intense intellectual interest yield to a condition of mental boredom. You will remember Naum Gabo saying that an artist's feelings and responses are in a more agitated state than those of the average man and that he is more personally concerned with them. But he did not say that it was only *through* such highly subjective experience that the painter, sculptor, or poet transcends ego and becomes impersonal and objective in the highest degree. In so doing the artist uncovers deep layers of his own being which are also central to our common humanism.

We have touched on the artist's personal experience from time to time. In discussing moments of vision, the presence of intuitive and unconscious forces driving his imagination has been stressed. Also, it was suggested that these forces constellate imagistically in consciousness and result in impressions which do not tally with the more rational sense-impressions of the world. Inspiration, therefore,

---

[7] *The Collected Writings of C. G. Jung,* ed. G. Adler, M. Fordham, and H. Read, trans. by R. F. C. Hull, Bollingen Series XX, vol. 15, *The Spirit in Man, Art, and Literature* (© 1966 by Bollingen Foundation), reprinted by permission of Princeton University Press, p. 101.

may be seen as the result of strong intuitive or unconscious mental processes which take over the rational consciousness and allow the artist to "think" and "feel" in terms of plastic forms without need of logical cause-and-effect reasoning. At this point, any artist writing on the subject may be reassured by a statement of Paul Klee's:

> Further, in order to avoid the reproach "Don't talk, painter, paint," I shall confine myself largely to throwing some light on *those elements of the creative process which, during the growth of a work of art, take place in the subconscious.* To my mind, the real justification for the use of words by a painter would be to shift the emphasis by stimulating a new angle of approach; to relieve the formal element of some of the conscious emphasis which is given and place more stress on content.[8]

It is, indeed, the deeper psychological forcefulness of the work we are stressing, in the belief that this often results when conscious deliberation has given way to more unconscious processes. Wassily Kandinsky puts it another way. He talks about "a prophetic power" possessed by works of true vision:

> There is another art . . . which also springs from contemporary feeling. Not only is it simultaneously its echo and mirror but it possesses also an awakening prophetic power which can have far-reaching and profound effect.
>
> The spiritual life to which art belongs, and of which it is one of the mightiest of agents, is a complex but definite movement above and beyond. . . . Although it may take different forms, it holds basically to the same internal meaning and purpose.
>
> The causes of the necessity to move forward and upward . . . are obscure. The path often seems blocked or destroyed. But someone always comes to the rescue — someone like ourselves in everything, but with a secretly implanted power of "vision."
>
> He sees and points out. This high gift (often a heavy burden) at times he would gladly relinquish. But he cannot. Scorned and disliked, he drags the heavy weight of resisting humanity forward and upward.[9]

In this statement Kandinsky puts the issue in a nutshell. He describes inspiration as a "secretly implanted power" and informs us that its purpose is to give men (by means of the images of art) a glimpse of higher and transcendent experiences.

---

[8] Paul Klee, "On Modern Art." (London: Faber and Faber, 1948.) Italics added.

[9] Wassily Kandinsky, "Concerning the Spiritual in Art," in *Documents of Modern Art,* vol. 5 (New York: George Wittenborn Inc., n.d.).

But how does inspiration happen? What events or sequence of events, external and internal, lead to such moments of vision? First, it is necessary to establish an important fact. The man who works in the plastic arts is dependent upon his visual sensations. Unlike the poet who uses words as living things imbued with an emotional charge, the artist uses form and space. For the painter, sculptor, or architect, solid shapes and spatial shapes are the vehicles which convey the range and power of his "secretly implanted" feeling and knowledge. Therefore, we should regard those organizations of form and space in the external world which attract the artist as potential catalysts, for they may initiate the moments of interior vision. It is often such a visual confrontation when out in the world that triggers the imagination. Or, in a routine act of drawing or otherwise shaping, the artist may suddenly discover the significance of a particular line, space, or shape, which has the same effect. The French aesthetician and philosopher, Henri Focillon, writes with great lucidity on the link between form and creative sensibility:

> . . . the idea of the artist is form. His emotional life turns likewise to form: tenderness, nostalgia, desire, anger are in him, and so are so many other impulses, more fluid, more secret, oftentimes more rich, colorful, and subtle than those of other men. . . . He is immersed in the whole of life; he steeps himself in it. He is human. . . . But his special privilege is to imagine, to recollect, to think, and to feel *in forms*. . . . I do not say that form is the allegory or symbol of feeling, but rather its innermost activity. Form activates feeling. . . . it is eventually to form that we must always come. If I were to undertake . . . the establishment of a psychology for the artist, I should have to analyze formal imagination and memory, formal sensibility and intellect. I should have to define all the processes whereby the life of forms in the mind . . . taking natural objects as the point of departure, makes them matters of imagination and memory, of sensibility and intellect. . . . Between nature and man, form intervenes. The man in question, the artist, that is, forms this nature; before taking possession of it, he thinks it, sees it, and feels it as form.[10]

On the occasion of his seventieth birthday, the Welsh painter David Jones was asked by a newspaper reporter to state what impulses and attitudes had driven him to devote a lifetime to poetry and painting. The artist replied, "All my working life I have been trying to make a shape out of the very things of

---

[10] Henri Focillon, *The Life of Forms in Art* (2nd ed.), trans. by Hogan and Kubler (New York: Wittenborn, Schultz, 1948), p. 47.

INSPIRATION

which I myself am made." Here is a contemporary statement confirming the basic thesis expressed by Focillon that the emotional colors and drives of the inner life become tangible when the artist can create or discover a corresponding form. As Malevich said, "This was no empty square which I had exhibited, but rather the feeling of non-objectivity. . . ." But how does the artist discover the equivalent form? Once again, because of the complexity of the issue, we can only make a general statement. We have already suggested that some men will draw with no particular natural object in mind and discover a particular shape or series of shapes which compel their interest. In developing these forms into a more complete image, the growing configuration itself acts as a catalyst and triggers further thought and feeling states in the artist; these new awarenesses will in turn cause the image to be modified as they are embodied in the growing design. Other men, however, may perceive an object in the world which, because of its particular form, releases thoughts and feelings hitherto unsuspected into consciousness. Of these two possibilities, the confrontation with form in nature appears to be the more common way of engaging vision. When this happens, it is difficult to know if the artist is already partly conscious of an enhanced range of thought and feeling moving within him and is therefore actively searching for the equivalent form, or if it is the sudden perception of the object's significant form which awakens an unconscious sensibility. But it seems that the latter event is the more usual experience.

The English landscape painter John Constable (1776–1837) writes on several occasions of the effect on him of an unexpected encounter with nature. He was particularly attracted to trees and the shape of clouds seen under changing conditions of light. He suggests that although on normal occasions a tree may be just a tree, there are times when a particular tree will capture his imagination so completely that he is moved by a surge of feeling for life which transcends all other realities. Other artists have described similar experiences occasioned by the emergence of a particular form. I use the word "emergence" deliberately, for at such times the significant object seems to detach itself from its context and stand isolated. Even though the man may have passed the same tree, or rock, or cow a dozen times during the previous week without giving it more than casual attention, on this special occasion it takes over the whole of his consciousness and the rest of the world fades away. I have described such a moment of vision in an earlier book while discussing the painting you see in Figure 5-3:

> A sequence of events of this sort resulted in the series of thorn paintings produced a few years ago by the British painter Graham Sutherland. . . . One day a common thorn bush, which the artist had passed by without notice on numerous walks, detached itself from its surroundings and demanded the painter's attention. For the first time he noticed the structural complexity of the object, the sculptural precision of its forms, and the organic vitality of its growth pattern. He experienced a thorn's sharpness without having to touch it, and wondered at nature's efficient and protective design. The imaginary pricking

61

FIG. 5-3   Graham Sutherland (b. 1903-   ).
Thorn Trees **1946. Oil.** Collection British
Council, London

> of the flesh stimulated a range of associated ideas and
> their mental images . . . the shrike family of birds which
> impales their victims on a thorn . . . the suffering and
> pain to which man is heir. . . . The thorn bush, so long
> unnoticed, became a motif for a series of paintings
> which symbolized all of these subjective experiences. . . .[11]

There is a curious *suddenness* to this kind of experience. Why it should happen
at some times and not at others is something of a mystery. But the evidence seems
to suggest that it occurs when there is a certain open receptive state to consciousness
occasioned by a slackening of ratiocinative control. And then, when the catalyst
or equivalent form appears, feeling and intuitive thought hitherto below the
level of awareness move into consciousness and merge with perception. When one
is walking with nothing in mind and noticing nothing in particular, lost in the
unhurried rhythm of the movement, it is possible to experience such moments
of vision. A scientist, as he walks, apparently without a thought in his head,
may suddenly have an inspired idea which he recognizes as the solution to a
particular problem. Yet if he were to be sitting at this desk trying hard to
concentrate on the issues, the answer would elude him. Similarly, the artist
whose concentrated work in the studio has failed to yield a significant image
may, while walking, be inspired by an object (because he thinks and feels
through form) to produce work of great plastic and psychological eloquence.

---

[11] Graham Collier, *Form, Space and Vision,* 2nd ed. (Englewood Cliffs, N.J.: Prentice-Hall,
1967), p. 184.

INSPIRATION

Even if the artist is searching more deliberately for forms which excite him, their discovery will still cause sentiments and thoughts hitherto unconscious to quicken and vitalize consciousness. The sculptor Henry Moore has sometimes found the germ for an important work to be contained in the shape of some leaf, small bone, or pebble, which acts as the trigger to release those interiorized images. Figure 5–4 shows a series of drawings of leaf forms which have become leaf figures. Ultimately, the drawings themselves have become transformed into

FIG. 5–4   Henry Moore (b. 1898–   ). *Leaf Figures* **1951. Pen, crayon, and water-color.** Private Collection. Courtesy of the artist

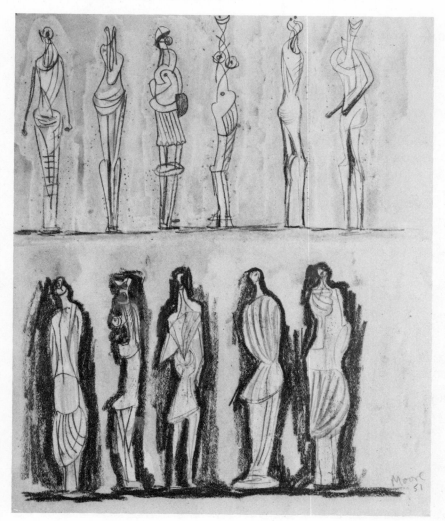

INSPIRATION

bronze sculptures, as you see in Figure 5-5. Thus we have an example of a first attraction to leaf shapes inspiring the development of a series of new and more significant forms. ("A palm tree can become a horse," says Picasso: We see also that a leaf can become a figure.) In one of his essays, Moore describes the attraction of nature's shapes for the sculptor:

> . . . . I have always paid great attention to natural forms, such as bones, shells, and pebbles, etc. Sometimes, for several years running I have been to the same part of the sea-shore — but each year a new shape of pebble has caught my eye, which the year before, although it was there in

FIG. 5-4 *Continued*

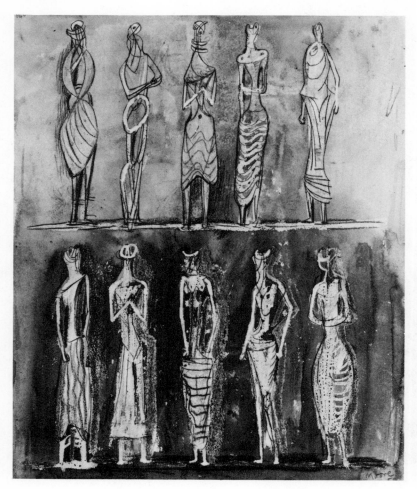

INSPIRATION

forms can trigger inspiration etc (handwritten note)

FIG. 5–5 **Henry Moore (b. 1898–   ).** *Leaf Figure No. 1* **1952. Bronze, 10".** Private Collection. Courtesy of the artist

hundreds, I never saw. Out of the millions of pebbles passed in walking along the shore, I choose out to see with excitement only those which fit in with my existing form-interest at the time. A different thing happens if I sit down and examine a handful one by one. I may then extend my form-experience more by giving my mind time to become conditioned to a new shape.[12]

Earlier in the same essay he writes:

The observation of nature is part of an artist's life, it enlarges his form-knowledge, keeps him fresh and from working only by formula, and feeds inspiration. . . .[13]

It is possible that some of the earliest images in the history of art were created as the result of such a perceptual experience. The paleolithic cave artists made their first drawings and paintings of animals on the rock surface of walls and roofs in

---

[12] Henry Moore, "Notes on Sculpture," in *The Listener* XVIII, 449, 1937.

[13] Henry Moore, "The Sculptor's Aims," in *Unit One* (London: Cassell and Company, 1934).

FIG. 5–6   Rock Surface. Photograph by Paul Zelanski

remote caverns. As a surface for drawing it was far from flat, showing different planes and textures, and marked by projections and indentations. Figure 5–6 is a photograph of such a natural, untouched surface. In flipping casually through the illustrations in this book, without reading the text, one may see nothing significant in this photograph. On the other hand, the viewer may stop at this page, intrigued by the configurations of tones, textures, planes, and cracks over the surface of the rock wall. As he regards the photographic image, certain forms may emerge from the overall ground as positive shapes and possess his interest. More than likely these shapes will suggest the form of an animal. When this happens, the perceiver is completing imaginatively the incomplete configurations of the wall surface. He is adding something of his own that is not visible to the senses. This action might be described as a minor experience of inspiration. Professor Giedion suggests that in some cases the paleolithic artists "found" their animal forms in this way and then completed them with an extraordinary graphic vitality. Giedion describes the image of the bison with the uplifted head (Figure 5–7), from the ceiling of the Altamira caves in northern Spain, in the following words:

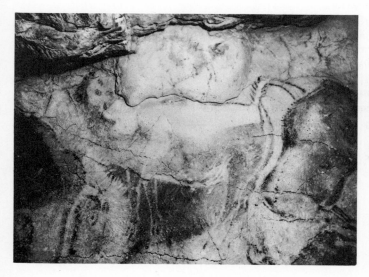

FIG. 5–7   Bison with uplifted head from Altamira. From *The Eternal Present* by S. Giedion. Bollingen Foundation, New York. Reprinted by permission of Princeton University Press

forms in most important /

The entire posture of this animal has been determined by the configurations of the rock. This bison also has its head upraised to bellow, a position *suggested* by rough irregularities in the surface of the ceiling, which even necessitated a certain degree of distortion. Both the uplifted head and line of the back are formed by a fine crack in the rock. The addition of some tawny color and a few engraved lines have simply strengthened the form that was already there. . . .[14]

The reader will appreciate that this example does not illustrate the more complete take-over of consciousness by the intense, imagistic thought and feeling previously described. But it does serve to illustrate how inspiration at the lower levels may be induced.

We know that Michelangelo believed in the power of *intelleto*, or the ability of the great artist to "see" the form of the image he was going to create already delineated in the raw material. That no one else could see this latent image he explained by attributing the vision to the inner eye, or eye of the soul. This faculty is the special endowment of the artist, for whom the eye of the senses is merely the first stage — the way *in* to the eye of inspiration — or, as Kandinsky described it, "the secretly implanted power of 'vision.'"

> The evening is cool and clear in this waning year of 1505. Idling on a high slope overlooking the Ligurian sea, a nervous, black-bearded man of thirty watches a distant craft. . . . He is dead-tired, *stanco morto*, both from his visits to the marble quarries of Carrara and from working on a statue. . . . Off shore the bark seems to be making little progress. . . . Mechanically he turns and contemplates two summits, upthrust like sentinels. . . . There is one especially high crag upon which his eye rests. . . . Instantly an idea overpowers his restless mind. It is an idea that has plagued him before. . . . In that alpine rock there is a hermetic form waiting to be released. A colossus stifles confined in his huge lithic prison, like a hamadryad in an oak or a *spirto in un' ampolla* ("spirit in a bottle"), awaiting release. If you look carefully, if your vision is true vision, you can already see the contours of the massive head and shoulders. The figure suddenly emerges so clear that it is impossible not to discern it. It was one of those giants that were to haunt him during his lifetime.[15]

One of these giants, sometimes described as the *Awakening Giant,* is shown in Figure 5–8. The form is emerging from the solid marble, freed as it were by the

---

[14] S. Giedion, *The Eternal Present: The Beginnings of Art,* p. 427. Reprinted by permission of Princeton University Press.

[15] Reprinted by permission of New York University Press from Robert J. Clements, *Michelangelo's Theory of Art,* © 1961 and 1962 by Robert J. Clements.

INSPIRATION

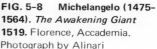

FIG. 5-8 Michelangelo (1475–
1564). *The Awakening Giant*
1519. Florence, Accademia.
Photograph by Alinari

sculptor's chisel once Michelangelo's "intelleto" or inspiration had espied it in
there, trapped, awaiting release. Professor Clements commences his fine book on
Michelangelo's artistic theory with the paragraph I have just quoted. It is fitting
that he should give an immediate introduction to the great sculptor's experience of
inspiration — the capacity for which Michelangelo attributes to God as an
endowment granted to the favored artist at birth. And it is interesting to note that
the author describes Michelangelo on this occasion as "dead-tired" and as turning
"mechanically" to "contemplate" the summits. The description indicates a
consciousness that is relaxed and receptive, uninvolved in objective or rational
analysis of the scene. It is a state with which we are now familiar, a necessary
prelude to the uprush of the unconscious.

INSPIRATION

In those cases where the artist is inspired to work from his own resources, without nature acting directly as a catalyst, we must distinguish between two ways of working and see a different inspirational buildup in each. Earlier in the chapter we quoted Piet Mondrian's statement that, "Intuition enlightens and links up with pure thought. . . . an intelligence which . . . feels and thinks." Mondrian spent many years closely involved with nature, always analyzing the structure of her forms. Ultimately he arrived at a position in art which has been described as a mode of plastic mathematics — an organization of linear and area proportions that are remarkably subtle and which create a harmony and unity pleasing to our sense perceptions. Although nature provided his original inspiration, after a certain point Mondrian needed no natural object to act as a trigger. It seems that his imaginative vision was stimulated by every new application of his aesthetic-cum-mathematical laws to a painting problem. We can see from a brief study of Figure 5-9 that Mondrian partly controls the process; when the theme is inspirationally delivered, it is then deliberately steered to reveal the abstract harmony and unity which is the crux of his vision and belief.

The second way of working in a completely abstract vein, without any particular external stimulus to inspiration, is illustrated by Figure 5-10, the work of the American painter Jackson Pollock (1912-56). Like Mondrian, Pollock was originally stimulated by nature's forms and ultimately was capable of being inspired from "within," without need of nature to trigger vision. But, unlike Mondrian, he was controlled throughout by the inspirational process, rather than controlling it after its initial manifestation. The process had hold of him, and he

FIG. 5-9   Piet Mondrian (1872-1944). *Composition in Brown and Grey.* **Oil.** Museum of Modern Art, New York

INSPIRATION

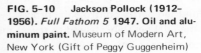

FIG. 5–10   Jackson Pollock (1912–
1956). *Full Fathom 5* 1947. Oil and alu-
minum paint. Museum of Modern Art,
New York (Gift of Peggy Guggenheim)

appeared to be completely at its mercy. He worked furiously, as if undergoing an
emotional catharsis. For Pollock, it seems that the inspirational theme continued
to develop as the creative action continued; that he gained inspiration from the
action itself — from surrendering to the necessity to give form to the living forces
within him. This is in contrast to Mondrian whose imagination was fed by an
inspired aesthetic theory which was complete at the outset. (And it is interesting to
see that the organic vitality of Pollock's images — in contrast to Mondrian's
geometric and mathematical constructions — suggests that the excitement of the
visual experience of nature still acted inspirationally for him at long range.) Yet
both men seemed to experience their moments of vision, one in contemplation and
the other in action, without help of an actual confrontation with nature. Therefore
we must suggest that the plastic imagination can be inspired also from within, out
of a state of "pure thought" or "pure feeling in action." The intensity of Jackson
Pollock's consciousness when inspired is described below:

> In a state of spiritual clarity there are no secrets. The effort
> to achieve such a state is monumental and agonizing, and
> once achieved it is a harrowing state to maintain. In this
> state all becomes clear, and Pollock declared the meanings
> he had found with astonishing fluency, generosity and

expansiveness. This is not a mystical state, but the accumulation of decisions along the way and the eradication of conflicting beliefs toward the total engagement of the spirit in the expression of meaning. . . . His action is immediately art. . . .[16]

If we were to try to define the spirit of man, we could not do better than to take Mr. O'Hara's suggestion that it is the element within us engaged in seeking for and expressing meaning. When its goal is achieved, the result is a "state of spiritual clarity." But is not this condition the same as Mondrian's pure thought, Malevich's nonobjective feeling, Kandinsky's secretly implanted vision, Klee's subconscious creativity, or Michelangelo's eye of the soul? It seems that ultimately, whichever way it works, we must relate inspiration to the creative faculty of finding meaning and value in existence; inevitably, such insights go beyond material and sensory realities to those more spiritual and abstract. We have seen that it is possible for the artist (who expresses this knowledge through form) to discover his inspiration in two ways. He can be moved by the sudden significance of an object confronted in the world, or he can gain this revelation through waiting on those intuitive or unconscious movements of the psyche which arise when consciousness is released from rational and objective involvements. In the latter event the artist may work contemplatively, as did Mondrian, to discover his laws of harmonious equivalence and relation, and Malevich to find his square representing the feeling of nonobjectivity; or he may throw himself into the kind of inspired action through which the form of the image is *discovered,* as did Pollock and other abstract expressionists. (This is the sort of spontaneous creation we discussed when describing the vitality of the predynastic Egyptian figurine in Chapter 2. As Shelley wrote in his "Defence of Poetry," "a great statue or picture grows . . . ." thereby implying the continuous interaction between vision and form as the image develops.)

THE SPELL OF INSPIRATION

Common to all inspired creative acts is a change in the artist's sense of the duration of time. This is too important an issue to treat briefly here. Let me just mention it in passing and say that Chapters 7 and 8 are concerned almost entirely with the problem of time in the artist's consciousness. Under the spell of inspiration the artist is often not aware of time. He is completely lost in the work. This total commitment has sometimes been described as "passion" or "fury." To say that an artist experiences a creative fury is another way of describing him as inspired. It does not mean that he is involved in wild or reckless behavior, but that he is heatedly and totally concerned with his work — so much so that, as Malevich said, ". . . the contours of the objective world fade more and more." This condition, in

---

[16] From Frank O'Hara, *Jackson Pollock* (New York, George Braziller, Inc., 1959). Reprinted with the permission of the publisher. Copyright © 1959 by George Braziller, Inc.

which the world is lost to sight, puts the artist at the service of his inspiration; or, as is sometimes said, he is visited by a muse or demon capable of extending his awareness to inspired lengths. It is a condition which allows the artist to feel an exaltation, an extraordinary sense of satisfaction and power. When he is not visited by the muse the true artist finds his work a burden and suffers a general feeling of discontent and frustration. Professor Clements writes:

> Croce felt that Michelangelo received the thrills of the rapid visitation by a muse or daemon. . . . Croce adds that this exaltation was not unknown to Michelangelo, who created "out of his nights without rest, out of his meditations, dreams, ecstasies. . . ." It is true that Michelangelo admitted that if he had not taken up the fine arts he would not always be "in such a passion."[17]

Michelangelo is not an exceptional figure in this regard. In reading the writings of artists and their biographers, we come to accept such experiences as commonplace for men of genius, from whatever source their inspiration arises.

There is a widespread belief that inspiration absolves the artist from using his reason, from the demands of normal mental deliberation. While this may be true for some, it does not appear to be the case for others. Eugéne Delacroix, for example, inspired to paint the large *Massacre at Chios* by the powerful feelings this contemporary event generated, made many deliberate changes as the work progressed. For him, the initial experience of vision was not lost because he exercised a conscious control as the image developed. Although the passionate intensity of the first urges to paint remained, the developing image itself demanded modification as it materialized. He was constantly appraising; re-painting the background one day, re-drawing a figure another, until the work was "right" and he knew it to be finished: it was a case of intense and inspired feeling uniting with a controlling aesthetic intelligence. The viewer regarding the large canvas can see no evidence of the mental anguish that Delacroix suffered in trying to achieve this balance. Color, drawing, and composition so perfectly express the illumination of the artist's feelings, and yet are so well realized formally, that one is not aware of Delacroix's struggle. The ability to effect this kind of integration and maintain inspiration over a long period is another mark of genius. On the other hand, there are men who are not aware of such a struggle, who work unselfconsciously when inspired. In Chapter 4 we quoted Mark Rothko, the twentieth-century American painter, as saying that the picture is, for the artist, "a revelation, an unexpected and unprecedented resolution. . . ." This statement confirms that Rothko was not consciously occupied with aesthetic or technical problems. On the contrary (although we know these problems exist in the making of any work of art), it must be that they are resolved so intuitively, or unconsciously, that the artist is unaware of the decisions he has made in developing the image. Consequently, although all

---

[17] R. J. Clements, *Michelangelo's Theory of Art,* pp. 44–45.

true artists experience inspired moments from time to time, we see that when it comes to expressing this heightened awareness, there may be differing degrees of conscious control.

ACCESS TO THE UNCONSCIOUS

Perhaps by now the reader recognizes that this discussion is, in part, an extension of our theories concerning the "reservoir of unconscious resources" which was the subject of Chapter 4. A clue was provided in our quotation from Paul Klee when he refers to "those elements of the creative process which, during the growth of a work of art, take place in the subconscious."[18] Possibly inspiration is, in some way, linked to unconscious resources. Once again it is necessary to draw attention to the distinct difference between the rational-deductive aspects of consciousness and those interiorized impressions which can come unbidden to arouse thought and feeling. When Mondrian talks about intuition becoming more conscious, instinct more purified, and the two linking up with pure thought, he is describing a mode of awareness which is pure because it is free from empirical elements. Inspiration engages the artist with a type of knowledge which invariably seems to lurk beyond the range of normal consciousness. In all of the examples cited, we have seen that the rational, cause-and-effect seeking consciousness must lose its grip on the individual if he is to hearken to what Delacroix called, "the little world man bears within him. . . ."

This world of the self, it seems to me, provides the chief motivation for the compulsive and all-absorbing quality of moments of vision or inspiration. We have discussed at length how the individual comes face to face with himself at these times, experiencing new levels of intensity and awareness. For he participates with his whole being, while at the same time contemplating his newly realized self with a proprietary delight. It is the joy of full possession of the self that gives the life-enhancing quality to the art that results from these moments. Nobody knew better than the poet Coleridge what this self-discovery or self-identification meant. Walter Pater, in his essay on the poet, quotes from a note written by Coleridge which reaffirms our thoughts in this chapter:

> In looking at objects of nature . . . as at yonder moon dim glimmering through the dewy window pane, I seem rather to be seeking, as it were asking, a symbolic language for *something within me that forever and already exists,* than observing anything new. Even when that latter is the case

---

[18] The word "subconscious" does not have the same meaning as "unconscious" in clinical or theoretical psychology. It refers to a deeper area of consciousness rather than to autonomous, completely unconscious processes. But a study of Klee's philosophy of art reveals his concern for truly unconscious processes, and I think we may assume that he is using the word in this sense.

yet still I have always an obscure feeling, as if that new
phenomenon were a dim awakening of a forgotten or
hidden truth of my inner nature.

I shall close this chapter with a short extract from Lancelot Whyte's historical
survey of the unconscious. Although not describing inspiration as such, the passage
does confirm the existence of a link between unconscious mental processes and
moments of heightened conscious realization:

> . . . . the American anatomist, essayist, and poet, *Oliver
> Wendell Holmes,* had been reading a paper to the Phi Beta
> Kappa Society at Harvard on "Mechanisms in Thought and
> Morals," which included the following wonderful passage:
> "The more we examine the mechanism of thought, the
> more we shall see that the automatic, unconscious action of
> the mind enters largely into all its processes. Our definite
> ideas are stepping stones: how we get from one to the
> other, we do not know: something carries us; we do not
> take the step. A creating and informing spirit which is with
> us, and not of us, is recognized everywhere in real and in
> storied life. It is the Zeus that kindled the rage of Achilles:
> it is the muse of Homer; it is the Daimon of Socrates. . . . it
> shaped the forms that filled the soul of Michelangelo when
> he saw the figure of the great Lawgiver in the yet unhewn
> marble. . . . it comes to the least of us as a voice that will be
> heard; it tells us what we must believe; it frames our
> sentences; it lends a sudden gleam of sense or eloquence . . .
> so that . . . we wonder at ourselves, or rather not at
> ourselves, but at this divine visitor who chooses our brain as
> his dwelling place, and invests our naked thought with the
> purple of the kings of speech of song."[19]

The language used is poetic, but there is no mistaking the implication that it is the
unconscious life of the psyche which shapes the wisdom of our more eloquent
utterances and invests our imagination with wings. And again we see this
inspirational activity described as the activity of spirit . . . as divine in origin.

> For the poet is a light and winged and holy thing, and there
> is no invention in him until he has been inspired and is out
> of his senses, and the mind is no longer in him; when he has
> not attained to this state he is powerless and is unable to
> utter his oracles.
>
> Plato, *Ion*

---

[19] Lancelot Law Whyte, *The Unconscious Before Freud* (New York: Basic Books, Inc., 1962),
p. 163.

INSPIRATION

VI
TRANSFORMATIONS

A few years ago a major London gallery mounted a comprehensive exhibition of Vincent van Gogh's drawings and paintings. It was a hot summer and I remember the discomfort of standing in the long queue of people patiently seeking admission. Inside, one painting in particular attracted large groups of people. It was the painting of a cypress tree on the road to Auvers which is reproduced here as Figure 6-1. A short time later I was in the south of France at Arles, the old Roman town

FIG. 6-1   Vincent Van Gogh (1835-1890). *Road with Cypresses* **1890.** Rijksmuseum Kröller-Müller, Otterlo

FIG. 6-2 *Cypress tree at Arles*

where van Gogh made many of his landscapes, when one morning I had a sudden desire to see the real cypress trees that had inspired the painter. My inquiry led me first to the local librarian and then to the curator of ancient monuments, before I found myself at four o'clock in the afternoon facing a "van Gogh" cypress. Figure 6-2 is my photograph of it. The tree appeared massive, tremendously solid and substantial, and I realized then how two-dimensionally flimsy and fragile was the painting. I thought how strange it was that thousands of people should wait in line to regard a flimsy image when they could come down to Arles and see the solid, real thing. But then the question arose: "Which is more real, the tree in the field or the image of the tree in the art gallery?" For there were no people waiting in line to see the tree in the field.

I have to admit that the tree in the stubbled wheat field was a disappointment. It had none of the fiery growth or dynamic color displayed in van Gogh's painting. Despite its concrete monumentality it was just a tree, whereas the painting was the tree plus something else. It is obviously the "something else" that draws the crowds to the art gallery to survey the image, rather than to the travel agency to purchase tickets to Arles. Once again I realized that art had misled me. It had given me a picture of a cypress tree that did not exist — or, rather, a cypress tree transformed. For the umpteenth time I realized that this transformation constitutes the magnetic attraction of art.

Art shows the world transformed. We do not really need a text to tell us this; all the images accompanying the chapters reveal well enough how the form of art differs from the form of nature. A generally accepted standard of criticism today is that when art strives to imitate an original model, however skillfully, it is not art. From our critical vantage point we can see that when, in the past, a major artist produced what *he* considered a naturalistic work, the final image always turned out to be more than just a faithful copy of the object. The work of the French Impressionists, for example, was an attempt to directly record the visual sensations of space and air, color and light. Painting outside, on the spot, the brush became an extension of the eye. And yet, Claude Monet, the greatest of the Impressionists, inevitably infused the natural scene with poetic mood and feeling in the painting. (See Figure 9-1, a painting by Monet illustrating the chapter on color.) It was, no doubt, these paradoxial aspects of Monet's work — the intention to faithfully record visual impressions, yet producing, nevertheless, a poetic transformation — that led Paul Cézanne to make his famous remark: "Monet is only an eye; but, my God, what an eye!"[1]

The phenomenon of creative or imaginative transformation has been our theme all along; in every chapter we have suggested how and why this artistic metamorphosis is achieved. Consequently, in focusing specifically on it here, we will recapitulate and consolidate the discussion. But the chapter will close by examining one new aspect of the transforming process which is central to the appreciation of the plastic arts. I am referring to the symbolic content of a work of art; to the emergence of images having symbolic power.

We made the statement in the first chapter that an image embodies two realities — the physical fact of the object as seen, plus its secret meaning for the artist beyond the truth of appearances. It was essential to establish at an early stage that the image represented both artist himself and object itself. This theme was developed in Chapter 2, using the seesaw analogy to indicate the range of such emphases responsible for shaping the image. We saw that at one end of the scale the work may show a marked perceptual faithfulness to the object — whereas at the other extreme it may have lost this, as the artist has worked under the influence of his imagination rather than his eye. And then, in the chapter entitled *The Compass Points of Consciousness,* Figures 3-2 through 3-5 were used to illustrate four basic transformations of an original object. Let us reproduce the first of these illustrations again to initiate the present discussion.

1. Graphic Transformation

Dürer's *Hare* (Figure 6-3), as a naturalistic drawing, shows the real hare apparently little changed. Yet it must be pointed out that even here the image is something more than a straightforward reproduction of the object. For the graphic process itself ensures a basic transformation that no artist can avoid. In recreating the object by means of lines and tones (areas of light or dark), the concrete reality

---

[1] Cézanne as quoted by Vollard.

FIG. 6-3   Albrecht Durer (1471-1528). *Hare* **1502. Watercolor.** Vienna, Albertina Museum

of the hare is lost. The creature in life is a material volume occupying a certain position in a contextual volume of space. It is not composed of lines as such; lines as such do not exist in nature. Even the hairs of the hare — if you will forgive the pun — are not lines but volumes having weight and mass. It is our way of seeing that imposes a linear definition to the form we regard. For in encompassing the mass of the object the surfaces of the form change direction in space, and the human eye cannot follow them around corners or over the other side. Light from surfaces in these positions does not strike the retina. Consequently, we see an edge or a limit to a plane or curved surface, which we translate graphically as a line when making a drawing. Also, we see a clear demarcation between shadows and lights as a line — and in drawing or painting, where these areas of different tone values meet, they automatically form a "line," although a line as such has not been drawn. Therefore, when drawing or painting, lines and tones become a plastic metaphor for our visual impressions of the real thing, and the image we make inevitably stands as a graphic transformation of the object. This transformation is common to all two-dimensional images.[2]

---

[2] Similarly in three-dimensional imagery — in sculpture or modeling — the translation of the natural object into even a facsimile involves the use of a different material, and therefore a plastic transformation is accomplished. But having said this, we must grant that the sculptural image occupies three-dimensional space and possesses mass and consequently represents less of a physical transformation than its graphic counterpart.

2. Perceptual Transformation

Dürer's drawing also embodies change of a higher sort, for this artist possessed a pair of the keenest eyes in the history of art. In addition he exercised a formidable concentration in his perceptual analysis of nature. This combination of visual and mental faculties produces a clarification of sense-impressions that, when realized in a drawing, give the image a larger-than-life credibility. For in the ordinary course of events most of us experience very general impressions when regarding an object. We receive an interrupted series of retinal sensations as our eyes blink and as we or it change position. And we rarely focus eye or mind intently enough to consolidate these generalized impressions into a coherent, unified mental image, allowing the form of the object to be indelibly imprinted on our mind in every particular. Consequently, when artists like Dürer, Leonardo, or Courbet present us with such a completely "seen" graphic statement — with the object now isolated in the illusory yet defined space-field of the canvas or paper — we see the image almost as if we were regarding the object itself for the first time. When this happens, a work such as the *Hare* represents a perceptual transformation of the object. It declares that the artist's eye and intellect have overcome the vagueness inherent in normal visual sensations to show us the hare crystal clear, so to speak, as a new experience. If you find that Dürer's drawing seems more real than any hare or rabbit you may actually have seen, this is a tribute to the perceptual clarification achieved by the artist.

3. Structural Transformation

Sometimes a painter or sculptor will go further than making the perceptual clarification we have just described. He is not content to render the surface appearance of the object, even though this does involve a considered appraisal of its structure and an intensive visual concentration. Instead, he will use his faculty of acute perception to discover some basic structure-shape characteristics of the object. With this knowledge gained he is free to structurally *re-form* the object in the making of a graphic or sculptural image. This sort of transformation satisfies certain demands made by the creative imagination. We have seen how the Greek sculptor Praxiteles re-formed the human body by modifying the proportionate relationships between the major structural parts and by refining the flow or articulation of these parts (see Figure 6–4). Yet Praxiteles could never have achieved these subtle changes if he did not already possess a firm knowledge of human anatomy. As we observed, the transformation effected by Praxiteles was the result of an ordering process, imparting a grace or plastic harmony to the sculpture which is not possessed by the figure in life. Thus the Greek sculptor satisfied an aesthetic need for certain visual "rightness" or perfection which is rooted in a need for order and which runs through art under many guises. The Greek attitude toward figure sculpture is but one rather special demand of this sort. Anthropologists have discovered that even primitive peoples seek their own kind of formal coherence in those art objects which

FIG. 6-4   **Praxiteles.** *Aphrodite of Knidos*
c. 350 B.C. Roman Copy, Vatican Museum

serve ritual and magic; if the image is well made and well structured, they believe it will work better magic. Running through many differing styles and periods is this search for a particular plastic, structural coherence. It is as if man seeks to establish through art a more absolute structural purity and permanence; and this represents his imposed order on the flow of multi-impressions received in a daily encounter with the world.

Such images represent a structural transformation of the phenomenological world which, at its most extreme level, reveals a dependence upon the elemental purity of geometric forms. We see this in Figure 6-5, a work by Constantin Brancusi. This piece is composed of only three highly polished, machine-like cylindrical forms. They represent the human torso which, in life, is that part of the body where the pelvis and the lumbar region of the trunk come together in a complex knitting of forms. It is most difficult to realize the subtle flow of these parts, as anyone drawing from the model knows. But Brancusi has dispensed with the problems of a biomorphic treatment in favor of a geomorphic simplicity. He has re-structured the body to create a cylindrical simplicity which has a visual

clarity and unity and at the same time conveys the poetic idea of the heroic youth in all of his slender beauty. The *African Dance Mask*, shown in Figure 6-6, reveals a similar transforming of the natural complexity of the face into the smooth ovals of more geometric elliptical forms. In this traditional example of primitive art the

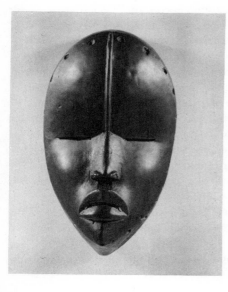

FIG. 6-6   **African Dance Mask, Ivory Coast.** American Museum of Natural History, New York

TRANSFORMATIONS

mask as face is completely depersonalized, becoming a design of pure volumes. This structural transformation of the head does not have much in common with the "cubist" transformation we see in Picasso's *Woman's Head* in Figure 6–7. Here, the re-forming magnifies and compounds the detail of plane and curved surface, exaggerating the bony thrusts of the skull against the skin. This new facial structure distorts and complicates the comparatively gentle "landscape" of the natural face into the steep-angled ridges and valleys of mountain country. Yet it does bring us to a positive realization of the head's structural dynamics through the exaggerated treatment of plane and curve. It would not take much to push the head made by Picasso into a completely geometric form. The planes would become triangled, squared, or trapezoid — the curved surfaces oval or circular. But Picasso maintains a nice distance between complete geometricization and organic plasticity, the same distance maintained, for example, between Brancusi's extreme cylindrical purity and the more organic variability of the oval forms shaping the African mask. In making this comparison between the African mask and the Picasso head, we gain some idea of how we respond to two differently structured forms. We should note how sensuously inviting are the swelling, smooth volumes of oval and cylindrical shapes — how they invite touch and are generally soothing to the feelings. In contrast, the sharpness of planes and angles stimulate a dramatic mood and are atactile, austere, and forbidding. (When mood and feeling can be aroused in this way, it indicates that the image is "expressive." We will discuss expressive transformation later in the chapter.)

Some twentieth-century painters come immediately to mind as specialists in the structural transformation of normal visual experience. In the sketch by Paul

Cézanne (Figure 6-8) we see that detail is eliminated in favor of simple, aggregate shapes. A tree, for example, becomes an organization of large, simply defined areas in which individual leaves are lost. Similarly, rocks, houses, or mountains assume an overall elemental simplicity of form, which again tends to the geometric. Cézanne's avowed intent is to realize his visual sensations of the world by creating an image in which transitory and vague impressions have no place. Bifocal vision produces an inherent confusion in seeing; for as two eyes converge on the scene, all that is within the cone of vision is seen relatively clearly, whereas things outside it are not. So we move our head in order to see more distinctly what is to the left or the right, above or underneath, and receive a new set of visual data. In thus scanning a large area we experience the scene as a *series* of visual sensations. There is a certain kaleidoscopic confusion inherent in this serialistic way of seeing which Cézanne wished to eliminate. To achieve this end through drawing, he sought to reduce objects to their essential shape — after considerable analysis — and to concentrate attention on those objects lying within a definite cone of vision built into his picture. But Cézanne goes further to structure his perceptions. He also treats spatial regions as positively as he does objects — as areas defined by the positioning and spatial extension of objects in space. This results in an image in which form and space are knit together in an almost frozen relationship. And we are pushed to the realization that in life our perception of the spatial intervals between objects is

FIG. 6-8   Paul Cezanne (1839-1906). *Landscape Near L'Estaque* 1882-85. Watercolor.
Zurich, Kunsthaus

vital if we are to perceive the objects themselves — that we distinguish the specific shape of a thing because the space surrounding it takes on the complementary shape of a matrix.[3] Cézanne's drawings and paintings thus assume an architecture of space, form, and color. They represent a structural reconstitution of nature, inspired by the need to know and define the world in a more concrete form than that presented by sequential visual sensations.

In 1911 the Dutch painter Piet Mondrian made a series of paintings of single trees. These images proceed from a naturalistic statement of paintings which grow increasingly abstract; for the artist ruthlessly strips the trees of superfluous detail to expose the basic skeletal structure.[4] In Figure 6-9 we see that Mondrian has, like Cézanne before him, treated the space demarcated by the tree's linear structure as part of the tree — as tree-space. He allows some of these regions to retreat into the background space, others to advance to the same plane as the tree itself. Once again we see nature transformed in the painting into an architectonic structure of form and space. The Cubist movement which originated in the first decade of this century also experimented in restructuring the appearance of things. But these artists had an unconventional attitude regarding the established way of looking at an object, refusing to be restricted to a single viewing position. There seemed no

FIG. 6-9   Piet Mondrian (1872-1944). *Horizontal Tree.* **Oil.** Munson-Williams-Proctor Institute Collection, Utica, New York

[3] Some of the issues of space perception are discussed more fully in Chapter 8.

[4] Mondrian's move to total abstraction is discussed in Chapter 11, and some of these tree drawings are reproduced there.

TRANSFORMATIONS

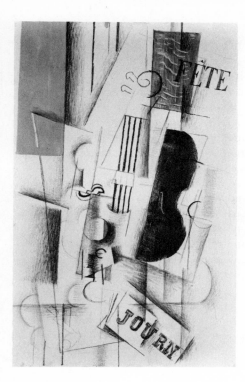

reason why they should not regard the object from as many positions as possible — from the back, front, side, underneath, above, inside, etc. — and show *all* these differing aspects in a single image. Of course, the object presented in the drawing or painting is not easily recognizable. We are accustomed to seeing it represented as viewed from one position at one moment of time; natural perception does not show us four or five different aspects simultaneously. Under the Cubist system, once the artist has gained his multifarious exposures of the object, he is free to restructure them in the image in any way he pleases. He is no longer bound by natural appearances, for he can now include in his drawing what he *knows* about the object, in addition to the single aspect he can see from one position. Figure 6-10 indicates the new plastic freedom gained. Georges Braque reconstructs his model, *and its spatial field,* to suit whatever intuitive attitude to formal eloquence moves him. It is not difficult to see that Cubism represents an extreme structural transformation of the physical world — one that will allow the artist to move easily into total abstraction.

4. Expressive Transformation

We come now to a mode of transformation which has been consistently present in the history of art, yet which has received the most complete and relevant

TRANSFORMATIONS

exploitation in the nineteenth and twentieth centuries in Europe. This is the way of *expressive transformation*. But I should make it clear that the word "expressive" is used with the broadest of implications; it is not just a specific reference to the well-known Expressionist movement of this century, but to a creative attitude seen in Primitive art, Etruscan art, Medieval art, Baroque art, Romantic art, and so on. It may be used simply to denote the expression of emotional experience.

We have talked constantly about the role played by feeling in an artist's life, and in Chapter 3 it was suggested that there are degrees of objective and intuitive feeling present in all creative acts — that all art embodies the emotional pitch of a man's life. What we will be concerned with here are those images which contain such a high proportion of "locked-in" feeling, so to speak, that they cause pronounced reverberations of an emotional sort in the viewer. For example, most of us would agree that the familiar Egyptian figurine (Figure 6-11) embodies a positive emotional charge which, in the eyes of some, is close to hysteria. In contrast, the perceptual and structural transformations we have just discussed appear very cerebral. The reader will know by now that I do not wish to set reason against feeling or sensation against intuition, but to suggest the totality of consciousness in all of its compass-like range. However, as far as the visual arts are concerned, I think Herbert Read was right in his belief that intuition and feeling rather than rational thought provided the original drive to make images — that a highly cerebral

FIG. 6-11   Egyptian Figurine (Pre-dynastic). 12" high. Courtesy of the Trustees of the British Museum, London

art was a later aberration, a Greek legacy to Western civilization. Writing about the year 2,000 B.C., an Egyptian essayist of the Middle Kingdom suggested that he wished to express from his body, feelings, the words for which were not in existence. In our own century, the German painter Emil Nolde has written:

> The artist knows the right moment, and also the
> relentless, tireless, depth-probing urge. The
> moment is a flashing spark, the relentless urge,
> the everlasting holy fire.[5]

Both of these statements, so far apart in time, reveal a common theme — the strength and drive of the feeling-mood when it possesses consciousness. So intense was this experience for the Egyptian that he found it could not be conveyed adequately in words. Curiously enough, in the phrase "to express from my body" he anticipates the contemporary development of *action painting* (see Chapter 11), when the painter lets the body itself act, dancing the emotions out and recording the action meanwhile on board or canvas in abstract line and color. (The reader will recall the short discussion of Jackson Pollock's action painting in Chapter 5, pages 69–71.) The statement by Emil Nolde conveys the same feeling of compulsion, the same sense of being driven, or, as we have previously described it in the case of Michelangelo, the fury and passion unleashed by the Muse. Nolde also implies, as did Michelangelo, that the ultimate values striven for are spiritual rather than existential or material. Wassily Kandinsky, another pioneering painter of our century, writes in the same vein in his essay *Concerning the Spiritual in Art* when he describes expressive art as "the art of inner necessity."

It is difficult to define feeling in nontechnical language and, therefore, we should think of it as a compound of mental and physical states; as the chemistry of mind and body conjoined to produce an intensity of thought, mood, and bodily excitation. Writing about the subtlety of poetic expression, Professor Wasson makes a statement that may be readily applied to the plastic arts:

> . . . . a matter of adjusting the line, the stanze,
> the genre to the particular nuances of the
> author's "felt thought," the contour of the
> poet's emotions responding to the inflections of
> the inner voice.[6]

Despite our original definition of the expressive element in art as "the expression of emotional experience," it is now necessary to say that emotion is not quite the same thing as feeling. We tend to think of emotion as the welling up of positive or negative passions on a day to day, hour to hour, or minute to minute basis

---

[5] Werner Haftmann, *Emile Nolde: Unpainted Pictures* (New York: Praeger, 1965), p. 37.
[6] Richard Wasson, "*Herbert Read Now: A Salutation to Eros*," *Journal of Aesthetic Education,* Vol. 3, No. 4 (1969), 20. University of Illinois Press.

FIG. 6-12   Emil Nolde
(1867-1956). *The Strange
Lady.* **Watercolor on rice
paper.** Courtesy Stiftung
Seebull Ada und Emil
Nolde

according to the sequence of events. Feeling, however, is a more constant attitude regarding those aspects of life which are always with us — those experiences which assume a positive quality in our consciousness and which stand out from the general flow of daily or hourly impressions. As life progresses we realize that our feelings have developed from the random emotional reponse; that they represent a more organized, stable, and trustworthy means of evaluating or appreciating the quality of an experience. In the small water-color reproduced as Figure 6-12, Emil Nolde conveys more than the flash fire of an emotional reaction. I feel he touches us more deeply and lastingly, arousing feelings concerned with the values we would attach to human existence. What are we to *say* when faced by such a painting? Are not our voices stilled because the visual expresses sentiments which tell us things so much more potently than words? Now we see how the use of carefully juxtaposed dark and light tones plays an important part in the expression of feeling, and is able to evoke sadness, tenderness, nostalgia, desire. . . . If we were to see this in color it would be more effective, but I must leave the discussion of the expressive power of color to Chapter 9 when color reproductions can be observed. Yet we can see that even in black and white reproduction, where tonal values alone provide the "color,"

Nolde does not depend solely on such values. He also creates mood by making slight changes in the natural proportions of the figure. The face and head of the principal figure are overly large in relationship to the body, thus drawing attention to the face wherein her feelings are mirrored. The large dark circles of eyes are pensive, if not expressionless; the mouth is slightly twisted. Nolde suggests through these shapings that this once young and beautiful face is now haunted and disillusioned. He eliminates detail in the figures, showing them as simple shapes of juxtaposed tones. The resultant looseness and vagueness of form works expressively rather than descriptively, imparting both mood and mystery to the work. The image thus exudes the dolorous scent of human travail and compassion.

We have been stressing all along that a positive relationship exists between form and feeling — that the expressive factor is always with us in art. Let us look at a few examples where distortion has gone to extreme lengths. Fashioned perhaps 20,000 years before the predynastic Egyptian figurine, is a piece small enough to be held in the hand and known as the *Venus of Willendorf* (Figure 6-13). Even if we grant that women might have been as rotund as this in those early days, the emphatic exaggeration of the sexual and maternal areas cannot be denied. It is difficult for us to comprehend the nature of primitive man's attitude toward human fertility and childbirth. With a high infant mortality rate and short adult life span, survival of the species depended upon a successful and rapid rate of reproduction. It must have been desired and expected that women would be prolific. Consequently, we do not find these early sculptors making images of individual beauties, although other pieces such as the Venus of Lespugue show a more positive symmetry and smoothness to the volumes. Rather, they are obsessed with woman as the source of

FIG. 6-13   Venus of Willendorf c. 15,000 B.C. Stone, 4-3/8" high. Original object kept in the Pre-history section of the Austrian Museum of Natural History, Vienna

life, as the swelling vessel that ultimately delivers the young in the awesome experience of childbirth. We will discuss the belief in sympathetic magic that probably lay behind the making of these images in Chapter 10; here I merely want to show how strong feelings for the erotic and biological aspects of the feminine are expressed in these burgeoning, highly tactile volumes. In my view, similar feelings are expressed in the life-size sculpture illustrated in Figure 6-14. Although the author of this work was a man of our own time (Gaston Lachaise died in 1935), these massive yet delicately balanced volumes contain a high degree of erotic feeling, which is enhanced by the sensuous flow and surface finish of the parts. Lachaise

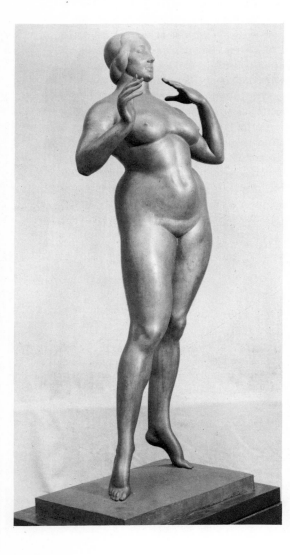

FIG. 6-14   Gaston Lachaise (1882-1935). *Standing Woman Called "Elevation".* **Bronze.** Albright-Knox Art Gallery, Buffalo, New York. James G. Forsyth Fund

also imparts a monumental grandeur to the figure of woman; she is the Great Mother, the personification of the feminine generative principle in life and nature. He expresses a feeling for this particular mystique of the feminine more self-consciously and more overtly than the sculptor who made the *Venus of Willendorf*.[7] Yet despite the greater naturalism of Lachaise's figure and its obvious sophistication, I feel that the image embodies intuitive feelings for the erotic mystique of the feminine as basic as those that inspired the fashioning of any primitive Venus. Even the abstract volumes of a sculptor like Brancusi suggest a sensuous distortion of the feminine figure and therefore express feelings of pleasure and comfort. (See Figure 6-15.)

In startling contrast is the distortion suffered by the figure in the hands of another contemporary sculptor, Alberto Giacometti (Figure 6-16). There are no sensuous physical volumes here to attract, no strong physical presence to provide a sense of security and comfort. Instead, the form is attenuated and almost immaterialized. With corporeal and existential reality so reduced, we are made to feel aware of the invisible mental and emotional tensions of man's life. It is as if

FIG. 6-15　Constantin Brancusi (1876-1957). *Le Nouveau-ne* 1915. Philadelphia Museum of Art: The Louise and Walter Arensberg Collection

---

[7]Yet it should be pointed out that Lachaise's literal treatment of the figure produces an erotic image which is more obviously physical or sexual than it is mystical. But with the *Venus of Willendorf*, the absence of feet, arms, and hands, and the lack of features to the face, do not allow one to dwell on the merely physical nature of erotic confrontations, arousing instead nonspecific thoughts and feelings pertaining to a more universal theme of the maternal and erotic feminine. For these reasons, the relatively a-natural form of *Willendorf* assumes the kind of symbolic transformation which is discussed at the end of this chapter.

FIG. 6-16   Alberto Giacometti (1901-1966).
Man Pointing **1947. Bronze.** Tate Gallery, London

Giacometti strips man down to the bare nerve, leaving us to pick up the vibrations. As these linear forms stand around, they cut through space rather than occupy space. This characteristic affects us in two ways. We feel the vastness of space as opposed to matter, and we feel the essential loneliness of each man as the fuse splutters briefly along the line of his life. Consequently, one way in which the volumes of Lachaise or Brancusi allow us to feel secure is by representing space dominated by the tangible and material. But we see with Giacometti that when space triumphs over mass we feel uncertain and even apprehensive. We can feel physically confident about life faced with substantial mass and volume but we become metaphysical and speculative and remember death when confronted by a void of time and space.[8] For mass remains earthbound, while linear and more open forms explore space and defy gravity. It is interesting to notice that massive forms whose surface is ridged in a complex of planes and curves with their accompanying edges appear more linear than those heavy shapes whose surface is undisturbed. As a result the former appear less weighty and less static. Notice how that great Italian sculptor of the Baroque period, Gian Lorenzo Bernini (1598-1680) enlivens an inert mass of stone through the linearism of sharp folds and angles given to the robe of St. Teresa in Figure 6-17. And observe how, in contrast, what we take to be the rounder, smoother volumes of the saint's body appear heavy and

[8] This argument is developed further in Chapter 8 when discussing the formlessness of minimal art.

TRANSFORMATIONS

lifeless. In this way Bernini is able to make the body float, for he reveals only a face, wrist, and ankle to suggest weight and so bear witness to the miracle of levitation. How well he expresses the tensions — both physical and psychological — that exist between the opposites of energy (spirit) and matter (body) as the saint experiences the inward rush of the Holy Spirit. But let us return to the expressive transformation of the object in painting. What kind of feeling for both the dream and the reality of

FIG. 6-17   Gian Lorenzo Bernini (1598–1680). *The Ecstasy of St. Teresa.* Church of St. Vittoria, Rome. Photograph, Alinari

TRANSFORMATIONS

the feminine lies behind the painting shown in the Figure 6-18? Entitled *Woman I,*
it belongs to a series of such images by the contemporary American artist Willem de
Kooning. The distortions employed here are extreme. The painter, in common with
the primitive sculptor of the *Venus of Willendorf,* employs gross and erotic volumes
to express feelings for the fecundity of woman. On the other hand, it is obvious
that this work also reveals an attitude of contempt for the feminine, for nobody
would call it a kind or even a neutral image. The short slashing lines are devoid of
rhythmic flow or grace, and work with the tensions of the spiky angular shapes and
the harpy-like visage to convey de Kooning's feelings for twentieth-century
American woman. The figure is even harried by the surrounding space which is
angled, fragmented, and restless. What a contrast when we turn to Henri Mastisse,
one of the great French painters of our time. Figure 6-19 shows a drawing so
antithetical in spirit to de Kooning's *Woman* that it is like a gentle love song heard
after a coarse tavern ditty. Matisse's feelings are joyous and serene — as serene as the
long-flowing line with its gentle yet voluptuous curvature, and as uncomplicated
and tension-free as the rounded figure breathing comfortably in its tranquil space. It
is important to remember that expression in art may be as much concerned with
feelings of serenity as with tension and drama. One feels that Matisse extols woman
while de Kooning is cynically critical. The Frenchman does not stress a primitive
erotic fertility, or a contemporary feminine neuroticism, but reveals a more gracious
and sophisticated erotic sensuousness. But let Matisse, writing in 1908, speak for
himself:

Expression to my way of thinking does not consist of the
passion mirrored upon a human face or betrayed by a
violent gesture. The whole *arrangement* of my picture is
expressive. The place occupied by the figures or objects, *the
empty spaces around them*, the proportions, everything
plays a part.[9]

It is worthwhile studying de Kooning's painting again after reading this
statement to observe how the whole arrangement of his picture is antithetical to
Matisse's point of view. Then a comparison of the two images will indicate the wide
range of expressive techniques at the artist's disposal for conveying the temper of
his feelings. Lines are obviously important — single long flowing lines or many
short, fighting angular lines — lines which flow over the surface, liquid and smooth,
or lines which bite and are jabbed down, sharp, broken, and rough. The shape of
form is important — angular shapes, spiky shapes, or rounded shapes — shapes which
are proportionate or disproportionate; shapes either grossly bloated or witheringly

FIG. 6-19.   Henri Matisse (1869–1954).
Kneeling Nude **1918. Etching.** The Museum of
Modern Art, New York

---

[9] Herbert Read, *A Concise History of Modern Painting* (New York: Praeger, 1962), p. 38.
(Italics added.)

emaciated. And then, as Matisse says, the arrangement of the forms is important, for this determines the shape of the empty spaces which in turn suggest the troubled or tranquil mood of the work. Forms can jostle each other and crowd the space, or breathe and relax spatially, as the artist desires. (Neither must we forget how color has been constantly employed for expressive purposes, and not only in the realm of easel painting. Stain and paint were used on Greek sculpture and Greek temples, on the high stone-vaulted ceilings of medieval cathedrals, and on the wooden sculptures made in the rococo style of the early eighteenth century.) Of course the sculptor and architect have all of these elements at their disposal no less than the painter. Color is again creeping into contemporary sculpture and playing a larger role in architecture. Also, both architect and sculptor can work with angled and linear forms, or with more rounded volumes. And both are involved with the design of space in and around the work — space volumes such as the "holes" in sculpture or the interior of a building which serve expression no less than the spatial intervals in a drawing or painting.

Figure 6-20 will serve to confirm this. The French architect Le Corbusier, a twentieth-century master, pits the vertical thrust of tent-like poles against the sideways sweep of sensuous curvilinear surfaces, thus producing an exciting structure in terms of stress and strain. This pavilion possesses a forceful sculptural form which, seen from the outside, hints at an interior space equally exciting. The *brio* or vivacity of the form cannot help but kindle a response in the viewer, quickening feelings of exhilaration, curiosity, and anticipation. I remember visiting the Brussels International Exhibition and coming, after a tiring day of walking, to Le Corbusier's Pavilion. My spirits rose and my step became lighter as I approached, for it appeared a joyous and celebratory building, defying gravity in its movements up and through space. This experience was in direct contrast to one a few weeks earlier when I took a photograph of that celebrated Greek temple, the Parthenon,

FIG. 6-20   LeCorbusier (1887-1966). Philip's Pavilion, Brussels International Exhibition, 1958. Courtesy Architectural Review, London

FIG. 6-21   The Parthenon. 448–432 B.C. Acropolis, Athens

atop the hill of the Acropolis. (This photograph is reproduced as Figure 6–21.) It was also late in the afternoon when I confronted and appraised the temple, and I use the word "appraise" to indicate the calmness or perhaps rational coolness of my attitude. Certainly I appreciated the Parthenon's dignity, even grandeur . . . the perfect balance and symmetry between parts and the whole and the serene, harmonious proportions of its linear and area mathematics. Yet I was not moved by feelings of elation, nor did I experience the physical response of my body to weave and dance a little, as happened before the Pavilion. Figure 6–22 helps to explain how the Parthenon calms rather than excites.

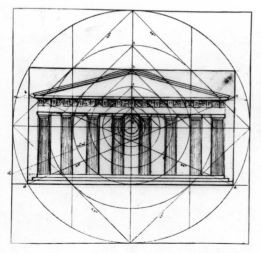

FIG. 6-22   Geometric Analysis of the Parthenon by Samuel Colman. Reproduced from *Nature's Harmonic Unity,* G. P. Putnam's Sons, New York

97

TRANSFORMATIONS

This diagrammatic analysis of the temple's structure reveals the calculated geometricism that gives the building its superb rationality. Conceived as a finely proportioned horizontal rectangle, we see how it is perfectly circumscribed by the circle whose horizontal and vertical axes pass through the geocentric and focal hub of the structure. Notice how the outer circle is proportionately diminished to the center and how the building grows concentrically from the inner to the outer circles. What a firm geometric control is exercised here — no eccentricity is allowed — nothing breaks out of the circular limits to strain the equilibrium. There is no pulling or pushing of forces to give the tensioned vitality that animates the Pavilion. I do not mean to imply that the Parthenon is so geometrically regular that it is dull. Like all Classical structures, the proportions of length, width, and height are subtly balanced yet have enough irregularity to give this balance a dynamic tilt. (The rules explaining this controlled formal vitality are described on pages 19 and 20 in Chapter 2, in the brief discussion of Euclidean geometry and the Golden Section.) However, we would surely agree that in contrast to the Pavilion, the Parthenon is a relatively static building, notwithstanding the satisfaction it affords our sense perceptions by virtue of its unity.

It is possible from this comparison to make some general statements about *expressiveness* which apply also to painting and sculpture. We are now aware that geometrically organized horizontals and verticals which maintain a 90° relationship satisfy a mental and emotional need for order and calm the feelings — they do not rock the boat of equanimity. Straight horizontal lines imply a gravity-like pull, a terrestrial equilibrium, which is emphasized when the overall organization of a design is horizontal and rectangular. The absence of forceful diagonals or straining curvilinear surfaces also help to tranquilize. A comparison of Leonardo's *Last Supper* (Figure 6-23) with Tintoretto's painting of the same subject approximately

FIG. 6-23   Leonardo da Vinci (1452-1519). *The Last Supper* **c. 1495-98. Mural painting.** St. Maria delle Grazie, Milan

FIG. 6-24   **Tintoretto (1518-1594).** *The Last Supper* **c. 1592-94. Oil on canvas.** St. Giorgio Maggiore, Venice

one hundred years later (Figure 6-24) demonstrates how these compositional factors work. Figure 6-23 epitomizes the contained dynamic balance of High Renaissance art, while Figure 6-24 confronts us with the diagonal-splitting compositional anarchy of post-Renaissance Mannerism. True, Le Corbusier's Pavilion is symmetrically organized — the two vertical thrusts on left and right balancing the central thrust point — but the dramatically curved sweep of the walls and the leaning angle of the poles overcome a potential static symmetry. In the Parthenon the vertical columns are subordinate to the dominant horizontality; in the Pavilion the three vertical thrusts positively oppose the horizontal. This opposition sets the lateral extension of the walls flowing downward from the thrust points and thus eliminates any true horizontal lines from the design. In their sweep from the supportive points, the walls sag in the center before rising to the next point of thrust and in this way follow the oval (less static than circular) ground plan. It is the tensions between horizontal and vertical, circle and oval, thrust and flow, upright and leaning, that we feel. The Pavilion is extremely plastic; it appears pliable rather than rigid, a breathing volume of contained space rather than a hard-edged and solid architectural mass. Thus the building has an organic vitality which is typical of Le Corbusier's work. Even though he may use a building material as harsh and as massive as concrete, his architectural forms seem to grow from the site and breathe. We can sum up briefly by suggesting that expressive vitality in architecture (as in painting or sculpture) depends upon motion and tension. If walls

99

or roof can be set in motion, swaying or diagonaling through space, a tension is created between inert mass (the material) and energy (the movement). Such an exuberant spatial extension of the ground plan and of the supportive structure in the shape of walls and roof produces the dynamic and exciting architecture which, when introduced in the seventeenth century, was called "baroque."

Now let us see how strong contrasts between light and shadow work to establish a mood. Compare for a moment two drawings. Figure 6–25 is by the eighteenth-century Italian painter Francesco Guardi, and Figure 6–26 shows a drawing by the nineteenth-century British painter John Constable. In Constable's drawing the dark tree forms and ground shadow give a strong, brooding darkness to the drawing; these are regions of mystery and ambiguity in which all detail is lost. Hence, the overall mood of the image is heavy, but some relief is afforded by the brief flashes of light which open up space, clarify something of the uncertainty, and herald the bright security of light after the darkness of night or storm. Constable maintains a complete contrast between black and white — there are no gentle transitions as in Guardi's drawing — and, as a result, the visual and the psychological tensions are strong. It seems fairly obvious that Constable was concerned with the dramatic visual effects of nature when he made the drawing. For these rapidly brushed-in forms do not appear to result from an objective deliberate study, but rather from the spontaneous overflow of feeling. The mood is elegiac, that is to say, one of foreboding and fascination before the elemental grandeur of nature. Guardi's drawing is the reverse side of the coin, showing a preponderance of light and gray tones rather than black. And here we see that an overall diffusion of light suggests a benevolent nature which sponsors human confidence and encourages a serenity of outlook. In contrast, shadow and darkness appear malevolent, tend to confine the body, confuse the mind, and turn the spirit in upon itself.

FIG. 6–25   **Francesco Guardi (1712–1793).** *Piazza in Venice.* **Oil.** Ca d'Oro, Venice

FIG. 6-26   John Constable (1776-1837). *Trees and Water on the Stour.* **Wash drawing.** Victoria and Albert Museum, London

In Guardi's brush drawing light floods the scene, all appears well with the world, and people stroll in confidence. Because a range of modulated gray tones separates white from black, the tensions of extreme opposition are lost. This overall play of light together with two other factors contribute to the optimistic mood of the drawing. Guardi employs soft or blurred edges to his forms; in addition, he has structured the scene horizontally and vertically and, as we know from past experience, such an organization imparts a gravitational stability to the work. Constable evokes his more rhapsodic mood by going to the other extreme. The edges of forms and shadows are brusque, broken, and in many places sharp; and the diagonal sweep of tree, ground, and sky creates a gravity defying turbulence. In conclusion, it should be mentioned that these two drawings represent attitudes toward nature which are typically Northern and Mediterranean. Landscape in Northern Europe often suggests man's unease in nature, displaying his sense of alienation before menacing mountains and threatening storm. But nature seems to become an ally when one descends (pictorially) to southern France, Italy, or Greece. Here the artist lingers among hills and trees, bathing in the light and enjoying the pastoral as home.

Now it remains for us to consider a form of expressive transformation which is capable of engaging a deep and sympathetic response without utilizing the more extreme means of exaggeration or distortion. It is a form in which passion and objectivity unite and are deliberately controlled to produce a taut feeling of suspense. We can do this best by comparing two paintings concerned with the same subject. They are both large canvases and were painted within ten years of each

101

FIG. 6-27   Eugene Delacroix
(1799-1863). *The Massacre at Chios*
1824. **Oil on canvas.** The Louvre,
Paris

other. Eugéne Delacroix painted *The Massacre at Chios* in 1824 (Figure 6-27), and Francisco Goya commenced painting *The Third of May* in 1814 (Figure 6-28). Both works were inspired by a contemporary event. Delacroix depicts the Turkish reprisal against the local people after a Greek uprising on the island of Chios. Goya shows a French reprisal against the citizens of Madrid for a similar resistance. In both of these works there is an intense saturation of human pathos, yet we see that Delacroix employs none of the more obvious means to achieve this. There is no blood spilled, no shrieking victims, and only a minimum use of violent gesture. Goya, however, shows the moment of killing, the bloody horror of the corpses, the faces of the victims distorted in their passion, the violent gestures of arms flung wide or covering faces. The figures reel and stagger, thrust themselves desperately forward on unwilling legs; the firing squad hunch aggressively over their rifles, their bended knees at a menacing angle. The night setting, illuminated by the glow of lanterns, aids the atmosphere of terror. We notice that Goya has painted the forms very broadly, paying little attention to detail of clothing or delineation of limb. The executioners appear as a subhuman species in their shapeless uniforms and square black hats; they are stocky and faceless. This looseness of handling helps impart a sense of unreality, as if the whole scene were a fleeting impression . . . a dream. And compositionally Goya organizes the design diagonally from bottom left to top right; the few horizontal movements are completely subordinate to the powerful diagonal thrust. This is a blunt, powerful painting in which the artist uses most of the expressive elements we have discussed to cry terror.

In comparison, *The Massacre at Chios* is mute. The horror does not explode in our faces and in our ears; rather, we experience an incessant inner weeping for the eternal tragedy of man's inhumanity to man. Delacroix's painting is more than a bloody happening in history. It reminds us once again that we distinguish the deeper, more profound feelings from the sentimental by the degree of tautness displayed. I do not mean to imply that Goya's painting is a sentimental work — far from it — but to suggest that the held-in agony of Chios may affect us more permanently than Goya's bludgeoning of our nerve. For there is an element of cathartic release with Goya that is not present with Delacroix. How does Delacroix achieve this kind of expressive intensity? First, it is obvious that in his drawing of the principal figures he is very objective. Their semi-nudity allows Delacroix to show an almost classical skill in delineating contour and shaping volume and proportion; even the clothing is rich in detail. Goya's figures are broadly treated — even impressionistic — the body itself lost in a shapeless bundle of clothes. Yet this very shapelessness is an obvious form of distortion which is strong in its expressive impact. Curiously enough, Delacroix's attention to natural appearances does not render his figures neutral as just naturalistic studies — as forms existing in their own natural right — although they possess this quality as a bonus. It is rather as if Delacroix's sympathy for the victims identifies him so completely in feeling with them that his desire to partly expose their bodies and reveal a noble physique is, in itself, an expression of his compassion for them. We should ask ourselves the question: "With whom do we identify most . . . Goya's victims or Delacroix's victims?" And perhaps another question should be asked: "Does the more blatant expressionism of Goya run to sensational reporting when compared to Delacroix's more naturalistic treatment?"

FIG. 6–28   Francisco Goya (1746–1828). *The Third of May* **1814. Oil on canvas.** The Prado, Madrid

I believe there is one lesson to be learned from the comparison of these two works. It is that the power of much expressive (or romantic) art lies in the degree of credibility it brings to the event; the image must establish this first, and then proceed to intensify or violate it in some way. This method is more effective than creating a completely imaginative fantasy, for we can tolerate the fantastic because it is not real within our matter-of-fact experience. The impact of early nineteenth-century romantic art, of which Goya and Delacroix are both great masters, lies in its ability to take real-life events and imbue them with the most intense feeling. But a study of Goya's works shows that he "escapes" to fantasy the more readily, while a similar examination of Delacroix shows him maintaining a hold on things as they are. Thus, in *The Massacre at Chios,* Delacroix moves us deeply without using positive gestures or distortions, without the aid of Nolde-like expressive colors, without the violent compositional movement of splitting diagonals or sweeping curves, and in the full security of daylight. Instead of exploiting any one of these possibilities, he creates a more subtle tension by playing several opposite factors off against each other. For example, the relatively sombre colors of the landscape and exposed bodies are opposed by the richer colors of cloth, uniforms, jewelry, and other objects. Compositionally, the work is organized essentially in a series of horizontal planes — and we have assumed that horizontal movements are passive in feeling — yet the two figure groups left and right of center form opposing pyramids, creating two diagonal movements which jar the horizontal pulse. Even these two movements are set against each other, for the taller right-hand pyramid formed by the rearing horse and rider produces a more threatening suggestion of diagonal force. Within this pyramid the figures twist and writhe — the only violent physical action seen in the foreground of the work. Contrasted with this, the figures on the left are still; in consequence, the frenzy of the nervously rearing horse with its rider twisting around to reach his sword, and of the struggling girl and attacking youth, gain a marked intensity.

Although the figures in the left-hand group appear to be individually still, Delacroix builds a tension out of their vertical-horizontal collective grouping as the pyramid collapses right across the forefront of the painting. The captive on the left is still on his feet, but those huddled around him sink to the ground, their bodies forming angled thrusts against the horizontal earth as they lose strength and will. This collapse of the composition from left to right is counteracted by the vertical body of the old woman who sits upright — a brief return to life and hope — before the movement sinks into the ground and expires in the horizontal body of the dead woman at the extreme right. And what an eerie, despairing last convulsion is imparted to this whole movement by the twist of the child's body as it lies on its mother. Light and shadow are in similar opposition; the painter emphasizes the movement we have just described by lighting the frontal figures, allowing the shadows behind to provide the necessary contrast yet also to shroud the guards in mystery as a threatening, unknown factor. Further paradox is supplied by Delacroix's treatment of the island context. For nature is quiet and benign, hardly ruffled by the smoke and flame from the distant town, unaware of the human drama being enacted. To set high tragedy against such an idyllic, peaceful backdrop of sea and sky can do nothing but sharpen the pathos.

We are led ultimately through a series of plastic and psychological polarities to *feel* the stillness of the victims. They do not clutch each other violently but huddle with a quiet desperation for contact, body against body. The rich stuff of their remaining clothes acts to remind us that life was good, and the contrast with their exposed bodies drives this point home. Physically speaking the figures of the left-hand group are not tense but resigned, yet we feel the depth of their mental and spiritual suffering. The central figure of the bearded man who reclines on one elbow serves as the silent spokesman for them all. His whole posture and the detachment of his gaze indicate a stoic strength of spirit in the face of imminent death. Yet even here Delacroix introduces an opposite note, for the fully dressed older woman who sits at his feet is rigid with fear. She sits tensely, her gaze not stoically resigned but fearfully expectant as she sees some danger approaching from outside the group. Again we see how juxtaposed opposites react to heighten each other's effect.

Goya or Delacroix; Delacroix or Goya. This is not the issue. The important thing is to see that a predominantly expressive work can make its point through a containment of feeling rather than by its extravagant release; that what we call expressionism in art does not depend upon the eccentric imagination and its high fantasy, but can be culled from the most obvious and real drama of all — from the fact that we exist, everything and everybody, participating in life, yet threatened by death. Here is the ultimate drama, the ultimate paradox.

5. Symbolic Transformation

There is much misunderstanding about what constitutes a symbol and what may be termed symbolic in the visual arts; and understandably so, for symbolic communication is a complicated phenomenon of consciousness. Therefore, we have avoided frequent use of the term thus far even though an image may have been aptly described as symbolic. Neither can we treat the implications of symbolism comprehensively here for it is far too vast a subject. However, if we can establish the basic nature of symbolic processes it will be possible in the remaining chapters to use the term when applicable and so develop an informed response to symbols in order to render the whole symbolic issue less complex and confused.

Symbolic transformation and expressive transformation are closely related, for they spring from a common soil — from the subjective life of man in the broad range of his thinking and feeling. The term "symbolic" is therefore sometimes used in a very general sense to define those qualities in a work which relate to the inner world of the artist, feeling and thinking alike. For we have seen that when a painter, a poet, or a sculptor looks at the world he brings to it something of himself — he invests the physical reality of the object with the psychological reality it assumes in his own consciousness. Yet thought and feeling are abstract and intangible events in the life of the psyche and, as such, have no concrete existence. Therefore, shape and color can never be formal replicas of ideas and feelings, but only allude to them in a correlative capacity. When art does manage to convey strongly the quality of our inner life, we realize that the forms employed go beyond their representational associations and tell us much about the nature of man's ineffable experiences. When this happens very positively we would describe the image as symbolic. The painter Wassily Kandinsky describes the nature of symbolic communication in a single sentence. He writes: "That which has no material existence cannot be materially crystallized."[10] William Blake, artist and poet, put it another way: "Our tangible, material experiences of the world can well be conveyed by analogy and metaphor; but the *essence* of life can only be conveyed by the symbol." Consequently, images that assume a symbolic power touch the deeper and more subjective areas of the self (rather than describing our more sensual, physically satisfying contacts with the world), for it is here, says Blake, that the essence of life is to be found.

All art is symbolic in greater or lesser degree — there is a man in his own essence behind every work of art. But it is necessary to move from symbolism in this broad sense and study it more specifically in those images which are powerfully and dominantly symbolic. This is no easy task, for it is difficult to distinguish the expressive factor from the symbolic; the two elements merge imperceptibly into each other. We gain a lot of help in understanding the implications of a positive symbolism from poets and artists themselves. I have already quoted in Chapter 5 from a note written by Coleridge and here quote from it again:

> In looking at objects of nature . . . as at yonder moon dim
> glimmering through the dewey window pane, I seem rather
> to be seeking, as it were asking, a symbolic language for
> *something within me that forever and already exists.* . . .

The fact that Coleridge would talk about "a symbolic language" for what he feels exists inside himself suggests that he does not positively *know* what exists. It is not something that can be categorically described even as a mental, a felt-thought event, much less be ascribed to any particular part of the body. This unintelligible aspect of the experience makes it impossible for the poet to know directly what affects him; he can only know it obliquely through the agency of a third thing acting to make it partly intelligible. So, for Coleridge, the glimmering moon becomes the third thing, the symbol. The reader will recall that in discussing inspiration in Chapter 5 we were concerned with the relationship between form and feeling, form and idea. We concluded that inspiration was essentially a moment of vision, an insight gained into the meaning and value of existence that went beyond the gathering of data and fact-finding activities of the rational intellect. Consequently, we now see that the objects which trigger moments of vision — the sea-shore

---

[10] W. Kandinsky, *Concerning the Spiritual in Art,* Documents of Modern Art, No. 5 (New York: George Wittenborn, Inc., 1947), p. 9.

TRANSFORMATIONS

pebbles for the sculptor Moore, or the thorn bush for the painter Sutherland — are themselves symbols. That is, they become more than themselves, triggering highly imaginative responses from the artist, rather than limiting him to an objective interest in their physical nature. The process comes full circle when the object is transformed into the work of art and so becomes the *created* symbol which now alludes more potently to the artist's inner life. In discussing the sunflower paintings of van Gogh the writer D. H. Lawrence describes this process as follows:

> When van Gogh paints sunflowers, he reveals, or achieves the vivid relation between himself, as man, and the sunflower, as sunflower, at that quick moment of time. His painting does not represent the sunflower itself. We shall never know what the sunflower itself is. And the camera will visualize the sunflower far more perfectly than van Gogh can. The vision on the canvas is a third thing, utterly intangible and inexplicable, the offspring of the sunflower itself and van Gogh himself. . . . It is a revelation of the perfected relation, at a certain moment, between a man and a sunflower. . . .[11]

Lawrence is saying that the sunflower is the symbol for van Gogh (as the moon was for Coleridge) which triggers the inner response. But in using the sunflower as the motif for his painting, it necessarily becomes transformed into the artistic or poetic symbol, for it embodies something of van Gogh which was quickened and realized at that moment of time when the relationship was perfected. Van Gogh himself describes the painter's problem in searching for the image which will convey the essential quality of such moments of self-revelation. In the year 1888 he writes from Arles to his brother, Theo, that he wants to paint so that:

> . . . . everyone with eyes to see can understand. To express the feelings of two lovers by a marriage of two complementary colors, their mixture and their oppositions, the mysterious vibrations of tones in each other's proximity. To express the thought behind a brow by the radiance of a bright tone against a dark ground. To express hope by some star, the ardour of a being by the radiance of a setting sun. . . .[12]

When van Gogh talks about "the ardour of a being" or "the feelings of two lovers," he is referring to human experiences of which we are all aware. Our consciousness is significantly changed when we are "in love," or at any time when our ardor for life is enhanced. On these occasions when everything takes on a different value, a person is moved to such a degree of self-awareness that he seems to be more completely identified with some principle of life. Van Gogh was concerned with how to express

---

[11] D. H. Lawrence, *Morality and the Novel: Selected Literary Criticism*, ed. Anthony Beal (New York: Viking, 1956), p. 108.

[12] Eugene Weber, *Paths to the Present* (New York: Dodd, Mead and Co., 1960), p. 202.

this identification so that everyone would understand it just by looking at a painting. You will gather from his letter that there are no simple solutions; two figures in an embrace would only describe the physical situation and not convey this new intensity of being, the essence of the experience. Instead, he talks about color and the "mysterious vibration of tones" which emanates from certain colors in juxtaposition. Similarly, he seeks to express a "thought" by the radiance of light against dark. He talks about wanting to paint "hope," but hope is not like a tree, a mountain, or an apple. It is relatively easy to paint a mountain for it has a concrete existence, but we cannot point to an object in the material world and say, "That is hope." Hope is merely the name we give to a human condition which is part feeling, part concept. Again, how would we paint a concept such as the *divine*? For the idea of the divine is an invention of our consciousness, not something tangible in the world. Yet art has attempted to visualize it for thousands of years. Van Gogh suggests that the creative solution to these problems is to discover colors and objects which imply or symbolize subjective and abstract realities — a star for hope, a setting sun for passion or ardor. In the same way the ancient Egyptians and many other peoples have used golden discs to illuminate the concept of the divine — we are all familiar with the golden halo in Christian iconography.

In the year 1886 Jean Moreas published a manifesto declaring that only Symbolism was "capable of logically conveying the contemporary tendencies of the creative spirit in the art." Although the manifesto was concerned with literature, its relevance to pictorial art was soon recognized and it was adopted by the developing Symbolist art movement. Paul Gauguin was the acclaimed leader of the movement, but it was the painter Odilon Redon who developed an art of total symbolism and inspired the Surrealists of our own century in their attempt to bring together imaginative dream and objective fact. It is interesting to see that the Symbolists — the first group to declare that art's prime role is a totally symbolic one — stressed, as Gauguin put it, "the mysterious processes of the mind." Maurice Raynal writes that Gauguin "no longer contemplated nature with an eye to reproducing it, but 'meditated' his picture beforehand. Of his *Christ in the Garden of Olives,* Gauguin remarked: 'It is imbued with an abstract sadness, and sadness is my vocation.' Another of his sayings was: 'What wonderful thoughts can be evoked by form and color!'"[13] Redon also declared the inspirational nature of thought translated into images to be the only justification of art, but we know that he was not referring to rational, cause-and-effect thought. Like the poets Blake and Coleridge, he uses the word "thought" as a synonym for that complex mental state known as poetic feeling, or poetic vision. We discussed this at some length in the chapter on inspiration and suggested how these imaginative reserves are tapped and what vital subjective realities spring from them. The paintings of Odilon Redon are symbolic transformations of the natural world, leading us mysteriously into his private dreams, his private cosmogony. And we receive further confirmation from Redon that these moments of vision — which can be best revealed not by description but

[13] Maurice Raynal, *Modern Painting* (Geneva: Albert Skira, 1960), p. 27.

by allusion — do not result from acts of reasoned and deliberate objectivity, but from states of surrender to the creative muse. He writes: "Everything takes form when we lay ourselves open to the uprush of the Unconscious."[14] The reader will not be taken unawares by this statement, for we have discussed the implications of the unconscious fairly thoroughly. But it is significant that the theory should crop up again in the context of symbolism, for it supports another conclusion. This is that genuine, powerful symbols cannot be deliberately or self-consciously produced; they can only be discovered in the unselfconscious involvement with the developing image. It seems that symbols develop from, and allude back to, those modes of apprehension which we attribute to intuitive or unconscious sources. Consequently, there is a degree of ambiguity or unintelligibility about the more powerful symbols for they are born from the deeper regions of the self, from beyond the fringe of reason. They give "intimation of a meaning beyond the level of our present powers of comprehension."[15]

The often-quoted phrase "to clothe the idea in perceptible form," was the proclaimed gospel of the Symbolist movement, and we can use it as a clue to distinguish between expressive and symbolic transformation. At the risk of oversimplifying the problem I would suggest that a predominantly expressive work arouses our feelings — our sympathy or revulsion, fear, anger, desire, and so on. Yet an image that is strong in symbolic allusion does more than awaken feeling. It involves us in speculation. We find ourselves wondering about things; about abstract principles and concepts such as those that occupied van Gogh when he pondered on the essence of human love or on the validity of hope . . . on the idea of a thing in the mind rather than on the thing itself. In our response to symbolic art we are generally led through feeling to thought. But we respond to expressive art much more simply and directly because our feelings can take us over, without benefit or need of meditation.

The selection of visual illustrations for this final part of the chapter has proved difficult; there are so many varied possibilities. Therefore, rather than diminish the impact by presenting several images, let us concentrate on one painting. Graham Sutherland's *Thorn Trees* (Figure 6–29) has already been reproduced in Chapter 5 as an example of how an artist experiences a moment of vision. Now let us look at it to see the symbolic transformation suffered by the natural thorn bush. It is not necessary to repeat the story of Sutherland's encounter with the thorns (see page 61) but rather to examine one's own responses to the painting. We are aware that the painter has created a design of twisted spikiness, the sharpness of which we can actually feel. He has almost made a sculpture of these sharp forms from his keen perception of nature's thorn bush. The pictorial space is trapped and menaced by the jabbing points, and while we realize that this is how thorn trees are — especially if one were to enlarge a small tangled section — the thoughts that finally come to mind may have nothing to do with thorn trees, and we may proceed

---

[14] Carl Jung, *The Spirit in Man, Art, and Literature,* p. 76.

[15] Maurice Raynal, *Modern Painting* (Geneva: Albert Skira, 1960), p. 29.

FIG. 6-29   Graham Sutherland (b. 1903-   ). *Thorn Trees* **1946. Oil on canvas.** Collection British Council, London

beyond feelings of apprehension or foreboding. Instead, one finds oneself thinking of the mystery of human suffering, of the unknown fate that awaits one beyond the portal of thorns, the frailty of the impersonal inevitability of nature and of death, and of the whole tragic sense of life. Different ideas will occur to others; sadists and masochists may have their thoughts turned in other directions, as may Christians or Mohammedans. But the important thing is that accompanying the feeling of apprehension, fear, or fascination, the mind will ponder the meaning and consequence of man and his place in nature. For many people the *Thorn Trees* stands as a symbol which engages and stimulates the imagination in its constant concern with our metaphysical problem.

> My work contains the whole soul of a man who has known
> the depths of life's mysteries, who has sought them as a
> lover, with joy, and reverence, and fear.
> Pablo Picasso

VII

THE IMAGINATION
AND TIME:
AN OBSESSION

The subject of time in art presents an enormous task in itself if treated comprehensively, and so I find necessary to devote two chapters to the subject in even this basic discussion. The present chapter and the next one are both concerned with the issue of time in consciousness. This arrangement enables us to discuss, first, what seems to be a fact of life for the artistic temperament, namely, a built-in obsession with time, and then to consider space and light as empirical realities which stimulate a further imaginative response to time. Even so, we can at best make only a cursory exploration of the fascinating yet inscrutable problem of time in the artist's consciousness. For although all men must experience the anomalous nature of time in their lives, the imaginative and creative man lives constantly with its changing intensities and pressures.

It will be obvious by now to even the most casual reader that there is a continuous pulse to the life of an artist — that his senses and mind move intently, like a radar scanner picking up signals. Even at those times when he may appear inactive, this inquiry into the shape of life and reality is still going on; the body with its visual and other senses is recording, the mind is making associations, and feelings and ideas are pursuing each other in a constant round. As Rilke wrote in a letter from Sweden:

> I have often asked myself whether those days on which we
> are forced to be indolent are not just the ones we pass in
> profoundest activity.[1]

And that prolific genius Leonardo was once compelled to explain to Ludovico Sforza, Duke of Milan, that when he appeared to be doing nothing he was really most active imaginatively. It seems that there is no rest for the creative personality. He is driven constantly by the psyche in a round-the-clock activity, and apparently

---

[1] C. G. Jung, *The Spirit in Man, Art and Literature,* p. 95.

there is nothing very much he can do about it. We gained a little insight into this situation in the earlier chapters when probing the nature of the artistic consciousness, the driving force of the unconscious, and the workings of inspiration. It is important to remember that the imaginative life is always going on with these men, that they are rarely, if ever, drifting unproductively. In his poem "In Railway Halls," Stephen Spender ruthlessly dismisses the ordinary man and his more mechanical consciousness in the following two lines:

> Time merely drives these lives which do not live
> As tides push rotten stuff along the shore.[2]

Now an aimless drifting through life may be very comfortable, but it is anathema to the dynamic yet constantly reflective mind of the artist. In the lines quoted above, Spender asserts that people who do not live in a positive way are merely pushed along by time, thereby implying that the man who lives intensely, that is, creatively, uses and exploits time to extract from it all he can. Time must be productive and valued rather than passively accepted or squandered. This attitude is echoed in the statements made by many different kinds of artists. They experience time as a force which drives them to work simply because they know there is only a certain amount of it available for any one life. Consequently, the man of sensibility regards time as both enemy and friend. It is the enemy because he dies from it; yet it is the ally because its brevity compels him to squeeze all he can from life. Thus the unremitting compulsion to produce which drives the artist results, in part, from an obsession with time unknown by the ordinary individual; the average man generally knows time as the mechanical sequence of intervals between routine places and events.

The realization that death is inevitable and is the end of one's personal amount of time lurks constantly in the daily consciousness of many artists. Some only experience it strongly during those creative moments when they are open to what Odilon Redon called, "the uprush of the unconscious." Michelangelo and Delacroix seemed to be thinking of it all the time; Paul Klee, on the other hand, was aware of it more compellingly during the last years of his life, through dreams, and in the special moments of creative vision. In any event, the effect of this kind of pressure on the artist is not easy to determine. But certainly a concern with death drives a man to produce works of art which will stand "in memoriam" to his life — to his aspirations and his vision. The writer James Baldwin exclaims:

> That is why he is called a poet. And his responsibility, which
> is also his joy and his strength and his life, is to defeat all
> labels and complicate all battles by insisting on the human
> riddle, to *bear witness* as long as breath is in him to that
> mighty, unnameable, transfiguring force which lives in the
> soul of man, and to aspire to do his work so well that

---

[2] Stephen Spender, *Poems by Stephen Spender* (New York: Random House, 1934), p. 60.

when the breath has left him the people — all people! — who search in the rubble *for a sign or a witness* will be able to find him there.[3]

Some of us may feel with Spinoza that "a man wishes to persist in his own essence," but even if a personal survival beyond death is not the issue — what Baldwin describes as the leaving behind of a sign or a witness — to be aware of death is to become doubly aware of being alive. As a result it is impressed upon us that all things change, that one experience must give way to the next in the flow of time. In fact, the reality of change is one reality we can depend upon and it forces us to ponder the transience of life, the significance of the fleeting moment. Yet one of the great satisfactions gained from creating a work of art is that a passing event has been "eternized," that some moments of joy, beauty, or pain have been withdrawn from the thrall of time and given a more permanent existence in the image. For example, I still remember the kitchenmaid painted so sensitively by Vermeer and as far as I am concerned, she is still going about her chores in her seventeenth-century Dutch kitchen. The urge to halt the remorseless passage of time by freezing it in the created image is, in my view, a powerful motivation for artists, and many have testified to the strength of it. "There is a passing moment in the world. Paint it in its reality. Forget everything for that," Paul Cézanne said. And Francis Bacon, the comtemporary British painter, has said:

> I would like some day to trap a moment of life in its full beauty. That would be the ultimate painting.[4]

Perhaps no other poet has expressed this power of art to withdraw life from time quite so poignantly as John Keats in his famous "Ode on a Grecian Urn." The personages depicted on the urn still live in the poet's imagination, for although they are physically dead, their joys, hopes, and desires are not lost or forgotten. The poem is Keats' tribute to art for the immortality it bestows upon the fleeting events of human life; for the figures on the urn, by their presence, posture, and silent dialogues, overcome time, the destroyer.

> Thou still unravished bride of quietness,
> Thou foster-child of silence and slow time. . . .

However, in the second verse a note of sadness creeps in. Keats acknowledges that art is not life and commiserates with the painted image of the youth long dead — for as an image he has gained immortality, but as an image he can never experience the existential fulfillment of love.

---

[3] James Baldwin, "Why I Stopped Hating Shakespeare," *Sunday Observer* (London), April 19, 1964, Sec. 2, p. 1. (Italics added.)

[4] Eric Protter: *Painters on Painting* (New York: Grosset and Dunlap, 1963), p. 246. © by Eric Protter, 1963.

Heard melodies are sweet, but those unheard
   Are sweeter; therefore, ye soft pipes, play on;
Not to the sensual ear, but, more endeared,
   Pipe to the spirit ditties of no tone;
Fair youth, beneath the trees, thou canst not leave
   Thy song, nor ever can those trees be bare;
Bold Lover, never, never canst thou kiss,
   Thou winning near the goal — yet, do not grieve;
She cannot fade, though thou hast not thy bliss,
   Forever wilt thou love, and she be fair!

Keats reminds us that "you can't have your cake and eat it!" To be immortalized by art is to be removed from time and desire. For if the young man is to know the pleasure of kissing the girl, he must proceed to the next stage of action *in time* and, in so doing, acknowledge that one event inevitably gives way to the next; thus even the first kiss will eventually become only a memory, and every fulfillment is a move nearer to his own death. The alternative is to eschew action, freeze time and life, and gaze forever on her face. So Keats recognizes and affirms that art is perhaps the only way we have to freeze the moment and arrest time's flow; but he laments that art exposes the ultimate tragedy of the human situation; namely, that when faced with meaningful events in life we lose the consummation if we stay the action, yet once we have acted, the consummate moment must inevitably pass. Art does stay the action and does render a moment relatively eternal. It feeds our need to know the continuity of human response; it relieves us temporarily from facing our destiny which is to die; but once we make art the reality instead of life then we are in the predicament Keats describes. Like the image of the Greek youth, the artist stands out of time wherein all events must be consummated.

    Of course the individual poet or painter recognizes that the creating of images affords at best a temporary and transpersonal kind of immortality and that consequently he must face a personal death and an end of time in his life. Yet he finds that a creative existence makes a good compromise, for in making every moment count through the practice of art, he not only discovers something of life's meaning, quality, and value, but also escapes the thrall of clock time. And yet in achieving this by constantly transforming life's experiences into art, the images in no way serve to prolong his own personal existence. Writing in his *Journal* on the nineteenth of August, 1858, Delacroix states that "one works not only to produce art but to give value to time. . . ." The same artist reveals the sense of frustration and oppression that besets him when time drags heavily and the work — or the inspiration — is not forthcoming:

> . . . The outcome of my days is always the same; an infinite
> desire for what one never gets; a void one cannot fill; an
> utter yearning to produce in all ways, to battle as much as
> possible against time that drags us along, and the
> distractions that throw a veil over our soul. . . .

It has often been said that certain works of art are timeless. What is meant by this is that they reveal an attitude toward life which strikes a responsive and familiar chord in others, irrespective of time or place. The ceremonies shown on the Grecian urn are not, in themselves, what Keats is concerned with. He is concerned about these happenings because they represent the constant and common ritual by which young people discover each other's attractions and begin to live their hopes and aspirations while they have the time. In the same way Vermeer was not just illustrating a mundane domestic event in the painting of the maid servant; if so, his work would have artistic value now only as an interesting record of period costume and furnishings. It is because Vermeer invests the scene with a familiar and unforgettable flavor of domestic serenity that the image lives on. And so we see that when Delacroix talks about giving "value to time," he means that in transforming events into art it is the special quality of the event in his consciousness that drives him to paint and, in so doing, to trap it and thus remove it from time's flow. Like the clairvoyant, the artist who is obsessed with time and value is totally involved with the nontangible world of psychological reverberations. He distinguishes the reactions which possess intrinsic value from those of lesser quality and, as his wisdom develops, he comes to know the essence — or ultimate quality — of Being, in and out of time.

Through countless years of evolution man has developed many concepts and sentiments which are his yardstick for judging the important values of existence. We talk about there being an inherent dignity or nobility to even the simplest life, about the power of love, the satisfaction of imaginative experience, the beauty of the countryside, the joy of accomplishment, the peace of God, and so on. Matisse spoke about "an art of balance . . . serenity . . . like an appeasing influence. . . ." Professor Giedion writes that "something lives within us which forms part of the very backbone of human dignity: I call this the demand for continuity."[5] Whatever statement is made about the various ways in which life assumes purpose or meaning, there is often the implication that this involves being aware of time as something more than a mere passing parade of impressions. For we can experience time in two ways — by duration of an event in consciousness and by the intensity with which it grips consciousness. Duration is normally thought of as the quantitative aspect of time, while intensity is regarded as a qualitative term. Time in duration is measured mechanically by the clock, the calendar, and other more sophisticated scientific instruments, but these devices tell us nothing about how intense or subdued is a portion of time in an individual consciousness. If we want to know this, then we do not turn to science or any of the chronologically-oriented disciplines, but to the arts. For it is the created image that captures an intense moment of perception, the days lost in dream, or the rapt involvement with an idea or revelation. The fact that an hour has passed in clock-time might mean nothing to a poet or sculptor, for the distinctive quality of a particular experience may have shortened the time to seem

---

[5] S. Giedion, *The Eternal Present*, p. 52.

but a couple of minutes. The reverse is also true. It is possible to experience just a few moments which are so charged with value that they seem to embrace all the experience of a lifetime. On these occasions, terms such as "beginning" and "end" have little meaning. When Delacroix complains about "a void (of time) one cannot fill," he is really describing a situation which he finds incredibly painful — when he is only aware of time as clock-time, as measured periods which assume no special intensity or change of pace because he is mentally and emotionally uninvolved. Mere physiological existence is anethema to a sensitive man.

Now this ability to experience time in terms of intensity rather than duration is not solely the prerogative of the artist — it is common to all men. But in today's world the pattern of life is so methodically and scientifically organized that time for most people is measured only in terms of clock-duration. That this is not a satisfying way to live is borne out by the number of younger people who adopt the artistic or uncommitted, nomad role in order to find time to give value to time. This faculty has never been lost to the true artist-poet. His ability to experience the present as a continuity of the past and as the herald of the future, due to a "telescoping" of chronological time in the intensity of his involvement, is a characteristic by which he has always been recognized. Writing about the number of possible dimensions of human awareness, the poet Robert Graves states:

> The fifth (dimension) is when we can control time as easily
> as a sculptor controls space.[6]

This statement brings us once again to face that difficult factor underlying the workings of the imagination, namely, the role of the unconscious; but now we confront it in terms of its effect on the artist's involvement with time. For the ability to "control" time seems to depend, paradoxically enough, upon an expansion of consciousness in which rational processes no longer play a dominant part. In discussing creative inspiration in Chapter 5, we were involved constantly with this phenomenon. And we saw that only when the rational processes of will and objective idea were transcended by an unselfconscious mental and emotional force did the artist experience the power of inspirational insight. It became obvious in that discussion that his sense of time underwent some change. Creative people in both the arts and the sciences have often declared that they are not always aware of time as a linear, measured progression from point to point, from a "beginning" to an "end." Instead, they talk about suffering noncreative periods of stagnancy when time drags unbareably along — witness Delacroix's "void"; but then they move from this extreme to the other — to periods of imaginative vitality when they are not aware of any long or short duration of time, for their consciousness of the linear flow is suspended. In fact, they sometimes talk of being "out of time." In the same way that the sound barrier can be broken if an aircraft's speed is sufficiently fast, so we can think of the time barrier being broken if the creative involvement is

---

[6] In a letter to the author dated November 2, 1969.

sufficiently intense. This comparison gives us a mental image of time in which the movement is no longer that of a line coming from the past, the forward end of which is the present, and the future the empty space into which the line is inching. Instead, it is as if the individual stands at the common *center* of past, present, and future, immersed in a *pool* of time and experiencing all three stages simultaneously.

Let me put this another way. If we think of time as a river in the linear sense of starting somewhere and flowing into an ocean of infinite size, we see the flow as relatively constant in one direction. This is how our normal and more mechanical consciousness is aware of time. But if some great force such as a powerful whirlpool suddenly appears in the river, it will interfere with the normal flow of water. Depending upon its strength it will suck in water from all sides, upstream and downstream, and one will witness the phenomenon of the lower stream drawn backwards by the force. Within the whirlpool itself, therefore, there will be water from upstream which has reached that particular point in the river for the first time; but there will also be water from downstream which had already passed that position. If we retain the analogy of the river as the flow of time, we see that the sudden appearance of the whirlpool has created a strange situation. For anyone who is caught at the center of this vortex will be immersed in three stages of time simultaneously. The present moment (the vortex center) will embrace time from the past (the water from upstream) and also future time (the water from downstream that was ahead of the whirlpool position). This mental image of a whirlpool of time may serve to describe those moments in an artist's life when he is, as Plato said, "inspired and out of his senses, and the mind is no longer in him." As the whirlpool interrupts the natural measure of the river's flow, so, it seems, the psychological force or intensity of creative involvement interrupts the natural measure of time's flow in consciousness.

Here lie the implications of Robert Graves' statement about controlling time. When the man we call the artist or poet is intensely involved with a significant event in his consciousness, he becomes a medium through which the whole range of the psyche's imaginative powers can flow. When Plato says that "the mind is no longer in him," he means that the rational intellect is no longer the policeman monitoring impressions in consciousness. And, as we have said many times before, this allows the artist to experience insights gleaned from intuitive or unconscious sources. A characteristic of this highly creative condition is that it seems to throw the man into the whirlpool of time we have described, thus allowing him to move back and forth in time as the spirit moves him. Consequently, Graves suggests that the person who is truly possessed of these creative powers has the means at his disposal to control time, to stand like the visionary and prophet in a simultaneity of past, present, and future. Is this not the experience of time which Paul Cézanne expressed so poetically when he said: "I breathe the virginity of the world. I am assailed by a sharpness of its hues. I feel as if I were aglow with all the hues of the infinite. I become one with my picture. . . ." Professor Clements describes Michelangelo's loss of a sense of time during his creative furies in the following words:

During these periods of intense immersion, when he did not eat
regularly and dropped off to sleep fully clothed, he lost all
sense of time. At these periods the necessity of dating a letter
became a minor annoyance. Thus, one reads such amusing
datings as "I don't know what date this is, but yesterday was
St. Luke". . . . "It's some date in February, according to my
servant girl". . . . These withdrawals from the calendar
coincided with periods of furious creativity, periods of what
he called *passioni* or *gelosie.*[7]

Many artists have talked about time in a way which supports the thesis developed in
this chapter, but two "modern" painters have made statements which are
particularly relevant. We have previously quoted from the perceptive writings of
Piet Mondrian, and now, in his essay *Plastic Art & Pure Plastic Art,* he has this to
say about time.

Both science and art are discovering and making us aware of
the fact that *time is a process of intensification*, of the
subjective toward the objective; toward the essence of things
and ourselves.[8]

Mondrian wrote this essay in 1937, and a year later the German painter Max
Beckmann gave a lecture in London in which he said:

To transform height, width, and depth into two dimensions
is for me an experience full of magic in which I glimpse for
a moment that fourth dimension which my whole being is
seeking.[9]

If I may be allowed to interpret these statements I find that they say virtually the
same thing. Both men have found a new dimension of time. Mondrian suggests that
some essence of the self is discovered when time is intensified through creative
action and that this, paradoxically enough, enables the artist to gain insights into an
ultra-personal reality — one in which truths pertaining to the nature of existence for
all things are revealed. Beckmann's statement is similar in implication, for he
suggests that in the creative act he discovers a timelessness which engages the
intrinsic self — the spiritual center which is beyond time and the world-oriented self
of the ego. It seems that these two painters have overcome the momentariness of
the "now" and discovered the whirlpool or continuum in which the time barrier, as
far as historical, linear time is concerned, is broken. In so doing they transcend a
point of existence in time and place and experience some kind of link with what we

---

[7] Robert J. Clements, *Michelangelo's Theory of Art,* p. 45.

[8] Piet Mondrian, "Plastic Art & Pure Plastic Art," from *Documents of Modern Art* (New York:
Wittenborn, Schultz, 1945). Introduction by Harry Holtzman.

[9] Max Beckmann, *On My Painting.* Published in New York by the late Curt Valentin in 1941. ©
Ralph F. Colin, executor, Valentin estate.

can only call the infinite (that is, if we may be permitted to take the mystical and necessarily symbolic nature of their words seriously). For myself, I believe that the artist's ability to adventure in time results largely from the operation of unconsicous forces underlying the creative imagination, and that his general obsession with the need to use time significantly and intensively before death is an inevitable consequence of his subjection to these forces.

The fourth dimension which Max Beckmann finds so magical is, of course, impossible to describe. But there is sufficient evidence to indicate that the contents of the unconsicous are not limited by, and do not belong to, the time dimensions of normal consciousness. For example, in our deeper dreams we traverse the centuries and find ourselves in strange places at different times in history. On waking in the morning it is the present time that seems unreal. When the artist is completely involved with his work, he is taken over by insights, images, and feelings which represent a transformation of consciousness. It is characteristic of this condition that the person experiences a transformation of time. All we can say is that his knowledge of time moves beyond the existential reality of the present, beyond his memory of time since birth, and he stands ageless before his work, a man of all seasons and of all time. It is not difficult to understand why Beckmann should describe this as a fourth-dimensional, magical experience. For it does seem to represent a breakthrough to another and mysterious level of our existence or being.

VIII

THE TRINITY OF SPACE, LIGHT, AND TIME

> The horizon was visible right round; beneath the sombre
> dome of the sky stretched the vast plain of empty sea. But
> immeasurable, unarticulated space weakens our power to
> measure time as well: the time sense falters and grows dim.

It is with these words that Thomas Mann, in his story *Death in Venice*,
describes the sense of isolation experienced on a sea voyage and inadvertently sets
the scene for this chapter. For although we have seen how the artist can be
psychologically involved with time in its own right, now we must try to show how
his unavoidable perceptual commitment to space and light feed this involvement.

It is not my intention to try to cover the wide range of artistic response to
space perception found in the history of art: This would require a book in itself
and demand the wisdom and patience of Methuselah. One would have to start by
discussing the curiously radial space-field of Magdalenian man that we see in
paleolithic cave art — a field where animals can stand on their heads as happily as
on their feet, and where no use is made of a horizontal line to suggest *terra firma*
or a related vertical line to indicate up or down. We would have to follow this up
by pointing out that it was 20,000 years later before Egyptian artists began to see
the world in this horizontal-vertical way . . . and that ultimately the Renaissance
science of perspective perfected an illusion of depth by utilizing a space-grid of
this sort. And then what about the claustrophobic jamming of space with forests
of columns that we find in Egyptian and Greek architecture; the superposing of
spatial regions vertically that occurs in Chinese and Japanese art; the flatness of
medieval art; the incredible open space of High Gothic architecture; and the
Cubist experiments with space and time of our own century? These are but a few
of the avenues that would be opened up in any reasonable survey of how space is
treated in art. Instead, I prefer to introduce the space-time issue by referring to a
few particularly significant examples of space-light composition — examples which
will, hopefully, reveal why space and light play such a fundamental role in an
artist's work.

In the operation of our consciousness, the perception of space and light is
the first step to achieving the concept of time. Space, light, and time act as a
trinity in our awareness of the world — they seem hardly to exist as independent

entities. As I understand it, this is the point of Mann's statement. In a void of empty sea and sky the ship's passenger cannot relate himself to a place or position and, consequently, loses the ability to gauge the passing of the hours. The implication is that a sense of time depends upon being able to differentiate one position in space from another, and upon recognizing the time-distance that separates them. Now as far as our perceptions are concerned we depend upon the presence of physical surfaces — of things or objects in space — in order to identify differing positions in space. But we should remember that it is only because light, in its travel through space, picks up the surfaces of things that we are visually aware of and can thus initiate any kind of positional or temporal orientation. Consequently, it is not difficult to appreciate the interdependence of space and light for our perceptual experience of the world. For space is the arena in which light manifests, and this manifestation permits us to discern the layout of objects. Only by perceiving the layout of objects do we become aware of the multidimensional shape of *space* between them and, ultimately, of the distances involved. Thus we are able to conceive of time . . . of how long it takes to get from here to there. We measure the travel of light in the universe in terms of light-years and our own movements in the world in hours or days, or in the three score and ten years of an average lifespan. Most of us will be all too familiar with the uneasy experience of being physically and psychologically lost in total darkness. For in the absence of light and, consequently, objects, it is easy to lose the sense of both time and place. Under these circumstances space and time cease to have shape or meaning.

This is the dilemma of the ship's passenger which Thomas Mann describes. Although it is not dark, space and time in the unarticulated void of sea and sky remain undifferentiated, and this brings about the feeling of isolation which most sea travelers experience from time to time. But with the sighting of land and the familiar forms of trees and hills, a feeling of security returns. For after a time in "immeasurable, unarticulated space" we seem to have a twofold need. First, to reestablish a time-position-in-space pattern which occupies our senses and our mind. Second, to inhabit spatial regions which, being shaped by tangible physical surfaces, are more in keeping with our own human scale. Some basic psychological surety depends upon our experiencing such interrelationships with the environment. Even if we grant that some of us seek the temporal and spatial isolation afforded by empty ocean or desert — because it allows us to identify with some abstract principle of the universe, or turns us back into ourselves to discover the reality of our own spiritual resources — only the saint or mystic seem to be able to stand it indefinitely.

In making a drawing, a painting, a sculptural piece, or an architectural design, the artist is involved in handling space to a greater or lesser degree. And whatever the size of the work, it is obvious that he is capable of organizing space on a more intimate scale than that of nature; a painting, for example, can become a very personal environment in which even the macro, unarticulated space of sea and sky is transformed into a scale which we can apprehend. I believe that the fashioning of a personal space-form-world (which is only another way of describing the creation of a work of art) satisfies an artist's conscious or unconscious need to "possess" or relate to space on human terms. For in doing so he affirms the significance of his perceptual experience of space in the world without which he would not be stirred by the phenomena of light, or speculate on the concept of time.[1] It may be that one artist will find himself fascinated with space and light at the expense of any interest in objects and, like Thomas Mann's traveler, lose contact with the world of time and material things. In the end I think it highly likely that such a man would become an artist-mystic. At the other extreme would be the artist whose concern with light and space is solely for the purpose of shaping and illuminating physical things — for providing a positive articulation between objects and space in order to impart some substantial physicality to the image. During the last few years the word "minimal" has crept into the vocabulary of art. As I understand the term, it is used to describe works in which physical statements such as graphic marks or sculptural surfaces are kept to an absolute minimum. The result is an image in which nothing can be clearly seen — in which, at best, there may be vague suggestions of physical surfaces disappearing or materializing. It seems, therefore, that an artist's creative response to the phenomenon of light and space can go in two directions. It can result in the conventional image of time-bound, substantial forms or the opposite, the minimal image of timeless, ambiguous space.

Let us therefore look at some works which illustrate these two possibilities. In our own time no sculptor has pioneered and explored the use of space more thoroughly than Henry Moore, and throughout the years the "reclining figure" has been a favorite theme which he has developed continuously. In first regarding Figure 8–1, the skeptical viewer may make a wry comment about a figure with "holes" in it. But if he will just give himself a little time, he will discover that the holes become positive *space-shapes* which hold his eye no less than the solid physical surfaces of the work. It becomes apparent that the holes are space-volumes which actually complement and help to define the material volumes by providing some spatial articulation; and that reciprocally the movement of the physical surfaces cradles and thus defines the holes as volumes which are sculpturally significant. If we move in closer — see Figure 8–2 — it becomes even more apparent that space and the light traveling through it play a vital part in allowing us to perceive clearly the sculptural plasticity of the figure. It is not long before the viewer has forgotten about holes as such and is responding to the spatial volumes as sculptural realities no less valid than the mass of the form. Yet while Moore has modeled a most articulate piece — that is, one in which the thrust of surfaces extruding into space and the flow of space intruding between surfaces serve to

---

[1] In his lecture, *On My Painting,* Max Beckmann describes the satisfaction gained by manipulating space on the canvas when he says: ". . . . thus to protect myself from the infinity of space."

FIG. 8–1 **Henry Moore (b. 1898–).** *Reclining Figure* 1953–54. **Bronze.** Courtesy of the artist. Photograph by Lidbrooke

"Knife Edge"   *Bloden 1962.*   *overhang*

FIG. 8–2 **Henry Moore (b. 1898–). Detail of Reclining Figure (Fig. 8–1).** Courtesy of the artist

heighten the definition of the figure — he has done more than provide us with an exercise in visual perception. For as light and space penetrate the form to produce pools of shadow and coruscations of brightness, it is possible to travel in time between the near and far surfaces as one becomes involved with the work. Although the physical scale of the sculpture is human, it assumes a canyon-like grandeur in the mind as the spatial volumes, play of light and flow of surface-flow work together to sensitize the onlooker to the relative issue of time. One of the curious things about this work is that it can assume landscape-like proportions in terms of time and space at one mental level, yet be intimate and more humanly inviting at another. As one peers into the spatial reaches of the figure, the darker recesses of space beckon, inviting our physical penetration of them as a comfortable and safe environment, a haven from the vastness of the world outside. They become the way of leaving the world of material things, objective experiences, and rational-analytical mental processes: like the hole in the ground down which Alice tumbled into the Wonderland of the unconscious, the darker sculptural tunnels draw us, offering us the same adventurous possibilities of a new space-time awareness in the inner world of the self.

If we describe Moore's *Reclining Figure* as a substantial image, it is reasonable enough to refer to Harry Kramer's *Torso 1964* (Figure 8-3) as a

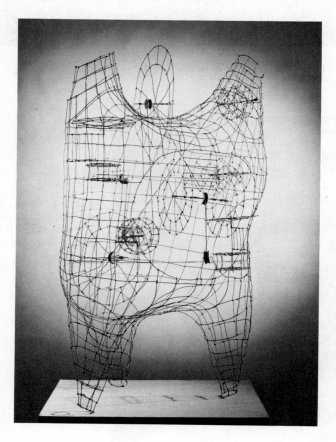

FIG. 8-3   Harry Kramer. *Torso* **1964. Wire.** Tate Gallery, London

minimal sculpture. For here the sculptural mass is reduced to the delicate linearism of a wire frame and, as a result, the spatial volumes have no three-dimensional firmness of enclosure. When mass becomes skeletal and attenuated to such a minimal level as this, it is not capable of serving as the matrix to space in the way achieved by the spreading surfaces of Moore's figure. Consequently, it is not easy to visually separate the interior space of Kramer's sculpture from the exterior environmental space; and, because of this, contained spatial volumes do not become a positively constructed part of the sculpture as they do with Moore. Instead, the insubstantial skeletal delicacy of *Torso 1964* allows external space to flow freely through the work without trapping any of it. The physical reality of the form is therefore more difficult to perceive, and one may even have doubts about its permanency. This piece is the complete antithesis of the Moore. In contrasting so positively, it affirms that our sense of the figure's time-space substantialness in Moore's piece is enhanced because we perceive the interior spaces as *part of the sculpture,* and not as part of the environment. But when physical surfaces are minimal, as in the Kramer, and space flows freely without being shaped and with little differentiation effected between inner and outer space, our ability to determine when and where something positively exists, is undermined. For neither positive space-volumes nor mass-volumes are apparent. Neither can light play its part by illuminating stretches of surface which stand in contrast to areas or pools of shadow, thus creating a sense of distance and a corresponding awareness of time. Kramer's sculpture may be a torso materializing or immaterializing . . . coming or going like some playful phantom. Standing before this image after experiencing the solidarity of Moore's space and mass volumes, we realize that Kramer is on the way to achieving a sculptural image which has something in common with Thomas Mann's thoughts about "immeasurable, unarticulated space." And because of this, it is difficult to experience a sense of time in one's imaginative involvement with *Torso 1964.* There is no triggering of those mental journeys through a sculptural landscape that one can experience before Moore's *Reclining Figure . . .* for with the minimal image "the time sense falters and grows dim."

Sculpture possesses the advantage of being physically three-dimensional and thus of occupying actual space in depth. Therefore, however minimal it may be, its spatial element is real rather than illusory. On the other hand, the drawing or painting which is made on a flat or relatively flat surface can only provide an illusory suggestion of space in depth. Figure 8–4 shows how the flat surface tricks the eye into seeing a three-dimensional space field. All that is required is for the surface to be marked by various types of line and stained by areas of differing tonal values. Li K'an, a late thirteenth-century Oriental artist, uses no structured system of geometrical perspective to create depth in this painting. Yet it can be seen that the brush marks (both line and area) seem to occupy different planes in depth. The marks which are heavier in weight and darker in tone come forward, while those which are less substantial in weight and lighter in tone move back. This is a natural perceptual phenomenon, for the eye seeks

to establish depth relationships no less than lateral or vertical ones when it is confronted by a varied range of marks or stains on a flat ground. Thus, in *Bamboo* the picture plane becomes an open space in which leaves and branches appear to float before and behind each other as the artist exploits a full range of tonal and weight values with his brush marks. Keeping this painting in mind as an example of the natural way we can experience the illusion of depth, it is interesting to study two works which represent opposing treatments of space (and therefore of light and time) — one completely structured or articulated and the other treated in the most minimal fashion.

To juxtapose Perugino's *Delivery Of The Keys* (Figure 8–5) and Reinhardt's *Abstract Painting* (Figure 8–6) may seem rather like going from the sublime to the ridiculous. But, as we shall see, this is far from the case. Perugino constructed his depth mathematically, using the newly developed Renaissance system known as perspective. Reinhardt paints what seems to be, on first glance, an all black canvas.[2] Perugino ensures that the surfaces of objects follow a horizontal and vertical alignment and recess diagonally "into" the picture plane. We can thus locate them positionally at left, right, above, and below, as well as in the foreground, middle-distance, or background. And then, by lighting his surfaces positively and employing a full range of color values, he cannot fail to render objects as solid and as quite distinctly positioned in space. Therefore, as in sculpture which is treated substantially, the clear presence and positioning of physical surfaces articulates space in the painting and we become aware of time and distance.

---

[2] It is not possible in black and white reproduction to show the color variations present in this painting. The artist discouraged reproduction for that reason. But in looking intently at the original the keen observer will notice rectangular variations of black, red-black, blue-black, and jet-black which are not immediately discernible.

THE TRINITY OF SPACE, LIGHT, AND TIME

FIG. 8-5   Pietro Perugino (1445-1523). *The Delivery of the Keys* 1482. **Fresco.** Sistine
Chapel, The Vatican, Rome

In stark contrast, Reinhardt's canvas brings us back to consider Thomas
Mann's "vast plain of empty sea," for it is an image that justifies description as
minimal. It is difficult to perceive any positive form or figure on the ground of the
canvas, and the only articulation of space is provided by the faint color variations
of black. The question then arises: "Do we see this as a painting of a more or less
solid form completely blotting out space — like the side of a wall for example — or
as a spatial void defined only by the sides of the canvas?" In seeing Reinhardt next

FIG. 8-6   Ad Reinhardt (b.
1913-   ). *Abstract Painting.* **Various
media.** Museum of Modern Art, New
York

to Perugino, some readers will be wondering what has happened to pictorial art — what kind of development after 500 post-Renaissance years does the contemporary image represent? Some of the questions raised by the wholly abstract art of our own century are discussed in Chapter 11, but the minimal painting we see here poses some interesting questions within the space-light-time context of this chapter. Obviously, I am not out to make any value-judgment comparisons between Reinhardt and Perugino, for this would be both impossible and ridiculous. Instead, I am concerned with showing a traditional attitude toward spatial problems in painting alongside a rather extreme contemporary one. For a number of years now, subject matter as such has not been of major importance for many artists. Yet even if we recognize this fact, Reinhardt's "nothingness" goes a step further. As an image it is almost formless, spaceless, and therefore timeless. Because of this lack of features, the viewer is forced to look hard to try to discover more of what he feels *must* be there. After all, it is a painting and the eye does not like to be thwarted. Even so it yields little save the slight presence of a cross motif. Other thoughts then come to mind, for a minimal image challenges the observer's imagination to make of it what he will. There is something hypnotic about such a neutral, ambiguous, minimal work. In my opinion, its dark and vague pictorial surface invites contemplation. After the visual confusion and clutter of our cities, the noise and the killing pace of modern life, such quiet emptiness can come as a great relief. Again, it has been said that ours is an age of apathy, when noninvolvement and noncommitment are the order of the day. Bearing this in mind it is possible to regard the bleakness of Reinhardt's image as symbolizing our loss of sensibility in those areas of commitment which are the particular prerogative of human beings; namely, an ability to respond to natural things with feeling and respect . . . to believe in love and commitment as principles in themselves, and to cultivate and trust one's values. These are but a few examples. To be more cynical and perhaps less perceptive, it may be said that the painting is a painting of nothing and means nothing — after all, an image cannot be any more minimal than that.

The reader may recall that in Chapter 5 we quoted the Russian painter, Malevich, on his experience of withdrawal from the world:

> . . . a blissful sense of liberating non-objectivity drew me
> forth into the "desert" where nothing is real except feeling.
> . . . This was no empty square which I had exhibited but
> rather the feeling of non-objectivity.[3]

In this statement Malevich is referring to a painting he made in the year 1913, which consisted solely of a black square on a white ground. But a few years later he produced a painting which goes considerably further in conveying "the feeling of non-objectivity." This is the famous *White on White* which was painted *circa* 1918 and which was probably the first minimal painting of this century. If we compare this (Figure 8–7) with Reinhardt's painting, we realize

---

[3] K. Malevich, "The Non-Objective World," in *Modern Artists on Art,* ed. R. L. Herbert, p. 94.

that the American artist has taken Malevich's nonobjective minimalism a stage
further. Yet in none of the statements he made about his painting does Reinhardt
mention "the *feeling* of non-objectivity"; instead, he tends to shun subjective
responses of this sort. He describes his "square (neutral, shapeless) canvas" as a —
"pure, abstract, non-objective, timeless, spaceless, changeless, relationless,
disinterested painting." Now although we would agree that these words apply to
his work, I think that the person looking at both Malevich and Reinhardt may
find them, on the visual evidence, very similar and regard Reinhardt as no less a
painter-mystic than the Russian. For it is relatively easy to perceive the configuration of a square in Malevich's painting — even though it is not possible to determine
whether it is square-mass or square-space — whereas it is more difficult to determine
any configuration in the Reinhardt. Therefore, we take the latter's painting to be
even more of a "desert" and, I feel, would be justified in regarding his withdrawal
from the environmental reality of objects in space as no less an ascetic experience
than that described by Malevich. For to be involved with "the timeless" and "the
spaceless" is surely to move closer to some link with the infinite and to transcend
levels of awareness which are usually concerned with the objective realities of
terrestrial and physical phenomena.

From these two examples we see that pictorial space can either relate us
to the world or take us from it. Perugino's solidly drawn objects (Figure 8-5)
articulate space and present physical surfaces to light in such a "real" way that
the painting appears to possess the solidarity of the natural world. But with
Malevich and Reinhardt this world has disappeared, as we saw it disappearing
with Kramer's wire-sculptured torso. With these two artists we face an ambiguous
surface where the illusion is not that of things materially existing in space and

time, but rather one of *no*thing in an unarticulated void of space and *no*-time. Our ability to perceive a spatial articulation through the intrusion of light-reflecting surfaces, to survey and estimate distances and so relate to a sense of time, is dimmed before these images. And I, for one, find myself moved to contemplate not the realm of Being, but that twilight dimension where all is in a state of becoming.

SYMBOLIC LUMINISM

At this juncture we can now confront the true father of minimal art, the British painter, James Mallard William Turner (1775–1851). Today we recognize Turner as a great painter-adventurer; a man of vivid and unusual imagination, caught in the grip of a vision which he followed faithfully to the end of his life. As Turner's work progressed from the romantic lyricism of the earlier landscape paintings to the spatial abstractions of the later years, he provided many shocks for the conventional London art circles. The figure of man, which he always treated so minute in scale against the vastness of space in nature, ultimately disappears in Turner's paintings; even objects lose their physical solidarity and are dissolved in space. In the canvases produced during the last 20 years of his life it is light and space that obsess him, dissolving the substance of the physical world to reveal the chromatic luminosity of the firmament. To gaze at *Sun Setting over the Sea* (Figure

FIG. 8-8   J. M. W. Turner (1775–1851). *Sun Setting Over the Sea* **1840–45. Oil on canvas.** Tate Gallery, London

8-8) is to embark on a space odyssey — to venture in the imagination into the uncharted dimensions of space and time in the universe. One wonders how Thomas Mann's sea voyager would have felt in this setting, for without even a firm horizon separating sea from sky he would surely be less able to orient himself to time and place. Like Reinhardt, Turner may be considered a minimal painter, inasmuch as objects in their concrete nature are lost in his later work. But there the similarities cease, for the light in Turner's painting suggests a cosmic energy which is completely lacking in the Reinhardt. Writing in 1816 the critic Hazlitt wrote:

> We here allude particularly to Turner, the ablest landscape painter now living, whose pictures are however, too much abstractions of aerial perspective, and representations not properly of the objects of nature as of the medium through which they are seen . . . They are pictures of the elements of air, earth and water. The artist delights to go back to the first chaos of the world. . . All is without form and void. Someone said of his landscapes that they were *pictures of nothing and very like.*

Whoever made the final remark to which Hazlitt refers, the statement is not surprising when one considers how modern Turner is today, and how avant-garde he was for his own period — even though few of his later works were exhibited in his lifetime. The anonymous critic is, of course, referring to the absence of objects firmly delineated by drawing. He is apparently not aware of the radiant energy which permeates the spatial sweep of Turner's canvases and through which all things are either forming or dissolving.

A simple equation to explain Turner would be:

$$Space + Light = Energy + Time\text{-}travel$$

In *Sun Setting over the Sea* we see a swirl of tonal values (embracing crimsons, ochres, and whites) which seem to traverse a macrocosmic region, suggesting waves of light and sound. To post-Hiroshima man, the energy generated seems sufficient to cause either the fission or the fusion of matter. In comparison with the orientally neutral, silent, nonlight, nonenergy blankness of Reinhardt's painting, Turner treats space dynamically and multidimensionally as the arena for cosmic happenings. Now the question is: "How does Turner's vision of light-filled space compare with the blank image of Reinhardt in terms of moving us to speculate on the infinite?" But this is a rhetorical question, for some of us will find that the active presence of light-energy is symbolic in itself, while others will respond similarly to space which is truly empty and nothing. Some religions, for example, have always used the image of intense light to symbolize the concept of the infinite and eternal; others maintain that in order to contemplate the absolute or infinite, it is necessary to eliminate sensory experiences of all phenomena. In the latter case, Ad Reinhardt's *Abstract Painting,* in its almost complete emptiness, might well help one to reach the desired state. The reader must come to his own conclusions about this problem and try to decide which of the two works best justifies the statement by the late Bernard Berenson that:

> Space composition . . . can take us away from ourselves and give us, while we are under its spell, the feeling of being identified with the universe, perhaps even of being the soul in the universe . . . this sense of identification with the universe is of the very essence of religious emotion — an emotion, by the way, as independent of belief and conduct as love itself. . . .[4]

We cannot look at one of Turner's later masterpieces without realizing how closely a sense of space is allied to a sense of time. In studying *Sun Setting over the Sea,* notice how the darker tones appear relatively solid and frontal — almost as if we are witnessing a transformation of matter into energy as particles are hurled forward with the speed of light. And it should be observed how necessary is the illusion of great distance present in the lighter areas — where the pictorial space seems to recede into a limitless vortex created by the fusion of sea and sky — for this effect of forward traveling light. It is from these spatial depths that the light energy comes, bursting forth into the more conventionally articulated horizon-cum-foreground space at the left. The suggestion of such limitless distances, of the speed of light as it traverses the firmament, and of the fission of matter in the darker forward regions, activates the imagination to ponder the eons of time in space. Such speculation and feeling turn one inevitably to the human issue — to the phenomenon of man occupying a brief span of time in the incandescent space-light of his own small solar system.

To celebrate the vastness of space and the radiation of light with the obsessive single-mindedness of a Turner implies that the need for the normal psychological security of which I spoke earlier — that of a more local, intimate, and clearly articulated environment — has been transcended. I think that Berenson implies that this kind of transcendence is what we experience when space-composition is capable of taking us away from ourselves, and allowing us a feeling of identification with the soul in the universe. He suggests that a confrontation with macrospace in art can push us to transcend the egocentric self, to forego the security of a terrestrial environment, and to identify with the universe almost in an abstract and impersonal way. Indeed, when we were discussing the insubstantial linear sculpture of Giacometti (Figure 6–16) in Chapter 6, it was suggested that we react with feelings of anxiety to the dominance of space over matter, especially when the object is the human figure. For when the human form is so overpowered, the ultimate significance of man in the cosmic scale of things is called into question. Facing this possibility, I suspect that the only imaginative move left by which we can restore some psychological security is to discover some symbolic aspect of space with

---

[4] Bernard Berenson, *The Italian Painter of the Renaissance* (London: Phaidon Publishers Ltd., 1952), p. 122.

which to identify. In doing this, the radiant presence of light has brought man some comfort. At least light allows us to see and to relate to things, which is denied us by the darkness. And depending upon the wavelength and the frequency of light, we see colors[5] to which we respond with feeling. A spatial void which is more dark than light seems to offer little hope of anything. The phrase "to bring light into the darkness" alludes symbolically to the positive role of light as a life-giving force redeeming the nothingness of the void; or to the presence of a knowing intelligence in the invisible reaches of the cosmos. It will therefore come as no surprise to the reader at this point when I say that Turner's paintings possess a certain religious authority — a symbolic power to stir the soul — in the visual confrontation with light-years, light, and space.

But light is not only present in art as a cosmic radiance; it is also the symbol of that vital thing we call the spirit of man. For in addition to the macro-light of "the beyond," there is also the micro-light of the "inner man." This is the light of the soul. Symbolizing the spirit are the lights of candles flickering on innumerable altars and the flames burning constantly on the tombs of unknown warriors. Christ is described as the light of the world, while Zoroaster was the prophet of the Lord of Light for the Persians. Many world religions refer to the *illumination* of the spirit, and in Aldous Huxley's novel *Time Must Stop* — an imagined account of after-death experience — there is a description of a gradual dissolving of the soul in a light so radiant that at first it was hardly bearable. But these two orders of light — the light of the cosmos and the light of man — are not necessarily antithetical. Many religious systems hold that the little light of man is but a part of the dazzling brightness of "the beyond." Aniela Jaffé, a clinical psychologist of extensive experience who has researched widely in mythological images to discover their psychological relativity to modern problems, writes:

> Actually the light belonging to the "inner man" corresponds
> to a "radiance" ascribed to the "beyond," for the "inner
> man" rises from that unknown realm which transcends life
> and consciousness. We know, for instance, that in
> connection with death and dying a bright light which is not
> attached to a human figure or to a ghost is sometimes
> mentioned.[6]

Thus we see that, symbolically at least, the light of man's spirit is linked with the light of the infinite cosmos. Therefore, after discussing Turner's cosmic light we should look at a painter whose concern was with the light of the inner man. I refer, of course, to Rembrandt Harmens van Rijn (1606–1669). Rembrandt painted all kinds of subjects for all kinds of occasions, and although his landscapes, civic group portraits, and great religious paintings all reveal the Rembrandt radiance, it is in the single portrait (Figure 8–9) that light assumes its great transcending power. Here we

---

[5] The relationship between light wavelength and color is discussed in Chapter 9.

[6] Aniela Jaffé, *Apparitions and Precognition* (New York: University Books, 1963), p. 70.

FIG. 8-9   Rembrandt van Rijn (1606-1669). *Study of a Man's Head* **(probably a portrait of Rembrandt's father). Oil on panel.** Mauritshuis, The Hague

see the glowing light of the human spirit. While Turner opens up the canvas into light-years of time and space, Rembrandt encloses a pool of darkness in which the head almost seems to float. Yet this ambiguous space gives us less sense of terrestrial security than does Turner's cosmic space, for it lacks light articulation. If we could see that the space around the head was part of a room or a garden, then we could come back to the familiar things of earth and time. But Rembrandt's purpose becomes clear when we face the man in the painting. For we see that the source of Rembrandt's light is the figure itself, the man portrayed. It is not a case of light from outside striking surfaces, but of an interior light glowing through the surfaces to render them visible. And this is the only light in the image, the only means of illuminating the mysterious space and challenging its unknown immensity. For myself, I see the subjects in the greatest Rembrandt portraits as quasi-substantial phantoms materializing, sustained, and illuminated in space and time only by the vital light of the spirit. Looking at them I am always reminded of that line from Edmund Spenser, the English sixteenth-century poet, "For soule is forme and doth the bodye mayke . . ." The portraits of Rembrandt find their parallel in this neo-Platonic assertion that the outer, physical form of man is shaped and sustained by the inner life of the spirit.

Therefore, I find the same kind of religious authority in Rembrandt as in Turner — "the light belonging to the 'inner man' [Rembrandt] corresponds to a 'radiance' ascribed to the 'beyond' [Turner]."[7] Although Turner is not a humanist as Rembrandt would be considered a humanist — his interest in a cosmic scale eliminates man — he and Rembrandt join forces in using light and space to move our thoughts and feelings beyond finite limitations. And although we can see other painters extending our notions of reality in a similar way, I believe that Turner and Rembrandt together are unsurpassed in this achievement.

IMPRESSIONISM

At the opposite extreme to symbolic luminists like Rembrandt and Turner are those artists who treat light and space as naturalistically and as sensuously as possible. The Impressionist painters of the late nineteenth century, led by Claude Monet, achieved impressive pictorial results in this direction. The color-light of Impressionist painting produces a completely "real" outcome. We feel the warmth, coldness, or humidity of the air and know the time of day and season of the year. (See Chapter 9 and Figure 9-1.) The finest Impressionist painting represents a glorious celebration of optical experience — a translation by means of brush and paint of the retinal sensations of light and air (space) directly experienced on the site. Claude Monet could paint some rather miserable little haystacks several times over in one day because the color and movement of light and the density of the air constantly changed. Monet was not searching for some enduring quality of the scene. He is saying plainly enough that the *changing face* of nature is the reality — that each aspect presented is as real as the next; that there is no point in seeking to abstract some nonvisual element from the scene. In effect, Impressionist "philosophy" suggests that the phenomenon of transitoriness or change is the only reality in life of which we can be sure. Obviously then, as far as time is concerned, Impressionist pictures are of the moment, *now.* I believe that this concern for the validity of the present assures the constant popularity of Impressionist art, for its sensory and existential vitality celebrates the living moment and allows us to escape briefly from the search for some more absolute truth about existence. Most so-called Impressionist or naturalist artists treat light and space as objectively as possible in order to intensify the pictorial illusion that the event is happening now, before your very eyes — that the light-reflecting and light-absorbing objects in their pictorial space are as physically immediate and credible as they are in natural space. Impressionist art is also a "local" art. The places we see are places with which we are familiar and in which we feel at home.

ROMANTIC SPACE-LIGHT

Yet there are ways in art to use the elements of light and space without approaching the extreme transcendent vision of a Turner or the naturalist

---

[7] A. Jaffé, *Apparitions and Precognition,* p. 70. (The insertions in the brackets are mine.)

objectivity of less mystical painters. And, in my view, some of the more interesting possibilities which embrace the time factor are to be found in that wide range of artistic vision loosely called Romantic art. For example, an expression which crops up constantly in discussions of romantic literature and art is "romantic distance." Now if we are to recognize one common theme running through the many diverse faces of romanticism, it is a preoccupation with distance in terms of time and distance in terms of space. It is characteristic of the romantic attitude to be concerned with more than the existential significance of the present and, in addition, to conjure up images of the past or to flirt with images of the future. There is a strong nostalgia for the past . . . a desire to capture the flavor of previous cultures or, as in contemporary science fiction, a desire to imaginatively explore the future. The romantic attitude sometimes seems to find both of these possibilities more attractive than savoring the present moment of time. Distant places assume a magnetic attraction because they are far away, and the unknown way of life offers the possibility of exotic and new experiences. In fact, images of Utopia are typical products of the romantic imagination. Even Greek and Roman writers described the remote and mountain-girt land of Arcadia in the Peloponnesus as a natural and rustic paradise. Dreams of an ideal communion with nature through the Orphic rituals are depicted in Greek vase paintings; and there are countless literary and graphic images of Gardens of Eden and even of Hells, where exotic delights or sufferings are to be experienced beyond the everyday world of time and place. A recurring theme in such imaginings is the idea of an island — a legendary isle to which man can escape and shed his mortality, enjoy timeless delights, and thus overcome the apparent physical limitations of mortal life. Antoine Watteau's *Embarkation for Cythera* (Figure 8-10) shows the start of a journey to such a magic island. The scene is diffused with a golden light, and even in black and white reproduction the haziness of the air is apparent, causing the mountain peaks of Cythera to loom ethereally over an ambiguous distance. It is indeed another world lost to time and place which beckons; and again, it is the quality of light that helps to create the dream. But the profundity of Watteau lies in the fact that we and they know the whole thing is just a dream. The jaded Parisians of 1717 will never set foot on the barque that is to transport them to Cythera; they are trapped by the real world of time and by the psychological inertia that results from satiated appetites.

The word "Utopia" was invented by Sir Thomas More as the title of a romance published in 1516. It is compounded from the Greek words for "not" and for "place" — hence no place or nowhere. To write at length about nowhere is the act of a highly romantic imagination. Yet the work of Thomas More has been followed in our own century by the utopian writings of H. G. Wells, Samuel Butler, George Orwell, and René Daumal . . . not to mention the new breed of science-fiction writers conjuring up thoughts of other communities in outer-space. It seems to be a mark of certain imaginative men living in a sophisticated, urban culture, that they experience a nagging desire for some time and place other than the present; a romantic longing for, as the French say, *je ne sais quoi*. In the

FIG. 8-10   Antoine Watteau (1684–1721). *Embarkation for Cythera* **1717. Oil on canvas.**
The Louvre, Paris

visual arts this interest in strange places and events where the experience of time undergoes change is seen particularly in the romantic attitude known as Surrealism.

SURREALIST SPACE-LIGHT

One of the established aims of Surrealism is to question what is normally accepted as reality; namely, that things are necessarily as our objective sense-intellect sees them. For we know how easily the fixed and familiar shape and arrangement of things may be lost with changes in the state of our consciousness. Well-known objects can undergo a metamorphosis and take on new form for a second or so; or the context can change abnormally — as when one might "see" a plush armchair in the middle of a deserted beach. As Picasso has said, "A palm tree can become a horse." Now it is not necessary to fall fast asleep in order for our normal view of the world to dissolve in dream. It only requires a certain intensity or preoccupation with one's own thoughts and mood — daydreaming as it is sometimes called — for some change in the concrete reality of the external world to be effected. At such times, the sentinel of reason, whose job it is to maintain an objective and rational consciousness, may be outwitted and the psyche freed to project its own images onto the world. So the palm tree may become a horse, windmills may change into giants, and the busy city street can become a silent, deserted, and foreign stage-set of a townscape. In dreaming during sleep such changes are taken for granted and are usually quickly forgotten with the light of day. But the Surrealists are not disposed to underestimate the importance of such experiences — either when sleeping or when awake — suggesting that they at least call into question the absolute credibility of so-called objective awareness. They hold that any total view of reality should encompass both objective impressions and those more subjective images which appear to be projected by the psyche itself. Hence the term "Sur-realism" — implying the combining of dream or imagined reality with the reality presented by the senses — in order to embrace a total view of what is real. Inevitably, the theories of Sigmund Freud concerning the nature of consciousness and its other side, the unconscious, had a considerable influence on the founders of the modern Surrealist movement in 1919.[8] Thoroughly disgusted with the "rational" and pragmatic attitude toward life which had turned Western Europe into the bloodbaths of the 1870 and 1914 wars and disillusioned with the belief that man is a rational creature — in view of the follies committed by the political, social, and commercial establishment — a few young men protested such folly masquerading as reason. Their names are now well-known — André Breton, Jean Cocteau, Philippe Soupault, Louis Aragon, and Paul Eluard — as the poets and painters who sought to discover a richer reality over and above conventional realism and logic.

Surrealism thus became a word signifying the redefinition of reality to embrace a broad spectrum of conscious states; and, as might be expected, one major concern was with our awareness of time — with the fact that we can shift gears in time depending upon the particular quality or condition of our consciousness. For it is natural enough to question the firm reality of chronological time when this time-structure can dissolve not only in dreams during sleep, but also when an intensity of mood or an involvement in imaginative speculation removes one far from the clock-bound world. Many of us have had to pinch ourselves on occasion to bring the mind back to the present because we had wandered off, and writers and poets describe how sudden flashes of recognition can make a new place seem strangely familiar — or how the "vibrations" of a historic site can push one back in time to live for a moment in another age.[9] We have noted before, that in the deeper dreams of sleep or poetic reverie, the time barrier can be broken, allowing our images to move freely back and forth in time and space. Consequently, as this chapter is concerned with space, light, and time, we should look at the Surrealists' space-light composition to see how they manage to suggest the illusory or ambiguous nature of time in their work. The example I have chosen antedates the Surrealist movement proper by a few years. Although its creator Giorgio de Chirico

---

[8] See André Breton, "What is Surrealism," in *Paths to the Present,* ed. Eugen Weber.

[9] See Henry Miller's account of a visit to the Greek amphitheater at Epidaurus in *The Colossus of Maroussi* (New York: New Directions Books, 1958), p. 76.

described his paintings of this period as "Metaphysical Art" — which in itself indicates an intention to move beyond material realities — they are the first manifestation of surreal vision in this century. As we look at *The Soothsayer's Recompense* (Figure 8-11), I think we are first impressed by the contextual oddities in the pictorial organization — by the juxtapositioning of solid and flimsy architectural arcades, reclining figure sculpture, and distant railway trains, all in the middle of a desert. For the train is not heading for any railway station in the town, and it is not certain if the space where the sculpture is sited is a town square or simply an extension of the desert. Something seems to be wrong in terms of our normal experience of such subject matter, and the bizarre spatial relationships contribute significantly to the enigmatic quality of the image. There is also something rather theatrical about the light in this painting, for it "spotlights" the sculptural piece very deliberately and forms pronounced shadows which are in strong contrast with the bright areas. Lighting of this sort always adds to the sense of drama and can transform mundane events into the realm of the extraordinary. Granted that this light represents the strong glare of the Mediterranean sun, it still misses the diffuse and airy quality of natural light and its effect is to create a silent stage-set of another world, another place — a world in which normal associations are no longer relevant. It is difficult to envisage the daily round of events and human contacts here, and the clock which marks the time as five minutes to two

FIG. 8-11   Giorgio de Chirico (b. 1888-   ). *The Soothsayer's Recompense.* **Oil on canvas.**
Philadelphia Museum of Art: The Louise and Walter Arensberg Collection

merely helps to strike a more paradoxical note. Can we really believe that this is just the hour of siesta? Or are we out of the material world and in the world of mental images which can suggest a different time-place reality? But these questions cannot be answered with any surety; all one can say is that the question marks of "when" and "where" hover over the scene.

In my view, this confusion of the time sense is produced by all important surreal images which utilize and exploit contextual paradox, bizarre spatial relationships, and dramatic light. For our ability to relate logically and experientially to the image is hampered by these factors. As far as the spatial relationships are concerned, one thing in particular serves to make them odd. It is the abrupt *demarcation* between architectural space which humanizes the scale and the impersonal openness of the abutting spatial distances. The sudden transition sets man's constructions against the emptiness of infinity; it questions his faith in the reality of time as measured by clocks; and mocks his conquest of distance by the bizarre appearance of mechanical vehicles such as trains. Both clock and train are purposely anachronistic in de Chirico's strange world. Strangely enough, the absence of human figures does not contribute much to the surreal effect. For in those paintings where figures appear, either singly or in groups, the surreal organization of the pictorial elements as we have described it invests the people also with the same dream-like quality.

CUBIST AND FUTURIST SPACE-LIGHT

But now we should leave Surrealist space, light, and time, and look briefly at the much more existential and perceptually oriented space-time impact of Futurism and Cubism. The Italian poet Marinetti's "Futurist Manifesto" of 1909 is, among other things, a glorification of the new age of the machine. These first years of the twentieth century saw the development of the internal combustion engine for use in powered vehicles and flying machines, the invention of the automatic machine gun, and the advent of cinematograph moving pictures . . . to mention but a few of the technical innovations. There was also the impact in 1905 of Einstein's relativity theory, which effectively quashed any lingering notions that absolute truths could be hypostatized. A few years earlier Charles Darwin's evolution theories had caused intelligent men to re-think their ideas concerning man's place in the universe; and Sigmund Freud, coming hard on Darwin's heels, had exposed some less attractive aspects of human nature which made it imperative that man take a more honest look at himself. All in all, it was rather difficult for informed men to adopt traditional philosophical attitudes or to act as if the old class values still had a great deal of meaning. The group of Italian artists and poets who founded the short-lived Futurist movement consequently rejected, in violent language, anything to do with the past — particularly those attitudes we would call humanist with regard to social, political, and cultural values. In fact, the *Futurist Manifesto* preaches rejection, violence, and destruction, and urges movement and action rather than contemplation and passivity, danger rather than security, the importance of youth rather than age, war rather than peace . . . .

> We declare that the world's wonder has been enriched by a
>   fresh beauty: the beauty of speed . . .
> There is no more beauty except in struggle . . .
> For art can be nothing but violence, cruelty and injustice . . .
> We want to glorify war — the only hygiene of the
>   world . . .[10]

Many historians have pointed out that the seeds of Facism which, as a political creed, later engulfed Mussolini's Italy and Hitler's Germany, can be detected in this document. But if we set its social and political implications aside, we are left with a naive and hysterical faith in the future because it offers new opportunities for physical action and excitement. Technology and the new machine age are going to provide escape from the mundane in terms of mobility, the exhilaration of speed, and the satisfaction gained from the beauty and efficiency of machines. Even the barriers of space and time will be breached as "we hurl our challenge to the stars!"

It is therefore not surprising to find Futurist artists seeking a way of expressing the sensation of speed and velocity in drawing, painting, and sculpture. Inevitably, as we see in Giacomo Balla's *Speeding Automobile* (Figure 8-12), two things happen to the image. Objects lose their physical solidity and unity — as they

FIG. 8-12   Giacomo Balla (1871-1958). *Speeding Automobile* 1912. **Oil on wood.** Museum of Modern Art, New York. Purchase

---

[10] Filippo Marinetti, "The Foundation of Futurism," in *Paths to the Present,* ed. Eugen Weber, p. 244.

do when glimpsed at speed in an actual situation — because the eye does not have time to bring them into focus; and the firmness of the spatial organization also breaks down, because perception cannot ascertain the layout of space if it cannot determine the physical actuality and firm position of objects. In Figure 8-12, Balla shows how firm perception diminishes as speed increases and illustrates the Futurists' efforts to develop a plastic structure which revealed the dislocation of both object and spatial interval when viewed at speed — particularly in the confined space of the city — yet which nevertheless allowed an aesthetic cohesion to be maintained in terms of pictorial design. As we see in the *Speeding Automobile*, it is difficult to distinguish what is object from what is space since the spatial intervals between objects are inextricably mixed with the fragmented pieces of objects themselves — yet the artist maintains a structural homogenity throughout the whole work. However, the sensation of rapid movement presented by this painting is not entirely dependent upon the breakdown of perceptual rigidity. We must also consider the way Balla uses light. The beams of light projecting from the speeding automobile cut arbitrarily through the form-space kaleidoscope and are the most positively perceived aspects of the image. The viewer's attention is thus drawn to the speed of light in its own right, and through this association the dynamic velocity of the work is considerably enhanced. The jigsaw puzzle appearance presented by dislocated form and space, bolstered by the firmer projection of light rays, is typical of Futurist art. It serves well to express an obsession with energy and the speed of mechanical things — to capture the sensation of the rush through space and the change in the duration of time as all becomes "now."

On first appearance a Futurist work looks rather like the Cubist experiments of Pablo Picasso and Georges Braque initiated in Paris about 1907. This is understandable enough for Severini, Boccioni, Balla, and others paid a short visit to Paris prior to their Futurist exhibition of 1912 and were considerably influenced by Cubism (and Severini had been living in Paris for some years). But as we turn now to look briefly at the space-time composition of the Cubists, it will be obvious that the Futurists, as exemplified by Balla's *Speeding Automobile,* introduced two factors not found in Cubism. These are: the pictorial dynamics of motion through space and the travel of light.

It is not my intention here to provide a comprehensive introduction to Cubism, but to suggest how it is significant for the theme of this chapter. Georges Braque's *Still Life with Violin and Pitcher* (Figure 8-13), belongs to the first phase of Cubism — the period known as Analytical Cubism — when the perceptual experience of objects was still the point of departure for making the painting. Yet, as you can see, the work does not relate to normal visual experiences of table tops, violins, and waterjugs. Obviously, Braque has taken some liberties with natural perceptual experience, for once again we face a fragmentation of objects and their spatial context which produces a special brand of pictorial plasticity. Now both Picasso and Braque have insisted on the *intuitive* nature of this painterly re-structuring of visual reality, rejecting the suggestion that it resulted from a deliberate attempt to create a new kind of analytical formalism. So what are we to

FIG. 8-13 Georges Braque (1882–1963). *Still Life with Violin and Pitcher* 1910. Oil. Kunstmuseum, Basel. La Roche Collection

say about the space-time-light implications of Cubist painting? Well, it seems fairly clear that Braque has not felt bound to observe his group from one fixed viewpoint or eye level. For while the tables are seen from above in almost a bird's-eye view, the pitcher and violin are viewed from a lower, more normal eye level. With every glance, new visual anomalies of this nature are discovered. In regarding the pitcher, for example, it can be seen that while the artist explores its spout and mouth as if looking into it from above, he nevertheless shows the body of the vessel as if seen from a lower eye level. The parts of the violin are treated in a similar way. As Braque breaks the instrument down into characteristic violin-esque shapes, he juxtaposes these parts in such a way that each part is presented as if seen from a different position — from the top, side, underneath, etc. Having gone this far in re-structuring the objects, there can be no logical reason against also re-structuring the space of the image. In fact, it is aesthetically necessary to do this in order to ensure that the work possesses a plastic homogeneity. Therefore, the spatial regions become shaped very concretely and are, in their turn, fragmented in a way that echoes the dislocated shapes of the objects. So space becomes violin-esque, pitcher-esque, or table-esque. We have said previously that the time element in a work of art depends upon the spatial illusions or suggestions of distance. What then is the time factor in a Cubist image where space becomes synonymous with form?

Normally, when we look at an object, we can see only that aspect of it which is visible from our viewing position. If we wish to see more, we move to scrutinize it from other positions. In order to see the half-dozen or so aspects of the violin presented in this work, it would be necessary to move either oneself, or the instrument, from one position to another; it might even be necessary to break the violin in order to see its internal aspects. The same is true for the pitcher. To regard it from the side constitutes one perception; but one cannot peer into the neck of the vessel without moving to another viewing position and experiencing this as a second perception. And this takes time. Now although our visual experience of the world constitutes a series of time-lapsed impressions, each one of which relates to a single viewing position only, there is no reason why an artist, being already familiar with many aspects of an object, should not design an image in which they are all seen *simultaneously.* In so doing, it will be obvious that a time factor is involved, for the image represents a speeding-up of visual impressions as different aspects of an event are seen together at one moment in time. Cubism (not really a very good title)[11] is the first full-scale movement of this century in which the artist breaks loose from the visual tyranny of the object. By this I mean that he exercises his freedom to re-structure forms multidimensionally in accordance with his knowledge of their several aspects — that he is not tied mentally and emotionally to his perceptual experience of them at one time from one position.

Generally speaking, Cubist images appear static, as if forms and spatial intervals are locked together in a state of deep-freeze. This static appearance is really inevitable when space is so firmly shaped and enclosed. But as far as a sense of time is concerned, to treat space in this way is to heighten the present immediacy of the work, the sense of "now." For the "cubing" of space imparts a relative flatness to the ground, eliminating illusions of near and far points. With distances thus reduced, any awareness of a range of time will suffer and the present will tend to dominate. This lack of movement through spatial distances imparts a frozen split-second appearance to the work which is even more pronounced when color is kept to an almost monochromatic level — when any light in the painting is gray and neutrally dispersed. In contrast, the Futurists achieve a dynamic pulse of movement and energy by using color which vibrates and strong light which moves through space. And because this light moves through space countering any rigid structuring that is apparent, it helps to keep space open and fluid rather than tight and enclosed. In my opinion, the overall form-space-light structure of Cubist art telescopes a series of visual events so thoroughly into one simple simultaneous presentation that time seems to have stopped. On the other hand, the form-space-light composition of Futurist art allows speed of movement to be briefly apprehended, but not arrested, as it moves on and beyond. I have always felt that Cubist time is time stopped, whereas Futurist time continues into the far reaches of space . . . into the future.

---

[11] Like many other names given to modern movements, this was a derisory title that gained currency after the critic Louis Vauxcelles spoke of "cubes" in reference to one of Matisse's works. (*Gil Blas*, November 14, 1908.)

THE TRINITY OF SPACE, LIGHT, AND TIME

CONSTRUCTIVIST SPACE-LIGHT

Cubism was the first group movement of this century to break the Western tradition of exploring the natural appearance of the world. As we have seen, one of its innovations was to treat space according to the dictates of a new and intuitive attitude toward the problems of plastic organization. We now recognize that this concern with space as an element to be shaped and positioned in its own right is one of the characteristics by which "modern" art generally can be distinguished. Therefore, it is fitting that we close this chapter by showing an example of an art which endows space with prime importance, namely, Constructivist sculpture, and let Naum Gabo, one of its great pioneers, describe its space ideology:

> It is only with the appearance of the constructive ideology in art that space has become of special concern to the sculptor and the painter. In the *Realistic Manifesto,* published in Moscow in 1920, there was a clear call to the artist to use space as a new pictorial and plastic element amongst the other visual elements, assigning to it the same importance that lines, shapes, and colors have, as basic means in the structure of a visual image. . . .
> Space in our vision is not the distance between far and near, not the above and below, not even the place which is there or here; it is penetrating, everywhere present in our conscious experience of vision. We are not interested in its material substance, or in its configurations as a generalized entity embracing the universe. Space is an ever-present reality in the visual experience of our world, without which no full image of anything can be conceived . . . it carries an experience of palpability equal to any conveyed by the tactile sense. In short, in a constructive sculpture space is not a part of the universal space surrounding the object; it is a material by itself, a structural part of the object — so much so that it has the faculty of conveying a volume as does any other rigid material.[12]

This statement is clear enough. After reading it we realize that the *form* of a work is as much spatial as it is physical, and we see that Gabo emphasizes what the perceptual psychologists have been saying for some time; that an awareness of space plays as important a role in our perception of the world as does an awareness of tangible objects. This formalist function of space is clearly seen in Gabo's *Translucent Variation on Spheric Theme* (Figure 8–14). In fact, the transparency of the media used allows the artist to suggest that space is the only positive element used, for when one can see through surfaces it is less easy to differentiate between the material and the spatial. Gabo takes light and air and they virtually materialize as formed space. Yet despite Gabo's insistence that such sculptured space — having

---

[12] Naum Gabo, *Of Divers Arts,* p. 99.

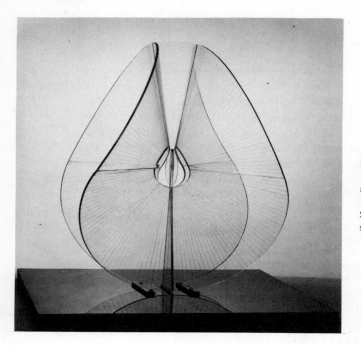

become form — is "not a part of the universal space surrounding the object," I believe that this very emphatic treatment of space in the image creates a unique relationship with the universal space outside. I find that one effect of Constructivist space is to give the illusion that the image is the center of plastic directions in space — a terminal, so to speak, shaping and focusing an infinite number of multidimensional directions. And when translucent media are employed, this illusion is intensified. What then, if any, are the implications of time in such Constructivist art?

If my suggestion that Figure 8-14 can visually allude to a space terminal is acceptable, then there is an implication of both time in *duration* and time in *intensity.* For to bring an infinite number of multidirections in space — which necessarily implies travel and therefore time in duration — to a "center" is to concentrate and arrest such paths of movement. In so doing, a time-space intensity is created within the space of the image and over its surfaces — an intensity which is inevitable when light movement and time become thus trapped and focussed in a whirlpool-like immediacy.

With these remarks we must end the space-light-time discussion. What we have said here merely introduces the trinity in the hope that the creative use of these elements in art may always be fully appreciated.

IX

COLOR AS SENSATION, EXPRESSION, SYMBOL, AND STRUCTURE

To write an all-embracing treatise on color would require a book in itself, and there are many such comprehensive works available for specialized reading. Therefore, in this chapter, I have selected for discussion only those aspects of color which relate more specifically to our overall theme — the significance of the created image as an act of consciousness. These aspects I see as:

1. the sensation of light and color
2. the expressive function of color
3. the symbolic function of color
4. the structural function of color

When discussing color in the context of the visual arts most people think primarily in terms of painting, and this is natural enough. Certainly, all of the examples in this chapter are reproductions of paintings. Yet it is not possible to talk about these or other paintings without discussing our perceptual response to color in the world, in order to see how artists are affected by their natural sensations. And we should not assume that color is only for painters to use. It has also played an important part in architecture and sculpture. (I have mentioned previously that the Greeks painted their statues and that the medieval builders colored the ceilings of their cathedrals.) It is difficult to imagine what life would be like if we possessed no color vision — if we saw the world only as black or white. If this were so, most of us would probably find that our visual experience would be less "rich" and our psychological reactions less subtle and complex. For we know only too well how strongly color can activate the visual senses and stir our attitudes and feelings. And I suppose that painters are painters and not sculptors primarily because color plays such an important role in their awareness of life and the world. We have talked a little about this before; it was obviously not possible to talk about painters and their work without referring to their use of color. In discussing expressive and symbolic transformation in

Chapter 6, we suggested how the color of Delacroix, Goya, and Nolde contributed to the power of their work; and we read an extract from one of Vincent van Gogh's letters in which he described how he could only achieve his pictorial aims through the symbolic allusions created by certain colors. It will be necessary to repeat van Gogh's statement in this chapter. However, we have already made an introduction to the theme of color in the last chapter through the discussion of *light* in its travel through space. For color is light; or, to be more precise, a particular color is the manifestation of a particular wavelength of light. In regarding Turner's *Sun Setting over the Sea* (Figure 8–8), we saw that its light-filled radiance results from the painter's use of particular hues, and that a manifestation of incredible energy accompanies such a revelation of light. Let us therefore talk a little about the physical nature of color and suggest how the artist can exploit its properties when he wishes to create a heightened sensation of color-light-energy.

SENSATION OF LIGHT AND COLOR

Light is one form of electromagnetic energy and, as a physical phenomenon, is the basis of our color vision. Light is the whole, of which each individual color is but a gradation in the spectrum. We should not forget that visible light constitutes only one part of the range of electromagnetic energy; that differences in wavelength account for the invisible energy phenomena we call gamma rays, x-rays, ultraviolet, infrared, and radio waves. Our light — the light by which we see — comprises those wavelengths of electromagnetic radiation which, acting on the eye, enable it to perform the function of sight.

Most of us are aware that when a beam of sunlight passes through a prism a spectrum of pure colors is formed which has a natural order. The seven major colors of the spectrum are violet, indigo, blue, green, yellow, orange, and red and they are observed in this sequence. This color separation of sunlight is explained by the fact that differing wavelengths present in the beam are refracted, or bent, to different degrees as they pass through the prism. Wavelengths that are shorter suffer a greater refraction than those which are longer, hence a separation is effected which allows us to see each wavelength individually as it manifests in what we call "a color." Thus it follows that color, or hue, is the visible result of a separation of light's wavelengths. This helps to explain why objects appear as one color or another, for an object will appear to be the color of the wavelengths of light which it *reflects*, and not those which it absorbs. An object that absorbs all light except that light with a wavelength of 5,700 A will be interpreted by the retina of the eye as yellow, for this is the wavelength of light that appears yellow in the spectrum. However, an object that reflects *all* wavelengths will be seen as white, for no separation is induced through the absorption of some wavelengths and the reflection of others. Conversely, an object that absorbs all wavelengths will be seen as black. Perhaps it should be pointed out that a wavelength is measured from the crest of one wave to the crest of the next, and that what we call frequency is simply the number of wave

FIG. 9-1   **Claude Monet (1840–1926).** *Le Printemps* **1886. Oil painting.** Reproduced by permission of the Syndics of the Fitzwilliam Museum, Cambridge. © by S.P.A.D.E.M., Paris 1972

FIG. 9-3   Pablo Picasso (b. 1881–   ). *The Tragedy* **1903.** Chester Dale Collection, National Gallery of Art, Washington, D.C.

FIG. 9-4   Paul Gauguin (1848–1903). *Maternité* **(II) 1899. Oil on burlap.** Photograph, Charles Uht. Private Collection, New York

FIG. 9-5 **Georges Seurat (1859-1891).** *Courbevoie Bridge.* **Oil painting.** Courtauld Institute Gallery, London

FIG. 10-1 **Two bison from Lascaux. Caisse Nationale des Monuments Historiques, Paris.** Courtesy Albert Skira, Geneva, and *Lascaux ou la Naissance de l'Art*

crests that pass per second of time. It will be obvious that wavelength and frequency interact significantly because the longer the wavelength, the fewer the wave crests passing in a second and, hence, the lower the frequency will be. On the other hand, the shorter the wavelength, the more the wave crests passing per second and the higher the frequency. This is rather important because the energy factor of color is involved; the energy carried by a particular wavelength is dependent upon the frequency of that wavelength. The higher the frequency, the greater the energy. The energy diminishes proportionately to the frequency; therefore, with colors of longer wavelength the energy or radiation factor will become relatively less.

I think it is important to understand these basic technicalities because they help to explain why we use terms such as "vibrant" or "pulsating" to describe certain color sensations. Also, some contemporary artists have deliberately exploited these physical properties of color in order to give the eye some surprises and new encounters in terms of color radiance and energy. They are called "Op" painters inasmuch as they create intriguing optical sensations with color mixing and juxtapositioning. It is interesting to study the approximate wavelengths of the spectrum's seven major colors. The unit which is used to express the wavelength of visible light is the angstrom (abbreviated A). It equals one hundred millionth of a centimeter, and a beam of light comprises wavelengths that range from about 4,000 A to 7,000 A. Here are the wavelengths of white light picked up by the eye in the spectrum:

4,100 A — Violet	5,000 A — Green	6,000 A — Orange
4,450 A — Indigo	5,700 A — Yellow	6,500 A — Red
4,670 A — Blue		

These figures show that red possesses the longest wavelength and so it follows that it will also have the lowest frequency. The sensation of red, as far as the eye is concerned, is thus much "quieter" than that of violet which, with its short wavelength and correspondingly high frequency, is vibrant and aggressive. The eye can become very tired of a prolonged involvement with the energy radiation of the violet to blue end of the spectrum . . . and in turning away to red it gains considerable physical relief.

Sir Isaac Newton was the first scientist to explore the prismic phenomenon of white light and to account for the fact that different wavelengths are refracted to different degrees as they pass from one medium to another. But we should not forget that some two hundred years earlier Leonardo da Vinci also observed the spectrum of color which results from passing light rays through a prism. Yet this did not cause him to paint in what we now call an "impressionist" way, by applying brush strokes of pure spectrum hues directly onto the painting surface, thus building up a pattern of color-light. We have to wait until 1874 to see the French Impressionists use the color divisions of the spectrum to paint sensations of light in this way. (This is discussed later in the chapter, using Claude Monet's *Le Printemps* [Figure 9-1] as our example.) Even though Leonardo the scientist was aware of the spectrum, he could not escape the traditional method of mixing the various colors required on some sort of palette before applying them to the painting surface, and making higher or lower tones of these colors by adding white or black. When lightening or darkening color in this way, it is necessary to keep putting back a touch of the original color into the mixture in order to maintain the chromatic quality of the new lighter or darker tone. If this is not done the mixture will deteriorate into a gray-black neutrality. As we are talking here about the traditional way of preparing colors for painting, it is perhaps appropriate to introduce three basic color terms.

> *Hue* is the chromatic quality which distinguishes one color from another — red from orange or blue from green. Hue implies a whole chromatic range.
> *Value* is the light-intensity of a color, that is, its chromatic intensity in terms of light saturation and purity.
> *Tone* describes a higher or lower light-intensity, or value, and can be compared to the sound-intensity of higher or lower tones in music.

Now the reason why many writers have said that it was the Impressionists who first showed us real color in painting is that these painters avoided mixing color in the traditional way. Instead of producing hues and tones by mixing colors on the palette, using black and white as lightening and darkening agents, they juxtaposed touches of purer, spectrum-like color directly onto the canvas in such a way that the eye does the mixing as it regards the surface. For if the retina picks up the light wavelength blue closely alongside the light wavelength yellow, it will tend to receive the impression of green. Such an impression is usually extraordinarily vibrant, made up as it is from the blue and yellow light which continue to persist in their own right. Also, we can now see that to mix colors together can only destroy the essential purity of each individual spectrum color — which is tantamount to saying that a color's light-intensity is diminished. Complex mixtures result inevitably in both dulled values and a diminished range of hue — in what that great English landscape painter John Constable called the "brown gravy" appearance of much traditional painting. (Of course, we know that the brownness of many old paintings results from the several layers of varnish with which they are smothered. And skillful cleaning has revealed in some cases color values and hues that look remarkably modern.) Again, to add black and white in order to lighten or darken the tone of a color can further reduce its value; and although the Impressionists would use white as a tinting agent or as a color in its own right, they tended to avoid black. Consequently, by keeping the actual physical mixing of colors to a minimum and by using purer hues of dark or light tone to model their forms, Impressionist painters did achieve a color revolution — a revolution that came as a visual shock to eyes unaccustomed to such chromatic purity.

Yet although Leonardo did not exploit his knowledge of spectrum color — at least not from the evidence of the few extant paintings we have — some artists working many years before the advent of full-blown Impressionism in 1874 did attempt to translate visual sensations of light and color directly into paint. I am thinking particularly of Vermeer and the seventeenth-century Dutch painters of landscape and town. They were aware that the bright value of a color is dependent upon the light-intensity of the moment; upon the density of the air through which light is filtered; and upon the spatial position of the color, near or far. They distinguished between what we call *local color* and *atmospheric color* — between the specific color of an isolated object seen under ideal conditions at close range, and the apparent change in color of the same object seen in different spatial positions under differing atmospheric conditions. Again, they knew that the local color of an object is affected by the context of objects in which it is seen — that the reflection of light from one surface to another reflects the color of one to the other. For example, a blue object next to one which is red may become blue-red or purple under the right reflective conditions. Other painters who treated light as color sensations come to mind. There was Velazquez, the seventeenth-century Spanish master, Constable, the English nineteenth-century landscape artist, Turner whom we have already discussed, the great French luminist Corot who was working at the same time . . . and one might even go back to Piero della Francesca in fifteenth-century Arezzo.

It is impossible to reproduce examples of the many types of painterly response to the sensation of light and color or, indeed, to discuss them all here. Therefore, I have chosen to discuss two artists whose work radiates light, or color energy: Claude Monet, the acknowledged leader and inspiration of the French Impressionists; and Josef Albers, one-time member of the German Bauhaus who came to the United States in 1933, and whose painterly research into both the retinal and psychological response to color has had a tremendous influence on recent painting in this country.

Paul Cézanne said of Claude Monet, "Monet is only an eye, but, my God, what an eye!" The implications of this statement could be discussed ad infinitum, but Cézanne was undoubtedly paying tribute to Monet's remarkable optical sensitivity towards light and color seen in the atmospheric envelope of air. Yet I have remarked previously — in using this statement by Cézanne to introduce the transformations theme in Chapter 6 — that Monet's art transcends a merely retinal sensitivity inasmuch as the poetic mood induced by his color and light is often deeply moving. For Monet, a particular quality of light could turn the most mundane object into a thing of beauty; and we should not forget this when regarding even his most apparently casual little paintings of haystacks. We have already talked generally about the painting methods of the Impressionists; now let us look more closely at *Le Printemps* (Figure 9–1), which Monet painted in 1886, and study its color-light composition. Surely what first strikes one is the sensation of being in the open air — of observing light dancing and flickering its way across surfaces, of sensing a certain density of atmosphere, and even of feeling the temperature of the air as a diffusion of early spring warmth infiltrates mistily between the trees. As far as the movement of light is concerned, it appears at first glance that the agitated vitality of the brush marks produces this illusion. But this is too simple an explanation; many aritsts have used a profusion of brush strokes without conveying the sensation of dancing light. It is necessary to look a little harder in order to realize that the brush marks encompass a particular range of hues and color values. As a result, it seems that every brush stroke is really a ray of light of a particular color wavelength. These color-light brushmarks are distributed, apparently spontaneously, over the whole area of the painting as if Monet's eye captured a host of spectrum break-ups of light simultaneously. Moreover, he does not seem to make any formal, structural organization of his brush marks; one is not conscious of the image as "a painting" in the traditional sense of regarding an organized painted surface which stops at the edges. Instead, it is as if a section of a natural view passes for a moment before one's eyes . . . a natural "happening" of color and light.

The hues, values, and tones of these color-light marks are all relative to the position and intensity of the light source at a moment of time — the moment of experiencing the optical sensation — and, in my opinion, no other painter has ever translated visual sensations so immediately and so convincingly into art. Monet's eye seems to take everything into account, even the various spatial positions of the surfaces reflecting the colors and the effect on surface color of reflected light from nearby color sources. You will notice that Monet does not produce his darker or lower tones by adding black or an earth color to an original hue, but employs hues which in themselves are lower in tone — hues such as blue, blue-red, or blue-green. In the case of the higher tones, he makes great use of the yellow end of the spectrum with yellow-greens and yellow-reds. Also, he will add white to higher-toned colors, and the paler values which result from the admixture of white and a color are known as tints. So we see blue-white, green-white, yellow-white, and red-white (pink) tints used alongside purer high-toned colors of the spectrum range. Much as he dislikes black, Monet is not averse to employing white. In fact, the painting is shot through with a few spots of absolutely white pigment which aids the illusion that we are receiving natural sensations of "white" light, despite the fragmented coloration of the work. It is characteristic of Impressionist painting in general, and of Monet in particular, that the hues and tints are juxtaposed freely and independently and that no attempt is made to model them into each other. As a result, the viewer's eye is subject to particularly vibrant sensations of color-light energy. Where a blue hue is placed next to a pink tint, the retina discovers a fleeting sensation of magenta or light purple which tends to oscillate between the two other colors. This Impressionist technique of brushing in fragments of differentiated hues or tints to lie side by side, and to be mixed by the eye into the resulting new color, is generally known as "divisionism." The word implies that light sensations are conveyed by breaking light down into its chromatic constituents on the canvas and that all the colors used, whether they be pure spectrum hues or secondary and tertiary colors, in whatever values and tones are required, retain their own independent existence in the image.

A pictorial technique such as this is obviously going to make considerable demands on an artist's natural or innate sensitivity for chromatic harmonies, even though the organization of the palette and the method of application may be fairly well standardized. In *Le Printemps,* I find that it is the reflection of color to color throughout the work which establishes an overall chromatic harmony and homogeneity. For the pink, blue, and violet colors of the water are picked up by the figures on the grass, changing the local colors of faces and dress. The man's white coat is "pinked" and "blued," and the girl's hat and dress also show the effect of pink and blue light vibrations. Yet if the technique of divisionism allows Monet to paint the movement of light, how does he manage to create a particular density to the air and suggest a certain air temperature? This is less easy to analyze and results from a combination of several painterly factors. Basically, however, I think that we can attribute these aspects of work to the overall "color-glow" emanating from the picture.

Let us discuss this for a moment. We are aware that every color, when seen in isolation, appears to have a certain temperature and humidity value. We say that reds and oranges are hot or warm and that blues and blue-whites are cold. The suggestion of humidity is dependent upon the opacity or transparency of the color. Opaque reds are more humid than translucent reds, while clear blues seem to be dry and become atmospherically progressively damper as the color loses transparency. But both the temperature and humidity of a color are affected when it is seen in a context of differing colors. Orange, for example, will appear warmer when it is placed alongside a cool blue than when it is placed against a hotter red; similarly, blue will appear cooler when seen juxtaposed to red than when alongside white. These laws of contrast play an important part in determining color dynamics, for a color's immediate color context not only conditions its temperature and humidity, but also modifies its hue, value, and tone.

Before returning to *Le Printemps* one more property of color must be mentioned. This is the space illusion of color. It is really not possible to lay down any absolute laws about color and space perception, for each particular organization of colors determines its own spatial result. But it can be said generally that if a hue possesses a strong chromatic intensity — a saturation of color which results in a strong value — the hue will tend to stand forward on the picture plane. Conversely, a dilution of chroma will cause it to retreat. The addition of white to a color weakens its chromatic intensity and therefore affects its spatial position accordingly. A tint will usually appear less frontal than the original hue. An opaque color will also usually stand before a transparent color, and tints tend to become opaque as a result of the whitening process. I suppose that artists have made more use of opacity and transparency factors than any other factors in order to position colors spatially. As far as tone is concerned, it is usually the case that the lower (or darker) the tone, the more frontally dominant the color; and the higher (or lighter) the tone, the more it recedes.

We can see that Monet uses all of these properties of color to produce the temperature, humidity, and spatial characteristics we sense in *Le Printemps*. By combining a warm (not hot) pink, a cold blue-white, a lukewarm blue-pink, a coolish green, and a yellow that varies between warm orange and a cool yellow-white,

Monet creates sufficient warmth to dispel the lingering chill of a spring morning. It is a most subtle temperature combination, being neither hot enough for summer, nor cool enough for winter. It is surely a spring afternoon. Yet in addition to suggesting a temperature range, this painting also suggests a certain humidity to the air. For there are no long distance vistas of clear, translucent atmosphere; instead, a milky "thickness" pervades the air which diminishes any three-dimensional clarity. Also, the chromatic intensity changes very little throughout the painting. Both color saturation and color value are more or less constant from foreground to background; and the colors are more or less uniform in tone, showing no great contrasts of light and shade. When these factors coincide with the "soft edges" of lightly brushed color marks, it is difficult to perceive depth in the image. The first impression is that the painting is all on one plane, for distinctions between space and form are difficult to apprehend, and it is only after further scrutiny that we discern the very subtle concave shape of the air space.

So, for Monet, the surfaces of things (leaves, grass, trees, figures) become the means of revealing the absorption and reflection of color-light which becomes the air — or space — of the painting. In my view, he reigns supreme among the Impressionist painters as the artist who most convincingly catches the sensations of moving light, seen at a particular moment of time through a certain screen of air, and translates them simultaneously into paint.

Now let us explore the color sensations experienced in looking at Josef Albers' *Homage to the Square: A Rose,* which was painted in 1964 and is illustrated here in Figure 9–2. We have talked about color energy and it is this aspect of color sensation which will dominate our discussion of the painting. Optical art ("Op" art), or retinal art as it is sometimes called, developed as an international movement as recently as 1964. Yet, as I have suggested, there is a long history of painters concerned with exploring optical sensations of light and color in air. In fact, what could well be the manifesto for the experimental Op art of the mid 1960s was written by Gauguin in a letter of 1899: "Think of the musical role which color will henceforth play in modern painting. Color, which vibrates just like music, is able to attain what is most general and yet most elusive in nature — namely its inner force." The energy or inner force of color to which Gauguin refers is the main interest of Op artists. Let me just describe a few ways in which this light energy manifests in confrontations with color. If we look with some concentration at a strongly saturated (vivid) red square for a few moments and then close our eyes, we may see a green square which seems to appear somewhere behind the retina. This mental-physiological phenomenon is called an afterimage and represents the appearance of a simultaneous contrast to the original color. It seems that the dominant spectrum hues continually interact with their balancing contrasts in our vision. For example, if we concentrate on red hard enough and then shut out any further light by closing our eyes, the green afterimage we see alleviates and relieves the intensity of the red experience, for the cool green is its balancing contrast. Again, if we place a blue square on a white ground and one on a black ground, we will notice that the blue on the white appears to contract while the blue on the black seems to expand. This apparent movement energy is due to the contrast provided by the ground which affects our perception of the blue wavelength; and obviously an artist can exploit such juxtapositioning to produce interesting effects of color energy. Yet even without the contrast effected by a second color or ground, the phenomenon of color energy operates. Color vibrates optically whether in isolation or in a context of other colors. This sensation of energy is, in part, explained by our own physiological response to color. For perhaps a hundred years scientists have told us that the retina gives off luminous sensations of its own when confronted by certain hues or combinations of hues, and thus we see more than is actually present — we add our own light rays to those we see.

However, as we have mentioned before, a color's energy is most obviously determined by its wavelength and frequency — its electromagnetic radiation. So Op artists will use blue for its shimmering vitality, which is the energy manifestation of its short wavelength and high frequency radiation. In contrast, red is comparatively still by virtue of its long wavelength and low frequency radiation. Therefore, we can suggest that two basic factors determine color energy: our own retinal response to color-light sensation, together with the wavelength and frequency of the color's radiation.

One important aspect of Op art is that it represents a concern for color in its own right — color freed from any associative or representational link with subject matter such as landscape, still-life, portraiture, and so on. It is reasonable to regard the Op artist as the color scientist of painting, for he researches color as a physical phenomenon, studies its effect on the eye as a sensation, and then experiments with the ways it affects us psychologically. An "optical" painting may bombard the eye with color sensations which induce such dizziness that one has to turn away from the painting. Or, conversely, it may drug the mind with such a subtle pulse-beat of energy radiation that one becomes almost hypnotically moved into a state of soporific languor. It is this latter effect which I suggest is created by Figure 9-2. The pulse of this painting is enticingly slow and steady. The squares of color advance and recede to a regular and stable "beat," for the brown-red, crimson, and brighter red colors constitute a family of reds which are chromatically and energetically homogeneous. It is this impression of a slow-beating red stillness which, with continued looking, ultimately engulfs one. How is this overall radiant energy pulse achieved? Many factors contribute to it. First, the bright red square is very red. By this I mean that it possesses a long wavelength of low frequency and beats accordingly as the major pulse. To test how red it is, look at it intently and then close your eyes and discover its green afterimage. The pulses of the other reds serve as reinforcing yet minor energy themes. There is also a temperature and weight difference between the reds. The bright red square is the warmest, the crimson square seems cooler, while the red-brown square appears the coolest. These implied temperature differences also create a pattern of energy movement. We discover some ambiguities in trying to determine color weight and realize that the size of color area is not as important as we might think. In gaining a number of reactions to this color-weight issue, it is the crimson square which appears heaviest to most people. It seems to act as an anchor for the major pulse of the bright red square. In contrast, the much larger area of brown-red is less heavy, for the color is more thinly spread, being dissipated by the canvas grain. This provides an indication that transparency and a dispersal of chromatic concentration make for less heavy colors. Most people agree that the bright red square appears to be lightest in weight. It seems, therefore, that both brightness and density have a lot to do with color weight. Generally speaking, a dark color which is opaque or dense will suggest heaviness, while a bright and transparent color will seem weightless. Yet a further study of the Albers will show that brightness is more important than density in determining the weight factor. For although the red square is about equal in opacity to the crimson one, it does not seem to possess as much weight. Its bright value, which makes it the most sensate light source in the image, negates its pigment opacity and renders it more energetic and correspondingly weightless.

All these factors contribute to the apparent spatial position of the three color squares in the environment created by this image. And we realize that the pulse-energy of the work is also aided by the fact that the spatial position of each color is not fixed or rigidly static. On first appearances, the bright red square projects strongly forward — it is a spatial characteristic of such reds to appear stereoscopically frontal in certain contexts. Yet the anchoring crimson square can challenge this frontal authority because its greater weight factor allows it to come well forward of the thinner red-brown ground. At times it appears to compete effectively for first place with the bright red, and the result is a coming and going between these two for the forward position. But even this situation is not absolutely predictable, for as one looks again, things have changed. Just for a moment, the red-brown, now subtly darker and denser at its base, dominates by virtue of its larger area and becomes a frontal plane *beyond which* we see two red distances; and, for a second, the bright red square becomes a red hole in this frontal surface. Yet although this persists only briefly, it is enough to vary the energy pulse of the work and prevent the eye from becoming bored — as opposed to hypnotized — with the languor of red's long wavelength radiation.

It must be stressed that all these varying sensations occur because Albers has created a color environment which fosters such contrasts and reactions. Although we are using it here primarily as an example of color sensation at just the optical level, it does pose many other questions. For example, what about the relationship of color to shape? What is the best shape for red? Is it square? triangle? circle? Because red tends to focus sharply (stereoscopically), is it best shaped in a square area? Because blue is a spacious color which does not focus so sharply, is the best area shape for it a circle? Can every color be shaped in such a way that its particular radiance is intensified as a visual sensation? Well, these questions you must ponder for yourself; they are the questions which artists like Josef Albers have been seeking to answer in their work, questions pertaining to the phenomenon of color as sensation. However, important as these questions are, there is more to Albers than just the optical factor. It is obvious that we cannot regard Figure 9–2 for long without experiencing a certain psychological response to red. What do we think about and how do we feel when immersed in a reddish environment? Such subjective responses to color — responses evoked by what we might call the expressive and symbolic power of color — will now be our concern as we leave this brief introduction to color as sensation.

THE EXPRESSIVE AND SYMBOLIC
FUNCTIONS OF COLOR

We remarked in Chapter 6 that it is somewhat unrealistic, and perhaps undesirable, to make a firm distinction between expressive and symbolic transformation. Nevertheless, we attempted to describe the differences. In talking about expressive and symbolic color, the situation is the same. The dividing line — if there is such a thing — is difficult to discover, and the problem of elucidation is made more complex because color can be expressive and symbolic at the same time. Therefore, the statements made here are in no sense conclusive; they are really meant to help stimulate the reader's response to color when faced by works which affect him strongly. At any rate, I think we have made it clear that the terms "expressive" and "symbolic" refer to images which result from, and allude to, the artist's subjective life — images which correspond to his moods and intuitions. As Kandinsky wrote, "In every painting a whole life is mysteriously enclosed, a whole life of tortures, doubts, of hours of enthusiasm and inspiration."[1] It is in paintings which answer to this description that color plays a most important expressive and symbolic role and speaks to us of the human condition.

Bearing in mind my reservations about making definitions, it is necessary for the purposes of this discussion that we try to distinguish between expressive and symbolic color in terms of how we, the viewers, are affected by such color composition. I think that the fine distinction which pertains can best be described in the following way:

> When the prime effect of color is to arouse recognizable feelings, such as happiness, sadness, elation, depression, anxiety, or serenity, the color is fundamentally expressive.
> If specific feelings as such are not clearly recognizable because the color touches some less tangible response in which imaginative thought, dreams, and stirrings of lost memories are mixed with feeling, then the color has symbolic power.

This distinction suggests that symbolic color evokes the most complex and profound experience for the viewer; yet I hope it also manages to indicate that the difference between the expressive and symbolic is one of degree. For in a particular context certain colors, as well as activating our more normal and conscious feelings, manage

---

[1] Wassily Kandinsky, "Concerning the Spiritual in Art," *Documents of Modern Art,* vol. 5 (New York: George Wittenborn, n.d.).

to sensitize deeper, unconscious responses toward life. Color which is so psychologically potent seems to contain, yet transcend, an expressive role as it assumes symbolic authority. It is therefore reasonable to think of all color as part expressive in function and part symbolic and to propose that it is within the particular context of a particular image that one aspect or another assumes power. I think it is certainly possible to suggest that when we experience the symbolic strength of a color we also experience an intensification of feeling, suggesting that the color has taken us through and beyond its expressive range. And even when the color of a work is primarily expressive, it can sometimes send out secondary, although much weaker, symbolic signals. Dr. Jolan Jacobi, in writing of the interrelationship between the objective sensation of color and our subjective response to it, discusses how easily human consciousness makes the move from accepting and recognizing color as a natural phenomenon to investing it with an elementary symbolic function:

> The correspondence of the colors to the respective functions varies with different cultures and groups and even among individuals; as a general rule, however, . . . blue, the color of the rarefied atmosphere, of the clear sky, stands for thinking; yellow, the color of the far-seeing sun, which appears bringing light out of an inscrutable darkness only to disappear again into the darkness, for intuition, the function which grasps as if in a flash of illumination the origins and tendencies of happenings; red, the color of the pulsing blood and of fire, for the surging and tearing emotions; while green, the color of earthly, tangible, immediately perceptible growing things, represents the function of sensation.[2]

It is possible to give many examples which support this statement. The most obvious example which springs to mind is the symbolic function of red, blue, green, and gold (yellow) in medieval and Byzantine religious painting. Blue, the predominant color of the Virgin's outer garment, stands for purity and lucidity; red alludes to human passion and earthly involvement; green represents fertility and the maternal condition; while gold is always used as the ground of the image to symbolize the divine. When we discussed symbolic transformation in Chapter 6, it was pointed out that long before the advent of Christian iconography the Egyptians created large golden circles to correspond to their concept of a divine power — symbols derived quite likely from the mystical aspects of sunlight and energy — and we know how Christianity has adopted similar golden circles as halos for their saints and martyrs.

In fact, the selection of yellow or gold as a significant color for religious use provides us with a good example of how the imagination reacts to the sensation of color. Many religions have one thing in common, namely, an involvement somewhere in their dogma with supernatural issues. We have said before that we

---

[2] J. E. Cirlot, *A Dictionary of Symbols* (New York: Philosophical Library, 1962), p. 50.

have no concrete, sensate evidence of the supernatural and so cannot describe it by means of normal analogy or metaphor. Christianity is essentially a supernatural and mystical religion and has always had to face the problem of discovering means whereby its mystical nature is forcefully communicated. This was particularly difficult in the beginning when employing the visual arts which traditionally made use of worldly objects and shapes, for the most effective symbolic forms are those not immediately intelligible in terms of normal associations. But as early as the sixth century the early Christians in Byzantium learned how effectively color — as opposed to forms — could serve their mystical needs. By spreading large areas of gold mosaic over the walls and vaults of their churches, they created what can only be described as an incredibly mystical atmosphere, a fact with which anyone who has stood inside a church such as St. Vitale in Ravenna would surely agree. For one becomes aware, in a completely nonrational way, that golden-yellow *expresses* man's feelings for religious experience, while at the same time managing to *symbolize* that which cannot be known.[3] Look at the glowing suns serving as halos in sixth- and seventh-century Byzantine images of the Virgin and try to imagine how you would respond if the halos were some other color. Would a green halo be as powerful in conveying the mysterious essence of the sublime? True, we have been conditioned to the idea of golden halos for almost 2,000 years and so perhaps cannot answer the question objectively; but the question is still worth asking. And one might go further and raise the question of a square halo's effectiveness. This involves an issue we have already raised: that of the significant relationship between color and shape in order to achieve the maximum expressive and symbolic reverberation. Perhaps a green, square halo would be more effective than one which is green and round?

At this point I would like to re-introduce the paragraph from Vincent van Gogh's letter to his brother Theo — the paragraph in which he states so well how he understood the expressive and symbolic role of color. He wrote:

> To express the feelings of two lovers by a marriage of two complementary colors, their mixtures and their oppositions, the mysterious vibrations of tones in each other's proximity. To express the thought behind a brow by the radiance of a bright tone against a dark ground. To express [symbolize] hope by some star, the ardour of a being by the radiance of a setting sun. . . .[4]

We have already discussed this statement in Chapter 6 in order to explain the significance of symbolic modes of awareness. It will serve here to reinforce our thesis that color is a vital element in conveying the artist's intention. It seems

---

[3] We should not go into another discussion here of what symbolism is and how symbols perform in consciousness. Instead, may I refer the reader to the section entitled *Symbolic Transformation* in Chapter 6 where some basic explanations are, I hope, provided.

[4] Eugen Weber, ed., *Paths to the Present,* p. 202.

quite clear that for Vincent the radiant energy of color was the only means of revealing both the strong surface emotion that two lovers share, together with the broader spectrum of psychic changes that results from "being in love." So let us now look at two paintings to see how color works in these ways. I have chosen for this purpose Pablo Picasso's *The Tragedy* of 1903 (Figure 9-3), and Paul Gauguin's *Maternité* (Figure 9-4) which was painted in 1896.

In both these paintings the figure is employed as the principal motif to suggest certain conditions of human life. Yet it will not serve our purpose here to discuss differences in treatment in terms of drawing, composition, or figure context. For although it goes without saying that the formal and stylistic elements give each work its distinctive character, I would like to try to bypass them and talk solely about the power of color to dominate our response. I would like to suggest that an all-pervading color mood emanates from each painting, and that we pick up this mood almost instinctively. This response may be more immediately experienced with the Picasso, for by using differing values of one hue throughout, the painter produces a saturation of "blueness" which does not have to fight any other chromatic competition. From a temperature point of view, blue is a cold color; it also suggests hardness, as when we talk about steely blue; and it is also a vibrant or energetic color, an electric blue as it is sometimes described. But by tinting the blue to create a range of blue-grays he allows the steely coldness to remain, while losing the energetic vibrancy of purer, more transparent blue hues. In this way the blue assumes a pessimistic, even threatening, role in the context of the painting. The figures do not stand in the clear light of a vast and universal sky-space, for this would suggest a more vibrant and even celebratory situation. Instead, the opacity and dullness of the blue environment reduces sky and space to more local dimensions, and suggests the despair and sadness of the personal blue world of human tragedy. Picasso provides no relief from the blueness. No warm or fertile hues intrude. In my view, the color of *The Tragedy* is primarily expressive. That is to say, it creates a particular mood by evoking a quality and range of feeling in terms of the given, existential situation — a mood that is communicated directly to the viewer. We feel the sadness, the loneliness and the hopelessness of the *dramatis personae* . . . we are pushed to identify with the particular situation in the painting in time and place. For myself, the symbolic implications of the work are secondary to its expressive power. There is no doubt that this weight of blue-gray also acts symbolically to lead our thoughts from the particular to the general, from the specific event as shown in the painting to the themes of isolation, despair, and death as issues in themselves. And it may be that for some people these symbolic undertones constitute the primary pull of the image.

I realize that in regarding Gauguin's painting (Figure 9-4) it is difficult not to be influenced somewhat sentimentally by just the theme of the maternal; and that also the exotic setting of the South Seas contributes a great deal to the romantic mood of the work. However, let us keep to the issue of color. In comparing this Gauguin with the Picasso, I think it is reasonable to suggest that the color impact of *Maternité* does not create the immediacy of mood which emanates from *The Tragedy*.

Certainly we will all recognize the feelings of serenity and peace breathed by the Gauguin, but we should ask how much of this is due to the color-mood and how much to the monumental nature of the design? My point is that in the Picasso the immediate effect of the color is to overwhelm the effect of the design; whereas, with Gauguin, we are aware of the expressive contribution his color makes to the mood of the image, yet it does not overwhelm and inhibit other factors affecting our feelings.

The first clue comes with the thought that this work seems timeless, that it transcends a particular event in time. I have suggested that it is the mark of strongly expressive color to pull one into the emotional intensity of an event now; that we cannot avoid sharing the moment with the three figures in Picasso's painting. Now I would like to suggest that when color acts symbolically it moves us to contemplate the essential and universal nature of the event or theme, *abstracted* from any particular manifestation or happening. In so doing it does not necessarily deny its expressive ability to convey the mood of the moment, as we see in *Maternité*. Yet in my view, such expressive undertones of Gauguin's color are secondary to their symbolic power. For I suspect that the colors in this work help substantially to impart a sense of timelessness — one before which the existential reality gives way and the normal feelings of involvement are transcended.

In any event, I would think that the theme of the "maternal" is going to challenge a painter's ability to discover the symbolic possibilities of color. For we have seen how firmly the several concepts of the feminine — the Great Goddess — persist in the mind as ideas that seem to remain eternally fresh, springing from some deep source feeding our imagery. If the artist is to do justice to such a universal theme, it is necessary that he find the effective symbols, and if he is a painter color may well be his most powerful ally in this respect. In order to embody such a complex and ineffable mental image, the artist must go beyond the expression of normal conscious feelings. To reveal feelings of tenderness, for example, may well be necessary; but it must be a tenderness that transcends a particular moment or a situational context and assumes a universal and atavistic significance. Although Picasso brings three figures together at a time of melancholia, nostalgia, or hopelessness, I do not think it is Gauguin's intention to represent a time-place-event with figures; and we should see whether it is not his color which causes our imagination to go beyond the local scene. We have already said a little about the symbolic role of red, blue, yellow, and green, and mentioned the special significance of gold-yellow; and we see here that Gauguin relies heavily on these colors. He uses three greens; the turgid dark-green of the earth is piercingly enlivened and rendered fertile by the yellow-green of the sky's light, while the lush green of the fruit suggests a synthesis of earth's fertility and light's energy. Green, as the predominant color of things that grow in the earth is, on the one hand, representative of the physical life of nature; on the other hand, while such greens directly represent the actual growth of specific things, they also allude to fertility as a principle in itself — as a force abstracted from the growth of any particular object at any particular moment of time. Fertility is but one aspect of the maternal, yet it is obviously a compelling and important one, and Gauguin conveys both its physical and metaphysical aspects through the expressive and symbolic power of green. We can see that the brilliant red skirt of the central figure plays a chromatic role as well as an expressive or symbolic one. It functions as a simultaneous contrast — almost an afterimage — to the greens and so helps to intensify their greenness; it also gives a deep and steady pulse to the work, against which other and more restless color-energy stands in contrast. The red assumes its symbolic significance in the context of the blue and gold-brown colors which are juxtaposed. Here it becomes the "color of the pulsing blood and of fire" and serves to symbolize the powerful drive of physical passions, the psycho-biological forces of human life. In contrast, the blue robe of the girl on the left, like the Virgin's robe in Christian art, conveys the idea of purity and innocence with all the archetypal flavor that the concept of the virginal and unspoiled brings to consciousness. Seen against the richness of these reds, blues, and various greens, the dusky golden color of the women's bodies assumes an important symbolic function, no less significant to my mind than the golden colors of Byzantium or ancient Egypt. I have always thought that Gauguin had no need of golden halos to impart the spiritual implications of his theme. The golden glow of the skin is enough to communicate something of the religious or mysterious element, which, for many cultures, is a natural part of the theme of motherhood. The nobility, grace, and inner peace which these figures suggest result as much from the symbolic significance of golden color as from the majestic drawing of their physical forms.

Three major aspects of the feminine-maternal are thus revealed, largely through the symbolic implications of Gauguin's color. The greens suggest the fertility of the earth — mother earth; the red stirs thoughts of the human passion which gives rise to the act of procreation; the blue implies all the virtues of innocence, the essential purity of the maiden. As for the gold, this almost seems to be a bonus, for it imparts a spiritual dignity to the figures which already possess a natural grace in the context of the painting.

I am aware of the dangers of separating color from the other elements that make up the painting, even for the purpose of discussion. But I hope that my reasons for doing this with Picasso and Gauguin will be understood. My intention is to introduce color as a psychologically potent experience in its expressive and symbolic roles, while recognizing that all the elements of a painting work together and complement each other in terms of the total effect. Yet separations of this sort are inevitably artificial and can perform a disservice to the work of art. Nevertheless, let me conclude by suggesting that very early in the history of art color was equally effective in stimulating the imaginative consciousness. If you will glance at Figure 10-1, which is reproduced in color with the illustrations for this chapter, you will notice how intense is the area of red coloration on the Lascaux bison. The red area encompasses those parts of the animal most vulnerable to attack, and it penetrates deep into the very heart of the creature. This patch of red is surely not intended as mere decoration. It is placed precisely and delineated carefully. In Chapter 10 we discuss the magical relationship between an image and the object it represents; I will not go into it here except to say that it seems likely that this coloration played an important part in the magic ritual involved. I would suggest that the life of the real bison was felt to be more firmly in the hands of the hunter if the red way to the vital organs was magically exposed in the image. This red, "the color of the pulsing blood and of fire," of the "surging and tearing emotions," may well have served to express paleolithic man's feelings and to symbolize certain mystical attitudes towards the animals upon which he depended for survival. In the heat of action during the hunt, with the real danger involved, the emotions would certainly be surging and tearing, and they would be well expressed by red when making ritual images. But more than this, I see the red as the *magic* color, or, if you prefer, the symbolic color.

Blood is red, and the spilling of blood results in loss of life. Blood is therefore the elixir of life, and it is possible that paleolithic man associated the color red with the life-giving and life-taking powers of blood. Thus, we can speculate that the color red took on magical properties for the cave painter, inasmuch as it corresponded to the life-force, to "spirit" powers that occasioned the physical manifestation of life or death. And then, as we shall see in the next chapter, the belief that the use of this color in the proper ritual enabled the painter to control the life-force of the creature accredits the artist with the powers of a shaman or magician. Certainly, this is what we would call a primitive or irrational belief. But it may be precisely the continuance of such pre-logical attitudes at unconscious levels that allows us to still experience the "magic" of color, or, in other words, the symbolic power of color. As we shall see in Chapter 10, nonrational mental experiences continue to play an important part in our lives, particularly in our responses to creative urges. My original definition of symbolic color suggests that it triggers unusual responses from deep within oneself. We know that what we conjure up imaginatively for ourselves does not always relate to what is called reality — meaning, of course, sensate experiences of things in time and space. Therefore, when we find that a color, or a context of colors, moves us subjectively to ideas which are not based on rational associations or relationships, we must grant that color works as a symbol. Most people have a strong personal preference for certain colors in their choice of dress and in the colors they will use in their homes. Whether or not they are aware of it, their choice is usually dictated by emotional or feeling attitudes rather than by rational deliberations. Most of us have experienced how uncomfortable and disturbed we feel with certain colors and how relaxed or excited we are with others. Consequently, I think it is very important when one views a painting to have not only an "open mind" but an "open heart" also, in order that the color — if it is fine color — can work its alchemy.

THE STRUCTURAL ROLE OF COLOR

It is possible to envisage the application of paint to a surface as a kind of deliberate "masonry." As each block of stone in a building performs a supporting role for each other block, and as the whole building is a composite structure of many small stone units, so every mark of the brush can build up the surface of the painting in an architectonic way. When taken to extreme lengths this method demands a conscious deliberation and calculation before making each mark; but at the other end of the scale, when the paint structure is loose, the brush marks may be more spontaneous and even opportunist. The French Impressionists provide a good example of a loosely structured brush-mark masonry. For although their color theories were systematic and the organization of their palettes relatively standardized, the brush marks of their paintings do not become uniform and dead; and although the divisionist technique of paint (light) application could also lead to a mechanically structured surface, this is avoided by the reflex-like immediacy of response to optical sensation which, theoretically at least, gives every brush mark a flickering vitality. A glance back to Monet's *Le Printemps* (Figure 9-1) will bear this out.

But we will concentrate here on a superb example which represents a more structured application of Impressionist theory — a truly structured, architectonic use of color-light. And we will see that such deliberate color building in the hands of a master does not become mechanical or "dead." In fact, the reverse is true; it is possible to intensify the optical excitement produced by color radiance, and maintain its expressive and symbolic qualities. A master such as Georges Seurat (see Figure 9-5) is able to make a structural warp and weft with his brush marks without in any way sacrificing either compositional or chromatic vitality. The structure of the painting in terms of the careful buildup of hues, tints, tones, and values has always been very important for some artists. As I write I think of Piero della Francesca at work on the frescoes at Arezzo in the middle years of the fifteenth century, and Mantegna working in Padua at about the same time. Both of these renowned Italian painters modulated their colors so carefully that figures and space seem locked in a sculptural solidarity which almost excludes air, while the light is uniformly dispersed so that we seem to be regarding a low-relief instead of a painting. Then there is Veronese (1528-88), a native of Verona, who came to Venice in his twenty-seventh year and stayed to paint for the rest of his life. He was an exquisite colorist, using gold, silver, amethyst, coral, blue, and olive green, all carefully modulated to produce a structural clarity which underlies the sensual richness of his images. The Dutchman Frans Hals (1580–1666) is renowned for the bravado of his brushwork, but it becomes obvious after even a casual scrutiny that each stroke and color is carefully placed to relate to the essential structure of the form in space. And Cézanne, who is probably the most pertinent example of a color structurist, was constantly inspired by Nicolas Poussin (1594–1665), the Frenchman who abandoned Paris for Rome and who was a great architect of paintings, drawing with color values and tones.

Cézanne put the color structurist point of view clearly when he said in 1887:

> One draws in the process of painting. Precision of tone gives
> at once the light and the shape of an object. The more the
> color harmonizes, the more precise becomes the drawing.[5]

---

[5] Henri Perruchot, *Cezanne* (New York: Presse-Avenir/Hachette, Courtesy Georges Borchardt, Inc., n.d.), p. 209.

Many such statements by Cézanne indicate that he regarded color and drawing as structurally indivisible, and that the harmonizing of colors gave an architectonic structure to the painting. He often used the word *moduler* to describe his aim in painting, and, in discussing Cézanne, Herbert Read writes:

> Modulation means . . . the adjustment of one area of color to its neighbouring areas of color; a continuous process of reconciling multiplicity with an overall unity. Cézanne discovered that solidity or monumentality in a painting depends just as much on such patient "masonry" as on the generalized architectural conception. The result, in terms of paint application, is an apparent breaking up of the flat surface of a color area into a mosaic of separate color-facets.[6]

So we see that the process of color modulation makes very precise demands on a painter. In terms of directional movement, the brush strokes must produce a thrust and counter-thrust which impart a firm yet vital balance to the work; horizontal, diagonal, and vertical movements must be homogeneously integrated over the whole surface. In addition, the value and tone of every hue must maintain an overall harmony of color orchestration which avoids discordancies or alien intrusions. Georges Seurat (1859–91), the "pointillist" painter whose work we are to discuss, explained such harmony of color orchestration in one of his letters. He wrote:

> Art is harmony. Harmony is the analogy of contraries and in the analogy of similar elements of *tone, tint,* and *line,* considered according to their dominants and under the influence of light, in gay, calm, or sad combinations.[7]

We have described the Impressionist technique of divisionism and recognized the advantages it possesses for the painter who wishes to suggest the movement of light over surfaces. The color architecture known as pointillism is a more deliberate and constructive application of the same divisionist principle — an application which seeks to impart a solidarity and sense of permanence which some painters felt Impressionism lacked. Cézanne was but one of several artists who were not content with catching the fleeting sensations of a particular moment, believing that such impressions were not, in themselves, profound enough as experiences to justify the aims of art. "I have tried to make of Impressionism something solid and abiding like the art of the old masters," he wrote on one occasion. Seurat held similar views. Like other painters around 1885 he had become interested in scientific literature dealing with the phenomenon of color and the psycho-physiological response of the visual sense. Consequently, he too wished to do more than paint the momentary sensations of light flickering over surfaces. And so he tried to "build in" light, in

---

[6] Sir Herbert Read, *A Concise History of Modern Painting,* p. 16.

[7] Eric Protter, *Painters on Painting* (New York: Grosset and Dunlap, 1963), p. 165. Copyright Eric Protter, 1963.

such a way that the color itself became the cause of illumination rather than the effect of it. Seurat painted in purer colors than Monet, keeping closer to the chromatic hues of the spectrum and making less use of tints and secondary or tertiary colors. Also, he applied his color by means of small brush-point dots, each carefully placed in order to derive the maximum value from its neighbor as the one complements the other. The resulting color structure appears very compact after Monet's free and apparently spontaneous brush strokes. Concerned with what Chevreul called "the simultaneous contrasts" of color, Seurat declared: "When two objects of different colors are placed side by side, neither keeps its own color and each acquires a new tint due to the influence of the color of the other object.[8]

Seurat's *Courbevoie Bridge* (Figure 9–5) reveals how such a patient buildup of small and contrasting color dots imparts a sense of structural permanence and regularity to the form of the image which, although appearing contrived, manages to convey the sensation of natural air and light. There is no doubt, to my mind, that Seurat manages to satisfy the Impressionist desire to paint sensations of air and light while at the same time satisfying Cézanne's dictum that "one draws in the process of painting." Yet apart from the architectonic significance of Seurat's color masonry, there is another aspect of his painting which makes a complete break from Impressionism. "Painting," said Seurat, "is the art of hollowing a surface." In other words, the three-dimensional problems of depth and distance are integral to the color structure of a painting and cannot be shelved because of a preoccupation with the immediacy of light sensations. This conviction led Seurat to create effects of distance induced both by color alone and by the formation of horizontal and vertical lines of color dots which act as space-markers in the image. A study of Figure 9–5 will show how the diagonal, horizontal, and vertical interplay of dotted lines of color gives the illusion of spatial divisions. And you can see how the chromatic intensity of the various dot-shaped regions and the tone values they possess allow them to occupy specific positions in depth. Imagine what would happen to this pointillist-structured space if a single stroke of bright vermilion were to be placed somewhere in the center of the river. It would appear so stereoscopic in its forward movement that it could only disrupt the regularly balanced "hollowing" of the picture surface which Seurat has constructed so painstakingly.

I think it would be difficult to find a more obvious example than this of how color may be used to impart an ordered structure to the form and space of a painting. But we should remember that color never became for either Cézanne or Seurat the structural monochrome to which it was reduced by the Cubist painters who followed them. For while Cézanne's color clarifies the shape of form and space, it is also expressive and engages strong feelings; and Seurat's color is so iridescent that the painting generates its own light.

Color as sensation; color as expression; color as symbol; and color as structure. These, I believe, are the four most important ways in which a painter can

---

[8] Eric Protter, *Painters on Painting,* p. 165.

exploit color in his work. As I pointed out at the beginning of the chapter, this is not a comprehensive treatment of the subject, but one that, I hope, serves the overall aim of this book, which is to stimulate the reader's imagination and interest in art. When face to face with a painting in a gallery, in a museum, or in someone's home, it is so easy to take the color of the work for granted as fulfilling a representational function (to nature), or as serving some vaguely "artistic" (decorative) end, that we often do not give it a chance to affect us in the ways I have described in this chapter. Perhaps this brief discussion will help to open a few eyes and quicken a new responsiveness to the color world of the painting.

X

PRIMITIVISM AND MAGIC: POSSESSION AND PARTICIPATION

Writing in Chapter 5 about those moments of insight which may be described as inspirational, we discussed Professor Giedion's theories about the beginnings of cave art. He suggests, as you may remember, that the uneven surface of the rock walls with their fissures, varied textures, and colorations, provided the configurations of ready-made animal forms. When seen in a dim, flickering light, these vague shapes on wall and ceiling took on the partial forms of animals in much the same way that a damp and stained wall surface will suggest the form of certain objects to us if we give it more than a passing glance. What we see there depends to some extent upon what we want to see there — images which are the projection of our desires, hopes, and obsessions. And while there seems little doubt that rock surfaces lend themselves to animal shapes (see Figure 5-6), it is also very probable that paleolithic man projected something of his own needs onto them. For as a man who lived by hunting he depended upon animals for his subsistence, and it is reasonable to assume that they became an obsession for him. In any event, his visual perceptions were engaged by these suggested forms to the extent that he was able to complete them by drawing, using a staining medium prepared from animal fat and mineral coloring agents. The effect of this visual manifestation on the imagination of the cave dweller is difficult to gauge. In all likelihood, this sudden "appearance" of an animal would have been quite overwhelming. It is characteristic of the primitive mentality to associate ideas freely, rather than to construct logically credible concepts based on the evidence available. Consequently, we might assume that paleolithic man would not rationally differentiate between the image materializing on the rock surface and the actual animals which he hunted. And the obvious fact that the visitation did not represent an animal in the flesh would imply to the pre-logical mind that it is the animal soul, spirit, or life force which is present. For the tendency to believe in an animal spirit is itself archetypal and one which persists strongly — witness the animal cemeteries in the United States today and the "sacred cow" rituals in modern India.

THE LINK BETWEEN IMAGE AND OBJECT

We can appreciate that the first thing to do on seeing the animal form suggested by the rock surface is to catch the ghostly visitant before it disappears; and the obvious way to accomplish this is to draw around it and into it with line and color. This accomplished, the vital life force of the animal is trapped and the hunter has thus gained some power and control over the creature's destiny. Drawing practiced in this way, for these ends, thus becomes a kind of wizardry. It is the magic ritual by which spirit forces become perceptible and subject to the will and control of man. One important result of such image-making rites is that it allowed early man to participate in the workings of nature's mysterious forces. Henceforth, he could feel less alienated, believing that through his magic he had some influence in the animal world and so could control his own destiny — he could modify natural events to his own advantage — particularly in the all-important matter of success in the hunt. So it is quite likely that in these early communities the artist was also the shaman or medicine man; for even at this early stage it would be recognized that he had the "gift" of seeing more than the average man and could cause images or spirits to materialize out of nowhere. The pre-logical mind would surely be very impressed with this performance. I suspect that even today the layman regards serious artists with a curious mixture of awe and suspicion for precisely the same reason. After all, serious art still plays a prophetic and visionary role in modern life.

The important thing to stress is that these early drawings or paintings were not made for aesthetic reasons — they were not intended as decoration or to give pleasure by virtue of their formal beauty. In the cave complexes of western Europe the images are found in the more remote caverns and corridors, not in the places used for domestic purposes. And in many instances these more remote areas would have been difficult of access. All of which tends to confirm that these "art galleries" were private places where special rituals were practiced. The use of such secret places for the performance of ritual or magic is prevalent in many cultures throughout history, suggesting that an archetype is at work here also. For there is a widespread belief that the magic will be more effective if carried out in places reserved for those initiated in the mysteries, and places which are reached only after some physical or psychological effort. (Think of how this archetype still operates in religious practices today — in the isolation of altar and sanctuary in Christian churches, an isolation which, in the Middle Ages, was visually maintained by the large screen separating the chancel from the nave — and in the long trek to Mecca so necessary for the Moslem if he desires to attain a spiritual goal.) Such archetypal attitudes cannot be supported rationally, but I believe we make a mistake if we think that modern man is a rational creature. While it is a mark of primitive man to respond directly to the non logical and less rationally defensible images projected by the psyche, similar primitive or elemental responses lurk behind the civilized facade of which we are so proud. For example, we might be somewhat amused by the cave dweller's belief that because he possessed the image of an animal he had gained some power capable of controlling the creature's life. But do we not believe something of the sort when we cherish the photograph of someone important to us and think carefully as to where it should be placed — where is the place we can contemplate it the most effectively? Can we honestly say that in possessing this image of a person we do not feel that some intangible link exists between us and them? And could we willfully and with passion deface the photograph without the irrational thought overtaking us that we had done some harm to the relationship and to the person concerned? That one might call such reactions superstitious makes little difference if the feeling persists and intrudes when we attempt to rationalize the incident.

Contact with societies which still function in this pre-logical way reveals that one important factor determines the efficacy of the spell cast by the image. It is that the image should be as convincing as possible — that it should capture some essential quality of the animal's physical and behavioristic characteristics — and that it should express the strength of feeling which comes when an artist strongly identifies with the object he is depicting. In other words, the effectiveness of the magical link between image and object is in direct proportion to the formal and psychological eloquence of the work. If this is so, I would have no doubts about the spellbinding power of the two bison painted at Lascaux which you see in Figure 10-1, included with the color plates. Keeping these two wonderfully vital drawings in mind, let me quote the learned French historian Marcel Brion on the nature of the prehistoric artist's involvement with the animal, for it would be difficult to better his appreciation of the sympathetic nature of these images:

> It is certain that this long familiarity with the animal due to
> hunting, a pursuit demanding attention, observation and
> concentration in the highest possible degree, created in the
> Stone Age artist the ability to produce something true and
> lifelike in a manner rarely equalled and never surpassed. It
> is possible to pick out detail where the eye and memory of
> the painter have captured an attitude, a movement, with
> the rapidity and precision of the cine-camera; caught as it
> was about to move, the animal's stance is what gives it
> character, at the same time peculiar to the individual and
> characteristic of the species. It is probable that the Stone
> Age artist managed to achieve this absolute truth only
> because he searched for it and painted it with such
> devotion. . . . Prehistoric art is suffused with love of form,
> of life and of the animal. It is possible that between the
> prehistoric hunter and his victim, because hunting was a
> vital necessity for him and not an amusement, recreation or
> sport, there grew up a sort of communion which is said to
> exist in the "hour of truth" between the torero and the bull
> that he is about to slay. . . .
> Prehistoric art is full of harmony, nobility and greatness,
> first because it is essentially based on truth, on that
> knowledge which comes from a sense of unity with its
> subject; perhaps also on a sort of spiritual brotherhood
> between man and animal. This is what makes it supremely
> religious. Never, or practically never, is there any trace of

savagery, the perverted pleasure of murder, or the ecstasy
of killing. Palaeolithic man seems to judge from his art to
have been more sensitive, more in harmony with nature, the
elements and the animal world than the modern hunter. . . .[1]

In the title to this chapter I use the words "possession" and "participation"
and the reader may now begin to see their significance. These bison are an eloquent
visual testimony to the keenness of the cave painter's eye, to the credibility of his
imagined possession of the animal, and to his ability to participate sympathetically
in the creature's life and fate; while Marcel Brion's statement constitutes a
contemporary response to paleolithic art which fully confirms one's own belief in
its creative sensitivity. I believe that an important truth about all genuine creative
expression is revealed in the prehistoric art in the caves of France and Spain — the
two principal regions in Europe where the finest work is to be found — a truth
which is suggested by the phrase *possession and participation.* Poets, philosophers,
natural scientists, and existential psychologists — to name but a few kinds of
inquiring and thinking men — have agreed (through the years) that a man's life gains
meaning if he participates in some way with the life of the world around him. To
do this he identifies himself at some level through some ritual with some aspect of
his natural environment. For example, when a painter constructs space in a painting
and an astronomer makes mathematical formulae after peering through space with a
telescope, both men are involved in a ritualistic act of identification with a
particular aspect of the universe by producing a creative construction — one plastic,
one mathematical. In his essay entitled *Morality and the Novel,* D. H. Lawrence
expresses this human need for identification in his own inimitable way:

> If we think about it, we find that our life consists in this
> achieving of a pure relationship between ourselves and the
> living universe about us. This is how I "save my soul" by
> accomplishing a pure relationship between me and another
> person, me and other people, me and a nation, me and a
> race of men, me and the animals, me and the trees or
> flowers, me and the earth, me and the skies and sun and
> stars, me and the moon: an infinity of pure relations, big
> and little . . . that makes our eternity, for each one of
> us . . . me and the timber I am sawing, the lines of force I
> follow; me and the dough I knead into bread, me and the
> very motion with which I write, me and the bit of gold I
> have got. This, if we knew it, is our life and our eternity;
> the subtle, perfected relation between me and my whole
> circumambient universe.
>   And morality is that delicate, forever trembling and chang-
> ing balance between me and my circumambient universe,
> which precedes and accompanies a true relatedness.[2]

[1] Marcel Brion, *Animals in Art* (London: George G. Harrap, 1959), p. 12.

[2] D. H. Lawrence, "Morality and the Novel," in *Selected Literary Criticism,* ed. Anthony Beal
(New York: Viking Press, 1956), p. 109.

After reading this it is not difficult to agree with Marcel Brion that "primitive" man "seems to judge from his art to have been more sensitive, more in harmony with nature . . . than the modern hunter"; and, one is tempted to add, to have displayed a more delicate morality. But the important understanding to which we come is that the artists of Lascaux and other caves like it, practicing perhaps 30,000 years ago, indicate right from the beginning that the making of images is a way of participating in life and of possessing, or making completely one's own, those events which are particularly significant because they reveal the quality of a true relatedness between ourselves and some aspect of the external world.

It is thus possible to see art as a therapeutic and ritualistic act, quickening, confirming, and grasping the psychological union of the self with some other thing. If we accept this proposition as valid for the cave painter, it seems to be equally true for his twentieth-century colleague; in which case it is necessary to ponder the fact that the relationship between art and the psyche has apparently changed little in 30,000 years. For Max Beckmann, an important painter of this century, made the following statement in his London lecture of 1938:

> My aim is always to get hold of the magic of reality and to transfer this reality into painting — to make the invisible visible through reality. It may sound paradoxical, but it is in fact, reality which forms the mystery of our existence. . . . One of my problems is to find the Self, which has only one form and is immortal — to find it in animals and men, in the heaven and in the hell which together form the world in which we live. . . . When spiritual, metaphysical, material or immaterial events come into my life, *I can only fix them by way of painting.*[3]

Beckmann's thoughts are very similar to those of D. H. Lawrence. Both men are talking about finding the soul or the self through discovering its relationship to things in the world. Lawrence writes of "achieving a true relatedness," while Beckmann talks of "getting hold of" and "fixing by way of painting" — two ways of describing a *participation mystique* in life and the accompanying feeling of possessing a hold on reality. For these men, reality resides in the heightened state of consciousness, and the resultant self knowing and feeling which accompanies an intense confrontation with events. In a lecture delivered at the University of Fribourg in 1897, the painter Ferdinand Hodler describes the experience in simpler language, using the word "love," which has connotations for us all. He says:

> One paints what one loves; that is why one gives preference to *this* figure rather than to *that* one. One reproduces that particular landscape in which one had been happy. For the painter, an emotion is one of the basic stimuli that cause him to create. He feels compelled to tell of the beauty of

---

[3] Max Beckmann, "On My Painting." Lecture published in 1941 by the late Curt Valentin in New York. Permission Ralph F. Colin.

the landscape, or of the human figure, that is to say, of that particular small part of truth which had "moved" him so profoundly.[4]

These intense "love affairs" which artists have with the things of the world go beyond the normal level of attraction to flowers, trees, and skies which most of us experience. As Herbert Read has often pointed out, it is necessary to remember the distinction between sympathy and empathy. The sympathy for nature which the average person experiences is a feeling *for* things; whereas the artist who is moved profoundly enough to create, projects his own feelings *into* things — an involvement best described as empathy. Surely it is the experience of empathy to which Hodler refers when he goes on to say:

> . . . . the deeper one has penetrated into the being of nature, the more complete is the experience which one is able to create.[5]

We know of artists who have had love affairs with some singular objects. Paul Cézanne obviously loved that dramatic peak just outside Aix-en-Provence known as Mont St. Victoire. He painted it on numerous occasions and was constantly drawn to it, finding there some fullness of being peculiar to him and the mountain. Vincent van Gogh was, for a time, passionately involved with the sunflower; and the offsprings of this relationship are to be found in numerous galleries and collections. Somewhat earlier, the English artist George Stubbs found his passion stimulated by horses, and I dare say no finer painter of horses has yet appeared on the scene. Also in the eighteenth century that most sensitive of painters, Jean-Baptiste-Simeon Chardin, created images in which the most ordinary household utensils are fashioned with loving care. Pewter mugs, stoneware pitchers, and copper kettles are invested with grace. They possess what the poet Robert Graves calls *báraka* — the quality of blessedness. Is it strange that an artist or a poet can love inanimate objects? Not really, if they are fine forms, or if you consider how they manage to symbolize the human qualities of the persons who have used them through the years. Unfortunately, the latter experience is lost to us today. In an age of planned obsolescence we rarely have anything about long enough for it to take on the patina and wear by which it becomes blessed. But artists treasure such things in their studios. They find it necessary to have such visible tokens of human care and continuity. A list of artists and their passions would be a long one. In the twentieth century alone one starts thinking of Braque with his mandolins and guitars, Picasso with bulls, Marc with all kinds of animals, Kandinsky with triangles, Moore with bones, Sutherland with thorns, and so on. Yet in every case I believe that through such involvements the artist participates in the life process and finds

---

[4] Eric Protter, *Painters on Painting,* p. 159. Copyright Eric Protter.

[5] *Ibid.*

some psychic reality which constitutes a truth — a truth which allows some meaning to emerge from the flux of time and the inscrutability of the universe. I have failed to mention the object which, more than any other, has constantly attracted painters and sculptors; namely, the human figure. It is not difficult to understand why this should be so, for this object represents ourselves and triggers important questions pertaining to our existence — of what we are and of what we would like to do with ourselves.

THE NEED FOR CREATIVE ACTION

Earlier in the chapter we talked about the magical function of cave art, suggesting that the making of images allowed man to possess the animals he depicted and thus be less at the mercy of nature's unknown and unpredictable processes. The magic of art was that it represented a *re-creation* of the visible world as man gave form to his own vision of reality. The psychological effect of such an act must have been profound. When man creates his *own* reality — be it only in images — external nature loses her omnipotence, for man feels his power to modify and even transform her. Man is no longer nature's creature in the sense that he accepts the world and her authority unquestioningly and blindly. It is in the creative act, in the construction of images whether they be of science or art, that he gains his independence, sense of purpose, and ability to live with uncertainty and fear. In reading the words of so many contemporary artists I am struck, over and over again, by the relevance of their statements to the ancient understanding of art as therapeutical magic. Pablo Picasso has probably expressed this attitude most strongly. In the following statement attributed to him, he refers to his reactions on seeing the first exhibition of African art in Paris:

> When I went for the first time, at Derain's urging, to the Trocadero museum, the smell of dampness and rot there stuck in my throat. It depressed me so much I wanted to get out fast, but I stayed and studied. Men had made those masks and other objects for a sacred purpose, a magic purpose, as a kind of mediation between themselves and the unknown hostile forces that surrounded them, in order to overcome their fear and horror by giving it a form and an image. At that moment I realized that this was what painting was all about. Painting isn't an aesthetic operation; it's a form of magic designed as a mediator between this strange, hostile world and us, a way of seizing the power by giving form to our terrors as well as our desires. When I came to that realization, I knew I had found my way.[6]

I think that these words would have made a great deal of sense to the animal cave painters of Lascaux. But the intriguing thing is that a great twentieth-century painter will make a statement of this sort. For it reveals that art is still a ritual

---

[6] Francoise Gilot, *Life with Picasso* (New York: McGraw-Hill, 1964), p. 266.

capable of satisfying man's psychological need to "seize the power" from nature, to shape his own mediating yet transcending images in terms of the reality *he* envisions. And this still holds despite the apparent sophistication of modern Western man.

Western countries have enjoyed a great boom in art since the end of World War II. This has not produced any visible increase in the numbers of men of real vision or genius, the aristocrats of art; but it has created a vast number of "middle-class" practitioners, ranging in quality of performance from that of the weekend amateur to the trained professional. There seems little doubt that art is very important to them all whether or not they reap any of the normal rewards. When one is involved in this popular marketplace of art, subscribing to it and asking questions as I have been for the last 20 years, it is possible to discern why the visual arts should have such universal appeal. It seems that any involvement with image-making today serves to satisfy a general need — a need to participate in the process of living at a personal level. Even if the involvement only takes the form of looking at works of art in galleries and museums, it can allow a person to glimpse a way of life that transcends the mundane and the impersonal. And the general availability of art for all, made possible by the tremendous proliferation of communication media, now makes what was once a ritual for relatively local consumption a viable experience for a much larger group of people, dispersed over a much wider area. That this popularization of art has happened at the right time goes without saying. It has, in fact, been a life-saver. For as this century has advanced, the way of life has become increasingly depersonalized, deritualized, and demythologized; which is to say that men have been cut off from the kind of psychological participation in life's processes which satisfies the spirit and the imagination. Living in a technocratic culture it becomes all too easy to accept a programmed way of life and a relatively predictable pattern of events. Our attitude and our behavior become regimented and we tend to distrust our more esoteric thoughts and feelings. We rely on what we call a "practical" response to life, emphasizing the rational approach over all others. But this can ultimately make for an unbalanced consciousness — one in which poetic and intuitive modes of awareness have little credibility — and results in the individual's inability to be nourished spiritually through symbolic means. Art, poetry, music, myth, and philosophical abstraction have not got much appeal for the practical man, whether he be part of a frontier society or a modern technological society which programs and regulates his life for him. Today, there are not many decisions an individual can make in order to determine the course of his own life; and in most Western countries this process of depersonalization has been accelerating since the beginning of the century. Unfortunately, the one ritual which might have supported the spirit of man, namely, a viable religious faith, has been slowly losing ground. World War II compounded the problem, exposing the dark and evil side of man in his ability to commit genocide and wreak wholesale destruction. It was difficult to find a way of affirming a belief in man and in life in those days.

Yet by 1950 it was noticeable that as the mechanical and technological pace increased, more and more people sought ways to realize some fundamental humanness or "wholeness" to life. There was a marked increase in the number of new religious sects that were established; in group activities which encouraged individuals to develop a feeling of identification with others and to pursue common goals of an idealistic nature; and in the proliferation of literature describing the Zen and Yoga ways to achieve states of "being" transcending the mundane. These and many other rituals satisfied a basic human need to participate imaginatively in life and to gain a sense of identity and meaning. It is my view that the widespread interest in "the arts" which we have witnessed represents one of the ways by which people have discovered the satisfaction of shaping experience for themselves — of realizing the complexity and depth of their own nature — and of developing empathy towards things of nature and the environment. There are those who believe that when the ultimate technological culture arrives, man will have evolved into a supremely rational creature. Only then will he be free of those nonrational demands of the psyche for the kind of participation mystique we have described. He will be free from art, poetry, religion, and all other magical rites which are the legacy of his pre-logical days. He will be sufficiently emancipated to live by the rational intellect alone, accepting things as they phenomenologically are and having no need to create the images of art by which natural events are transformed to embody human sensibilities. Well, as far as I can see, there is little evidence at the present time to suggest that we are moving in this direction.

I would like to close this chapter by affirming that the rites of transformation and participation, so well defined by Marcel Brion in his description of paleolithic art, are still with us. Although they may be well disguised under various labels such as "cultural" pursuits, it is my opinion that those acts of the creative imagination we call art serve the same human need to participate in life and to possess it as they did 30,000 years ago. When such acts cease to be necessary, I think it will be necessary to redefine the word "human" and to rediscover the spirit in man.

XI

FROM ABSTRACTION TO THE ABSTRACT

The term "abstract art" is now part of the jargon of art history and criticism and is taken pretty much for granted; but it is not always understood. Because it is used so often as a general label to describe so-called modern twentieth-century art, the layman receives the impression that abstraction in art is a contemporary development; whereas the truth is that all art is abstract in one important sense of the word. Therefore, I think we should discuss how the word "abstract" applies to art in general and then see how certain evolutionary processes of abstraction have fashioned some of the important art of this century.

When one is in any doubt about the meaning of a word it always helps to go to the dictionary to discover how the ambiguities are defined and then to select the particular definition most apt for one's present purpose. Following this procedure, I found "abstraction" defined in Webster's dictionary as, "a withdrawal from worldly objects." This is an ideal definition because we can interpret the word "withdrawal" to mean either a complete rejection of worldly objects, thereby describing the emergence of a nonobjective art, or to imply that one's conscious awareness withdraws some truth or reality from the object. This latter possibility supports the important premise that:

> an image is something "withdrawn" or extracted from the
> object — something standing apart as a mental and plastic
> reconstruction of the object — something that is inevitably
> abstract because it does not comprise the essential, natural
> elements of the object.

All images are abstract in this sense. In Chapter 6, which was entitled *Transformations,* but which might well have been called "Abstractions," since to transform is to abstract, we discussed some of the essential reasons why images are not, and cannot

FIG. 11-1   Albrecht Dürer
(1471-1528). *Hare* 1502.
Watercolor. Vienna, Albertina
Museum

be, replicas of worldly objects. We saw that even Dürer's *Hare* (Figure 11-1), surely as "like" the real thing as any image in the history of art, represents an abstraction (transformation) of the object in two essential ways. First, the hare we see on the paper possesses only a graphic reality — it is but an abstraction of the living object by means of stains and lines. Second, the act of perception which produced it is, in itself, a limited form of awareness, giving us only a certain amount of information about appearances and their underlying structure; perception alone can never tell us what being a hare in the flesh is really like. Consequently, any mental construction we make *after the fact* of the hare as an "outside" physical phenomenon, whether it be a verbal, mathematical, biological, or graphic construction, must inevitably be an abstraction for it cannot replicate the object itself in the wholeness in its being. Therefore, if we grant that all image-constructions are essentially abstract in this way, how are we to differentiate degrees of abstraction — that some are more abstract than others? It is my job in this chapter to try to lay down some guidelines for this process of differentiation — hence the title "From Abstraction to the Abstract." For I want to suggest that abstraction is a general term applying to all created images, but that when we talk about "the abstract" we are referring to a created form which displays one fundamental characteristic; namely, that it bears *no* representational affinity to any worldly object. Such an image would indicate a withdrawal from worldly objects in the sense of a rejection of them as necessary points of departure. For example, as far as we know, pure geometric shapes such as circles and triangles are human inventions which owe little representational allegiance to natural objects, and we refer to them quite properly as abstract forms. Consequently, we can postulate a scale of abstraction in art. At one end would be an image such as the hare in Figure 11-1, while at the other would be something like Wassily Kandinsky's *Abstract Composition* (in watercolor) of 1910 (Figure 11-2).

FORMULATING A SCALE OF ABSTRACTIONS

We have already stated the case for accepting Dürer's watercolor as an abstraction, yet we see that it does not constitute a withdrawal from the object in the sense of rejecting it. Kandinsky's painting, on the other hand, does represent such a rejection, for no objects can be recognized. It is thus a totally abstract image — one that signifies what we mean when we talk about "the abstract." If we take these two works as representing the two extreme positions on a scale of abstraction, it is not difficult to place other images on the scale relative to them. Such an assessment is a visual matter. It becomes a question of recognition. For we can see how far a particular image has moved from representing the natural appearance of the object — to what degree it shows the object rejected. From this point of view Dürer's watercolor is completely representational; there is no rejection — we face a superbly naturalistic image. But we can recognize nothing in

FIG. 11-2   Wassily Kandinsky (1866-1944). *Abstract Composition* 1910. Watercolor. Mrs. Nina Kandinsky Collection, Paris. Courtesy, Albert Skira, Geneva, and *Modern Painting*

Kandinsky's painting; the question does not even arise as to whether an object has been distorted or transformed in some way. The object, apparently, was never there. Thus we regard it as a totally abstract work. Using these criteria, it is possible to select at random any illustration in this book and determine the degree of abstraction it represents. Where, for example, would you place the Cubist painting shown in Figure 8-13? Or our old friend the predynastic Egyptian figurine (Figure 2-2)? For between the two extremes of naturalism *par excellence* and the total disappearance of a natural object lies a whole range of possible abstractions.

The appearance of a work like Kandinsky's *Abstract Composition* raises an important issue. For it seems that we can no longer only consider a work of art to represent a *transformation* of the world in the sense that an object provides a point of departure. In the case of abstract art it appears that the artist does not withdraw an image from worldly objects, but that he rejects objects as unnecessary. He finds that he possesses an imaginative ability to create form without reference to objects as such. Yet I suppose he will admit that without the memory of all previous visual experience of the world, his abstract creations would be inchoate and perhaps perceptually meaningless. Figure 11-2 is reputed to be the first deliberate abstract painting of this century, and as Kandinsky has written extensively about his work we should let him describe how it came about. He tells how he would become immersed in the sensation of color and space experienced in the rich evocative atmosphere of Russian and Bavarian churches, and in the lamp-lit rooms of Russian peasant homes; how, in becoming part of these floating impressions, the concrete reality of the scene dissolved. He writes about the paintings which followed:

> I did many sketches — these tables and different ornaments. They were never trivial, and so strongly painted that the *object dissolved* itself in them. . . . I have for many years searched for the possibility of letting the viewer "stroll" in the picture, forcing him to forget himself and dissolve into the picture.
>
> Often, too, I have succeeded: I have seen it in the observers. From the unconsciously intended effect of painting on the painted object, which can dissolve itself through being painted, derived my ability to *overlook* the object within the painting. Much later, in Munich, I was once enchanted by an unexpected view in my studio. It was the hour of approaching dusk. I came home with my paintbox after making a study, still dreaming and wrapped up in the work I had completed, when suddenly I saw an indescribably beautiful picture drenched with an inner glowing. At first I hesitated, then I rushed toward this mysterious picture, of which I saw nothing but forms and colors, and whose content was incomprehensible. Immediately I found the key to the puzzle: it was a picture I had painted, leaning against the wall, standing on its side. The next day I attempted to get the same effect by daylight. I was only half-successful: even on its side I always

recognized the objects, and the fine finish of dusk was missing. Now I knew for certain that the object harmed my paintings.

A frightening depth of questions, weighted with responsibility confronted me. And the most important: what should replace the missing object . . . ?

It took a very long time before this question . . . received a proper answer from me. Often I look back into my past and am desolate to think how much time I took for the solution. I have only one consolation: I could never bring myself to use a form which developed out of the application of logic — not purely from *feeling* within me. I could not think up forms, and it repels me when I see such forms. All the forms which I ever used came "from themselves"; they presented themselves complete before my eyes . . . they created themselves while I was working, often surprising me.[1]

Kandinsky's account of forms creating themselves while he was working — forms which resulted purely from feeling within him — is as good a description as one will find of the kind of painting now commonly referred to as Abstract Expressionism. In Chapter 6 we referred very briefly to *action painting* as a form of expressive release when "the painter lets the body itself act, dancing the emotions out and recording the action meanwhile on board or canvas in abstract line and color." And in Chapter 5 you may recall that we discussed the action painting of Jackson Pollock, perhaps the greatest American Abstract Expressionist of the post-World War II period. It can be seen now that there is very little difference between Kandinsky's abstract expressionist innovations at the beginning of the century and Pollock's highly skilled action painting in mid-century. As the name implies, it becomes a question of the kind of action involved. For both men gave themselves up to that transitory and intense state of being when feeling finds counterpart in form and color, and the intuitively created form and color finds its inner echo in feeling. There is a simultaneity to such action and reaction that defies cause-and-effect chronology. As I see it, the kind of painting action involved is determined largely by the size of the surface to be painted. The larger the surface, the more energetic and extensive is the bodily movement required to cover it as the forms create themselves in the working. Consequently, physical action necessarily plays an important role in the production of a large image. Kandinsky's watercolor (Figure 11-2) measures approximately only 19" x 25". Pollock's *Number 27*, which you see reproduced as Figure 11-3, measures 49" x 106". Yet despite the greater size there is no loss of nervous excitation, of spontaneity of feeling, in the lines and stains which form the Pollock. It is every bit as vibrant and as passionately lyrical as Kandinsky's painting. Yet I think there is no doubt that to maintain this intensity over the larger area requires a ballet dancer's agility of every limb of the body. Hence, the name action painting; or, Abstract Expressionism writ large. In

---

[1] Wassily Kandinsky, "Reminiscences," (Berlin: in *Der Sturm,* pub. by Hermuth Walden, 1913).

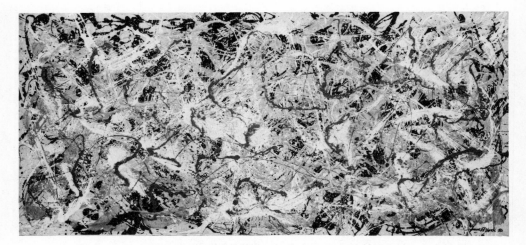

FIG. 11-3   Jackson Pollock (1912–1956). *Number 27* **1950. Oil on canvas. 49 x 106.** Whitney Museum of American Art, New York

my view, Jackson Pollock and the other action painters are the inheritors of Wassily Kandinsky's discovery that the object harmed his paintings and that he could only dissolve into his work when feeling and action became one, unimpeded by considerations of object representation.

Most of us have grown up in this century with what is known as *nonobjective* art. This art of free invention has taken many paths, more than we can follow here, but the important thing is that we no longer expect a work of art to necessarily show us some aspect of the world of objects. Instead, we have grown accustomed to regarding images as works of pure plastic invention — as imaginative statements in a plastic and visual idiom which spring from, and correspond to, significant states of consciousness — and which can affect our sensibilities in a similar way to that achieved by the most abstract of art forms . . . music. Curiously enough, Kandinsky's first intention was to be a musician and throughout his life he never lost a musical sensibility. He used musical analogies from time to time in his writings and was a good friend and supporter of the innovative twelve-tone composer Arnold Schonberg whose a-melodic works — in comparison with traditional, eight-tone melody — were as new to the ear as Kandinsky's paintings were to the eye. Music and architecture have always been considered truly abstract art forms, whereas painting, sculpture, and poetry have constantly been thought of as more descriptive — more tied to experiences of worldly objects and events. The reasons for this are not difficult to understand. Architecture is essentially concerned with the shaping of space for functional and aesthetic ends, and the architect is free to apply himself imaginatively without conscious reference to, or stimulus from, nature. Nature does not provide many examples of ready-made spatial constructions which man can inhabit and call "cathedral," "house," or "law court." For such designations represent concepts of space which are essentially human and abstract rather than natural and visible. Similarly, musical composition is not an art which represents a re-creation of sounds auditorily perceived in the world. The sounds of mountain streams, ocean tides, rushing winds, or cuckoo calls have not in themselves shaped the musical form of a symphony or sonata. The mathematical basis of tonality on both the eight- and twelve-tone scale represents an intellectual creation of the human mind, rather than a system for recording sensations picked up by the ear from the outside world. Also, that fundamental element in music we call rhythm rests on a mathematical base, as do the dynamics of musical sound. The whole structure of a musical work springs from man's creative faculties rather than from his ability to imitate; there is little in nature, except perhaps that marvelous silence which we "hear" sometimes, to inspire the musical forms of a Beethoven or a Gershwin. Music is thus the most abstract of the arts; even as an event in time and space it is ephemeral, for when the sounds have died away all that is concretely left is the score.

I suppose it has rarely occurred to anybody — even to the most naive and musically ignorant listener — to ask what a piece of music is meant to represent. But the question is asked constantly of a painting or a work of sculpture. We are less able to accept a visual configuration which is totally abstract than we are an auditory one. Surely this is because our sense of sight is the dominant way through which we are aware of the world? Our cognizance of its physical surfaces and the spaces which surround them is almost completely dependent upon visual perception; and, as we have seen, a work of art also exists by virtue of our perceiving the elements of material surface and space. It is therefore only to be expected that because the elements of form and space are necessary for both our perception of the world and a work of art, we expect to recognize something of the former in the latter. Music does not suffer from such perceptual associations, for the sound-shape of nature does not enter into music as her sight-shape inevitably enters into art.

The abstract art of Kandinsky and others represents a cutting loose from this natural tendency to expect some recognizable association between the form and space of the image and that of the natural world. Indeed, it has often been suggested that Kandinsky's abstract works should be viewed as "visual music," if this kind of mental association can be achieved. For when we listen to music it is the structure of sound in its own abstract right — divorced from memories of the world's sounds — that moves us. The suggestion is that we should be similarly divorced from memories of the world's objects when we look at art; then we may be more easily moved by the structure of form and space as a plastic language in its own abstract right.

TOWARDS TOTAL ABSTRACTION

Although I have used Wassily Kandinsky as a prime example of the move to the abstract early in this century, other individuals are also responsible for pioneering other paths to total abstraction. We have seen that Turner was painting almost totally abstract images as early as 1840, and that by 1900 Paul Cézanne's landscape paintings were growing increasingly abstract, and were destined to influence Picasso and Braque in developing their late Cubist abstractions of 1912. Then there was Kasimir Malevich with his own brand of nonobjectivity which he called Suprematism, implying the supremacy of feeling over all material or objective experiences (see Chapter 5). There were the brothers Naum Gabo and Antoine Pevsner, whose Constructivist ideology produced some of the first totally abstract sculpture of this century (see Chapter 8). There was also Piet Mondrian. If we regard Kandinsky as the forerunner of Abstract Expressionism, we have to think of Mondrian as his opposite number — as the pioneer of an abstract painting style which was not concerned with finding a plastic equivalent for feeling, but for those universal laws on which mathematical logic is based. Sir Herbert Read describes these two abstract extremes as follows:

> Kandinsky himself, in theory if not in practice, was always to remain faithful to what he called "the principle of internal necessity." But largely on the basis of Kandinsky's practice other artists were to come forward with what might be called a principle of *external* necessity. The whole purpose of this alternative principle was to escape from the internal necessities of our individual existence and to create a pure art, free from human tragedy, impersonal and universal. . . .
> The painter who was to develop to its logical extreme the objective concept of abstraction was Piet Mondrian.[2]

So we find that two alternatives exist within the realm of the abstract itself. There is the freely formed, irregularly flowing image such as Figure 11-2 which, as Kandinsky says, springs directly from the artist's feelings; and there is the image which represents a pure art, an art of absolutes, inevitably impersonal and structured according to the laws of reason, logic, and mathematics. This you see in Mondrian's *Composition C* (Figure 11-4). Yet despite the carefully thought out ratios and horizontal-vertical harmonies, Mondrian manages to avoid a mechanical geometricism. For there is a rightness or inevitability about the subtle juxtaposition of these variations on a rectangular figure that constitutes a truth, or that strikes us as true. In such a work all oppositions and tensions are reconciled in an ordered plastic scheme which satisfies one of the great human dreams — the intuition of a cohesive, purposive, and dynamic principle of unity underlying the apparent polarities and diversities of man's experiences of the world.

If we label Kandinsky's free compositions as Abstract Expressionism, what are we to call Mondrian's structured images? Does Herbert Read's term "objective abstraction" manage to convey the full flavor of a pure Mondrian? I think not; but one is hard pressed to find a better label. Yet words such as objective or subjective

---

[2] Herbert Read, *A Concise History of Modern Painting,* p. 195.

184   FROM ABSTRACTION TO THE ABSTRACT

FIG. 11-4 Piet Mondrian
(1872-1944). *Composition C*
1920. Oil. Museum of Modern
Art, New York

must be redefined when used to describe totally abstract images. For we saw in
Chapter 5 that Mondrian did not consider himself to be a calculating logician, but
talked about the enlightening power of the *intuition* to produce a creative
intelligence which feels and thinks. But the result of such imaginative experience
for Mondrian was to bring him to the realization that:

> . . . there are *fixed laws which govern and point to the use
> of the constructive elements, of the composition and of the
> inherent interrelationships between them.* These laws may
> be regarded as subsidiary laws to the *fundamental* law of
> equivalence which creates *dynamic equilibrium and reveals
> the true content of reality.*[3]

One wonders how Kandinsky would react to this statement, for by his own
admission he could never bring himself "to use a form which developed out of the
application of logic — not purely from feeling within. . . ." Of course, what we see
in comparing the statements and the work of these two abstract painters is the
difference between the classical and the romantic imagination. Mondrian searches
to discover an abstract plastic language through which to shape certain insights of
the intuitive intellect — insights concerning the permanent laws which maintain a
viable balance between opposing forces. In so doing he follows the classical

[3] Piet Mondrian, "Plastic Art & Pure Plastic Art," in *Documents of Modern Art* (New York:
George Wittenborn, n.d.).

FROM ABSTRACTION TO THE ABSTRACT

tradition of imposing on (or extracting from) life a hypothetical order and cohesion. We might coin the label Classical Abstraction to identify his work. Kandinsky, however, on the evidence of *Abstract Composition* (Figure 11-2), is a full-blown romantic. It is the living moment, and knowing the moment intensely through the quality of feeling accompanying it, that constitutes the true content of reality for him. The special kind of contemplative objectivity that is required to bypass personal feelings and passions in order to postulate impersonal and universal laws concerning the abstract nature of reality is anathema to the romantic personality. As Herbert Read says, "Kandinsky . . . in theory if not in practice, was always to remain faithful to . . . 'the principle of internal necessity'. . . ."[4] And we know from Kandinsky's other writings how personal, intense, and fundamentally spiritual was the content and flavor of this internal necessity. So we see that abstract art also can go in two opposite directions. For we see the purity and dynamic harmonies of classical forms which possess their own spiritual implications in terms of the ideal systems they create — systems which transcend the individual. And we see the vigorous and individually anarchic character of romantic forms which testify to a personal spiritual struggle — a way to truth which must be found by playing out the private drama of the psyche's feeling and knowing impulses.

We have recorded how Kandinsky lost the object in his painting through a sudden and unexpected encounter in the half-light of his studio with a work which was leaning on its side. At this moment he responded to the sight of shape and color as one would to the sound of music, with no distracting references to worldly objects getting in the way. The nature of this revelation was in itself romantic, being undeliberate and chance-like, although it must be said that Kandinsky's landscape paintings before this show a movement up the scale towards total expressive abstraction. Mondrian came to the abstract more deliberately and more systematically. Oddly enough, his earlier works were no less expressive than those of Kandinsky and his principal subjects were also architecture and landscape. The color in these paintings is gloriously evocative of all kinds of mood, and the drawing is lyrical and free. However, around the year 1909, a change occurs. Mondrian starts to reduce the complexity of natural forms to a simpler statement of their essential structural characteristics. There are images of this period in which the artist, searching for a common and basic shapeness among a wide variety of objects, imposes geometric simplifications over naturalistic drawings of butterflies, flowers, and plants. Yet it was trees that seemed to fascinate him above all; and by studying his images of trees, made over two or three years, we can follow the sequence of reduction from the naturalistic to the abstract.

I believe that the five works reproduced here as Figures 11-5 through 11-9 speak for themselves, especially in view of what has already been said. There are other tree drawings and paintings that come, chronologically, between these five, and which reveal other stages of abstraction; but I think that these examples illustrate the general development well enough. It is also interesting to see how the

---

[4] Herbert Read, *A Concise History of Modern Painting.*

abstraction of the 1912 *Flowering Appletree* (Figure 11–9) has moved to a completely nonobjective abstraction in *Composition C* (Figure 11–4), a painting made in 1920. Although the tree has virtually disappeared in the former work, a tree-like curvilinear and organic liveliness remains in the way Mondrian treats the movement of line and the flow of space. But in Figure 11–4 this expressive vitality has disappeared and the organic world of tree movement and tree space has given way to the closed, invariable, and essentially more abstract world of pure geometry. Perhaps if one is proceeding from lyrical and expressive images to what Mondrian called "pure plastic art," this move from the organic is inevitable. Kandinsky lost the object by dissolving himself into the emerging image in a surrender to feeling. Objectivity, either towards the world or towards self, cannot be part of such an experience. Mondrian, however, lost the object through a series of analytical steps, whereby it became reduced to a few basic lines which represented its simplest, and

FIG. 11-5   Piet Mondrian (1872–1944). *Tree* 1909–10. **Drawing.** Collection Haags Gemeentemuseum, The Hague

FIG. 11-6   Piet Mondrian (1872–1944). *Tree* 1911. **Oil.** Collection Munson-Williams-Proctor Institute, Utica, New York. Photograph, Courtesy Sidney Janis Gallery, New York

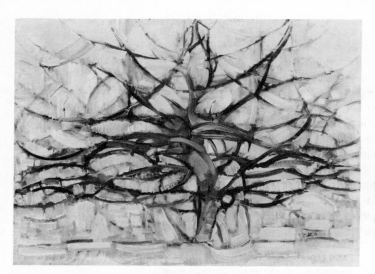

FIG. 11-7 Piet Mondrian (1872–1944). *The Gray Tree* 1911. Oil. Collection S. B. Slipjer, Haags Gemeentemuseum, The Hague

FIG. 11-8 Piet Mondrian (1872–1944). *Trees in Bloom* 1912. Oil. Private Collection, New York

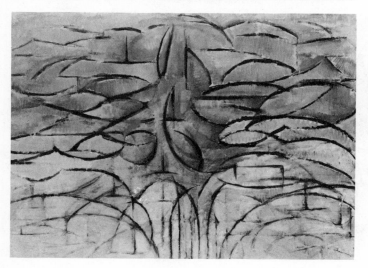

FIG. 11-9 Piet Mondrian (1872–1944). *Flowering Apple Tree* 1912. Oil. Collection Haags Gemeentemuseum, The Hague

thereby purest, form. Such activity is truly objective, both towards the world and oneself, for one has a logical aim in mind and tries hard to achieve it. It is perfectly reasonable therefore to label Mondrian's later work as Objective Abstraction. Before leaving Mondrian's five tree pictures it is interesting to note that once the artist ceases to regard the details of the tree's natural appearance as sacrosanct — as Figure 11-6 — he is free to concentrate perceptually and analytically on the space which the tree inhabits. In fact, if he is to eliminate inessential physical detail in favor of overall tree rhythms and proportions, it is absolutely necessary that he be aware of the *shape of space* which the tree's presence creates. For without the perception of tree-space it is not possible to assess the directional movement of a single limb from beginning to end or to visually comprehend the rhythmic and proportionate conglomerate pattern of many limbs which comprise the whole tree. When Mondrian begins to show us the shape of tree-space as he does in Figure 11-8, it is a curious thing that even though the physical surfaces of the tree limbs are reduced to a linear abstraction, we still apprehend the general "treeness" of the image. It is proof of the fact that in our perception of the world, the ability to apprehend the shape and positional implications of the space field is just as important as the ability to discern the physical surfaces of objects — even though we concentrate on the latter more consciously. And I would go so far as to say that when the artists of this century turned their attention to shaping and organizing space as a plastic element in its own right, the physical details of objects lost the traditional and authoritative attentions lavished on them for 600 years in Western art. For the *Flowering Appletree* of Figure 11-9 is no longer an image of an apple tree, but of appletree-space. In my view, this is the great lesson to be learned from Mondrian; that space, which is abstract and no thing, may be so purposefully used as the major element in an image that we respond to the beauty of its dynamic equilibrium in terms of its two- and three-dimensional organization.

It has been said by more than one person that architecture is "concrete music." Such a statement makes a great deal of sense. Think of musical form as a sequence of sounds organized around intervals of silence. The sounds comprise a range of various tones, sustained for various lengths of time and possessing various strengths from very loud to very soft. The silences, or spaces, also vary as long or short intervals between the sounds. The permutations that can be made on these musical elements would seem to be almost infinite. It is not difficult to see the relationship of music to architecture — to think of architecture as solidified music — if we compare the elements comprising architecture with those of music. The solid surfaces of an architectural ensemble can suggest a high or low sound value, depending upon their vertical or horizontal emphasis — high or low, they can be sustained for various lengths of time until their spread is interrupted by space; and they can be loud or soft in impact according to their frontality or recession, their textural quality, and their brute strength or delicate fragility as mass. Similarly, as the intervals of space or silence in music articulate the stream of sound, so the spatial element in architecture articulates the spread of surfaces. But whereas music is essentially linear and relatively two-dimensional, architecture is volumetric and three-dimensionally substantial. Space or silence are omnipresent; but in order to be perceived they must be shaped, and the sounds which shape them positively in music are physically short-lived and fade away — hence musical space as an auditory experience has no concreteness in the sense that it endures. However, the physical surfaces which shape space positively in architecture persist by virtue of their material nature — hence architectural space endures. Whether the substantial elements of architecture can be subjected to the vast number of permutations possible in shaping the elements of music is another matter. Technical and physical limitations would seem to be against it. Yet the concept of architecture as "frozen music" provides much food for thought.

I mention this analogy of architecture to music because it may help us to comprehend and appreciate abstract or nonrepresentational possibilities of form and space in the visual arts. I mention it also because I want to close this chapter by showing two works of sculpture which will reinforce our discussion of Mondrian's classical abstraction and Kandinsky's romantic abstraction. At the same time they should illustrate and confirm the musical analogy in terms of abstract sculpture. We saw in Chapter 8 the important role played by space in Constructivist theory and sculpture. The effects have been widely felt throughout the whole field of contemporary sculpture. Space has become an element to use in a positive manner, and the new techniques of welding, brazing, laminating, plastic-moulding, and casting have helped to make this possible. Consequently, the sculpture of our day has developed a close affinity to architecture, for it is a prime function of architect and sculptor to shape space through the disposition of surfaces. In the end, the differences between architecture and sculpture become a matter of intention, function, and scale. It is not difficult to envisage the kind of architectural space that would result from the partial enclosure of the sculptural space in Figures 11–10 and 11–11. Therefore, if it is possible to talk about architecture as frozen music, I think it is possible to make the same analogy for space-conscious contemporary sculpture.

Georges Vantongerloo's *Sculpture in Space: $y = ax^3$ minus bx^3* (Figure 11–10) is a work in which the rectangular spatial regions are carefully modulated in terms of major vertical and minor horizontal themes. The artist has carefully controlled the respective ratios of these sculptural spaces. If one were to assume that the image seen here is a basic motif or unit around which extensions into space are to be developed, it is inconceivable that the development would take a form which does not follow the proportionate spatial modulations already established. If the aesthetic rightness of the piece is to be maintained, then the homogeneous and proportionate relationships already established must be maintained. The linear ratio between vertical and horizontal is approximately 8:2 throughout, and any volumetric enclosure of the space would have to follow the same proportions. In other words, we can determine the structural laws which account for the form of this work — laws which are manifest because the dynamic relationship and logical equivalence of part to part is constant and can be seen. In contrast, the structural laws which may explain the form of Laszlo Moholy-Nagy's *Plexiglass and*

FIG. 11-10   Georges Vantongerloo (b. 1886–   ). *Sculpture in Space:* $y = ax^3 - bx^3$ **1935.** Kunstmuseum, Basel. Emanuel Hoffman-Stiftung

Chromium-rod Sculpture shown in Figure 11–11 are not so obvious. Although the spatial regions follow a general elongated elliptical shape, their three-dimensional interrelationship is not clear, and neither the area nor the linear ratios follow the kind of logical or predictable relationship we see in Figure 11–10. Moholy-Nagy's piece seems to have come into being much more fortuitously, discovered, so to speak, in the act of working. If it were to be extended into space, the artist (or architect) would have considerable freedom to move in any direction and to

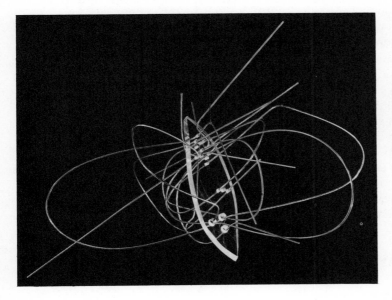

FIG. 11-11   Lazlo Moholy-Nagy (1895–1946). *Plexiglass and Chromium Rod Sculpture* **1946.** Solomon R. Guggenheim Museum, New York

employ virtually any proportionate length or volume. There are spatial oppositions and tensions in this sculpture which are not present in Vantongerloo's piece, where a *harmony* of equivalent and predictable relationships reigns thoughout. It seems that we are back to the classical and romantic proposition again. And I suppose it is fairly easy to see that Vantongerloo's work could be taken as a Mondrian painting translated into three-dimensional sculptural terms, while the Moholy-Nagy may be seen as the sculptural equivalent of Kandinsky's first abstract-expressionist painting. In any event, the arguments we have presented in discussing the abstract images of Mondrian and Kandinsky respectively would serve equally well to describe the two space sculptures we see here.

But what about the analogy to music? While discussing the Greek Aphrodite and the predynastic Egyptian figurine in Chapter 2, I suggested that Aphrodite may be likened to a Bach fugue and the figurine to a blast of Wagnerian sound. I think a similar comparison may be made for these two sculptural pieces. The proportionate contrasts between major and minor themes which are maintained overall in Vantongerloo's sculpture are nearer to the musical structure of Bach than to that of Wagner. For we experience a Bach fugue as a contrapuntal organization of theme and variation in which, despite the obvious presence of a major motive, a classical balance is maintained. Although this statement briefly describes a musical form which we hear, it makes just as much sense if applied to Figure 11-10 which is a plastic form to be seen. But it is not possible to associate such a contrapuntal balance of sound with the visual characteristics of Moholy-Nagy's piece, where a crescendo of space-sound diminishes, in the course of its diagonal sweep, to an attenuated murmer and is not counterbalanced by any reciprocal space-sound minor theme. In fact, the major theme which is shaped by the chromium rods has little, if anything, to do with the minor theme which is shaped by the Plexiglass. Neither the position nor formal appearance of this secondary theme can be justified logically — it is an intruder, a seemingly aberrant and intransigent form not formally integrated with the dominant theme of the work. Therefore, I associate Figure 11-11 with a burst of orchestral sound which exists independently of what has gone before or of what is to come after — with those magnificent romantic gusts of which Wagner was so fond.

Kandinsky declared that the object harmed his paintings. It was a prophetic remark, for since then the art of the twentieth century has been preponderantly nonobjectively abstract. Because of this we have all had to try to learn a new plastic and visual language. We have had to respond to the sensuousness of line, surface, space, and color as autonomous visual experiences and to refrain from asking the question, "What is it?" The object harmed Kandinsky's painting because the problems of graphically representing it impeded the spontaneous flow of his feelings, and because its presence prevented him from discovering the abstract form best suited to express these feelings. It seems that the creative imagination has come full circle — from feeding on the stimuli afforded by the world outside, to generating its own classical or romantic abstract inventions.

The question is, "What now?"

XII

AN ART OF NEGATIVE
CAPABILITY:
DADA AND "POP"

> What is beautiful? What is ugly? What is great, strong,
> weak? . . . What is "I"? Don't know! Don't know! don't
> know, don't know![1]
>
> Georges Ribemont-Dessaignes

With the foregoing quotation we are pushed headlong into the problems of
our own century. It was not my intention to bring the book to a chronological end
for, as I said at the outset, we are not concerned with a linear, historical survey of
art; and, indeed, we have not dealt with our subject in this way. Instead, the
particular theme of each chapter has determined the art forms to be introduced. As
a result, we have ranged fairly freely over the whole field, juxtaposing for discussion
images of our own time with those of periods far removed. Yet despite this lack of
chronological development — or perhaps because of it — we have been able to
constantly support one basic proposition to explain the human activity we call art.
It is that image-making is a necessary and purposive creative act. However much I
may have been sidetracked by my own prejudices and persuasions, I think it has
been possible to consistently maintain that *art serves to shape consciousness,* first
for the individual and ultimately for us all. I have the feeling that in this final
chapter it will be necessary to continuously bear this in mind. For now we are to
confront an art which seems to deny and violate artistic necessity and human
purpose — as we have previously understood these terms — an art which, in its own
time, has been described as anti-art.

A BREAK WITH TRADITIONS

The well-known label "modern art" has not been used in these pages to
signify the images springing from a twentieth-century consciousness. I have avoided
it deliberately. In fact, it is antithetical to another of this book's major propositions;
namely, that certain imaginative themes and certain plastic treatments keep

---

[1] Georges Lemaitre, *From Cubism to Surrealism in French Literature* (Cambridge, Mass.:
Harvard University Press, 1947), p. 69.

cropping up throughout the history of art and that much of what we call modern, meaning new, is not new at all. (You may remember that in Chapter 4 I referred to a fairly recent exhibition in London which was entitled, "40,000 Years of Modern Art.") Again, we have had no need of a blanket term to denote twentieth-century art in general because we have selected particular movements for discussion out of their chronological context. In this way we have been popping in and out of the twentieth century all the time, discussing "modern art." Symbolist, Cubist, Surrealist, Expressionist . . . are twentieth-century styles with which the reader is already familiar. The opening sentence to this chapter therefore seems irrelevant, if not downright misleading. To say that here is a quotation which pushes us "headlong into the problems of our own century" implies that we have not been here before and also suggests that we have come to the end of a chronological trail. However, neither of these suggestions is true. Therefore, it must be that there is something rather special about what I call "an art of negative capability" — something that makes it peculiarly an art of our time, yet ensures that it is sufficiently unique to merit individual treatment. This, as I see it, is the problem presented by Dada and its more recent derivative, "Pop" art. For while one can chart the path of its evolution, and even find its antecedents in the art of some primitive cultures and in odd sporadic outbursts of eighteenth- and nineteenth-century eccentricity, it does make a violent break with the aesthetic and ritualistic traditions of art.

It is the task of these final pages to try to account for Dada as art, and to do this by applying the kind of values with which we have been concerned all along. On first appearances this task is not going to be easy. It is difficult to see how Marcel Duchamp's *Fountain* (Figure 12-1), a "readymade" urinal, can be said to represent a shaping of consciousness in any positive sense. It is especially difficult because we have said constantly — as a fundamental justification for art — that through the insights of his creative imagination the artist shapes the more profound, meaningful, and possibly spiritual aspects of his confrontation with life. Well, a urinal, after all. . . . Duchamp produced this "readymade" in 1917 and since then

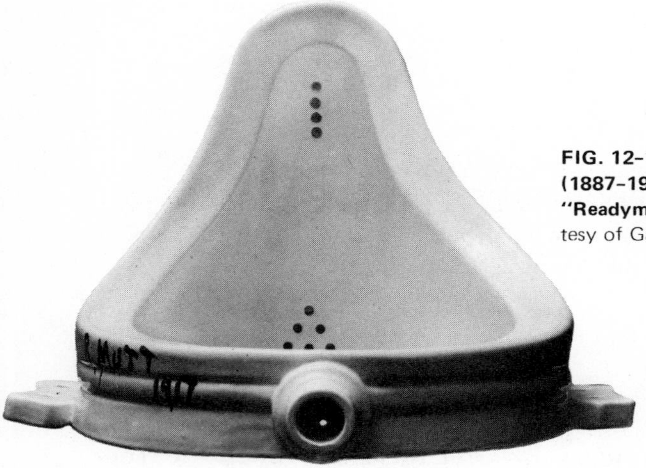

FIG. 12-1   Marcel Duchamp (1887-1969). *Fountain* 1917. "Readymade" Photograph. Courtesy of Galleria Schwarz, Milan

we have grown accustomed to all kinds of artistic oddities. Of more recent fame we recall the *Flat Iron with Metal Tacks* and the *Metronome with cutout photograph of eye* . . . by Man Ray; the images made by Alberto Burri which utilize pasted down sacks and rags; the scrap-iron "junk" sculpture of César and Stankiewicz; the clinker and sponge figures of Jean Dubuffet; the boxes containing unexplained oddities by Joseph Cornell; the Campbell soup cans and Brillo boxes mass-produced by Andy Warhol; and the painted models of giant hamburgers by Claes Oldenberg. These are only a few of the bizarre and unconventional art objects that have set the fashion for galleries and collectors during the last 50 years.

The creative innovations of Cubism, Futurism, and proto-Surrealism (de Chirico's Metaphysical Art) all occurred within the first decade of this century; and the sculptural and pictorial breakaway they represented was positive and quite abrupt. In introducing these various movements earlier I hope I was able to imply that at the turn of the century — say 1890 to 1905 — the time was ripe for a new spirit of artistic invention. For it was 600 years since Giotto's achievements in the Scrovegni Chapel at Padua (c. 1303) — 600 years spent in pursuing aspects of visual reality, or what some writers have called "the truth of appearances." These involved all the problems of spatial representation, the solidarity and weight of bodies, and movement through space. They are issues concerned with our perceptions of the natural world. In 1874 the first exhibition by the so-called Impressionists was seen in Paris, and with its advent the last frontier in the task of translating visual experience onto a two-dimensional painted surface was reached. I refer to rendering the appearance (sensation) of light and air. It is both interesting and significant that the two men who create the bridge between the old art and what is to come — Paul Cézanne and Vincent van Gogh — were both involved with Impressionism and yet could not be contained by it. With the problems of visual representation apparently solved, these painters turned to examine consciousness itself; Cézanne to order his sensations and reconcile them with feeling and mood, and van Gogh to give himself up to, and express, the passionate nature of his feelings for life. With the example of these two men serving as inspiration there was no going back for the creative spirits of the new century. By 1906 Picasso, Braque, and Kandinsky were involved in the search for a new visual truth — one which depended entirely on the artist's intuitive ability to create plastic relationships of form and space independently of any recourse to the appearance of the world. And, as we know, Picasso and Braque invented Cubism while Kandinsky invented Abstract Expressionism. With their appearance the final "holdfast" bonds with the past were broken.

It is not intended that this chapter should relate the history of twentieth-century art, but rather that it should raise the issue of twentieth-century artistic *freedom* and say just enough — or perhaps not enough — about the evolution of this freedom so that we can focus on the phenomenon of Dada, an art which represents the ultimate in freedom. In studying this question it becomes clear that, following the consolidation of Impressionism, the forward-moving artists of the twentieth century sought a threefold freedom. There was a need to be free from the traditional expertise in using staining or modeling media, particularly oil paint; a need to escape the dominance of subject matter dependent upon the natural appearance of objects; and a need to be free from traditional ideas about how art should look and what constituted its function. These deductions are borne out not only by the appearance of the new works themselves, but also by a scrutiny of the manifestos, writings, and statements which accompany them. Everything bears witness to the new directions sought by the European creative consciousness at this time. In his account of twentieth-century "assemblage" — the art of incorporating scraps of everyday things such as theater tickets, mirrors, sacking, or other "found" objects into painting and sculpture — William Seitz collects an impressive amount of evidence to support this change in the artist's intuitive attitude toward the creating of images. If I may, I will borrow from him here to illustrate what the pioneers of "modern art" were thinking and so set the stage for the advent of Dadaist anarchy.

> Guillaume Apollinaire was the first of the twentieth-century figures — Marcel Duchamp and André Breton were two others — who served as accumulators of avant-garde ideas. . . . His defence of collage and *papiers collés* in *The Cubist Painters* published in 1913, far surpasses in boldness the cubist painting of that year: "You may paint with whatever material you please, with pipes, postage stamps, postcards or playing cards, candelabra, pieces of oil cloth, collars, painted paper, newspapers."[2]

The preceding statement reveals a strong element of Dada in the way it shocks by touching on the absurd, for to paint with candelabra is an obvious affront to reason. Yet it is through such extreme proposals that Apollinaire makes his point. Even taken as a purely rhetorical pronouncement, it is indicative of how "far out" a spokesman of Apollinaire's reputation would go to uphold the artist's right to do what he wanted to do, in whatever way he wanted to do it. But let me continue with further evidence from Mr. Seitz.

> Picasso, Braque, and Gris all indicated, at one time or another, a distaste for the slickness of oil paint.[3]

> Because Gris' seemingly realistic images were arrived at deductively, from arrangements of geometric forms, because his art was more self-consciously philosophical, and because he explained his method, the use of collage is less problematical in his work than it is in that of Picasso and Braque. For him, Kahnweiler asserts, it was only a means of getting real details, of abolishing "tricks of brushwork and of replacing the 'handpainted' surface by the 'readymade.'"[4]

---

[2] W. C. Seitz, *The Art of Assemblage* (New York: The Museum of Modern Art, 1961), p. 14.

[3] *Ibid.,* p. 22. (originally from Kahnweiler, *Juan Gris: His Life and Work*; New York: Valentin, 1947.)

[4] *Ibid.,* p. 22. (originally from Kahnweiler, *Juan Gris: His Life and Work*; New York: Valentin, 1947.)

According to Kahnweiler, Picasso wished to "debunk the
idea of 'noble means,'" and thus romantically and ironically
to "display the pre-eminence of the creator's personality
over his creation."[5]

Futurism's "beautiful ideas that kill . . . ."[6]

The first major freedom was gained, as we have seen, by Cubism; it not only
represented an escape from natural perceptual experience, but also released the
artist psychologically so that he was free to let the intuitive aspect of his creativity
come into play. Yet Cubism still relied upon normal drawing and painting
techniques. But it was not long before even these well-established methods were
infiltrated by new possibilities. For example, in 1912 Picasso introduced a piece of
oil cloth into a small cubist painting in order to simulate the cane seat of a chair;
and, for a frame, he encircled the work with a length of rope. This little oval
"painting" was called *Still Life with Chair Caning.* Other collage and assemblage
images soon followed. Juan Gris was one of the group associated with Picasso and
Braque in Paris as early as 1908, and we have noted already what Kahnweiler the
dealer had to say about his collages. But here is Gris speaking for himself:

> You want to know why I had to stick on a piece of mirror?
> . . . Well, surfaces can be re-created and volumes interpreted
> in a picture, but what is one to do about a mirror whose
> surface is always changing and which should reflect even the
> spectator? There is nothing to do but stick on a real piece.[7]

Such is the nature of artistic innovation before the outbreak of the World
War I in 1914. That it represents a major break with tradition is patently obvious,
yet at this point in time we can understand and appreciate its evolution.[8] But what
about Duchamp's *Fountain?* Well, I am leading up to this. For although it appears
to be completely irrelevant, and irreverent, in the mainstream of art — even to the
art of collage and assemblage — I think it is necessary to suggest that it owed its
birth as an art object to the prevailing spirit of artistic freedom established before
1914. Duchamp's use of a ready-made urinal is but a further step along from
Picasso's use of a ready-made piece of oil cloth. In my view, it is not possible to

---

[5] *Ibid.,* p. 23. (originally from Kahnweiler, *Juan Gris: His Life and Work*; New York: Valentin,
1947.)

[6] *Ibid.,* p. 25. (originally from *The Initial Manifesto of Futurism*; London: Sackville-Gallery,
1912.)

[7] *Ibid.,* p. 22. (originally from Kahnweiler, *Juan Gris: His Life and Work*; New York: Valentin,
1947.)

[8] Yet even this form of collage had been practiced a long time before the twentieth century.
There are thirteenth-century paintings of the Pisan, Sienese, and Umbrian schools in which
pieces of colored glass are incorporated to represent "real" jewels in robes and mitres. And even
Botticelli is not above using a real medal — instead of a painted one — in his Portrait of a Man
with the Medal of Cosimo the Elder of c. 1473–74.

discuss Dada without first establishing the kind of innovative climate that encouraged the visual arts at this time, for this is the aesthetic background to Dada. Now we must look briefly at other climates — spiritual, moral, social, and political climates — which had been developing for some time, possibly since the French Revolution, but which attained their full implications in the consciousness of sensitive and thinking men during that great disaster known as World War I.

World War I (1914–18) put an end, at least geographically, to the cross-fertilizations that were going on between Futurism in Milan, Cubism in Paris, and Expressionism in Munich. But, more than this, it was responsible for crystallizing an attitude toward life which, I believe, has been with us ever since. As Albert Camus, Samuel Beckett, and others have expressed it, we have to confront the possibility that human life is absurd; that the evidence of history — and particularly the history of the last 50 years — does not support the view that man is a spiritual and moral creature fulfilling some divine, or even natural, purpose. The Christian church had been losing ground for some time, ever since the seventeenth century put forth its "Age of Reason" and delivered the Newtonian theory of the universe. Further reversals were suffered in the nineteenth century. Social revolution, industrial revolution, and economic revolution . . . all conspired to undermine a conventional faith and put the spotlight where perhaps it belongs, on man. This was also the first age of science as we know it, and it gave rise to an optimistic belief in the ultimate power of science to conquer all human problems — a belief which has been shrinking steadily since World War I. Also, the nineteenth century produced Charles Darwin and his theory of evolution and natural selection. It is difficult from our position in history to comprehend the full effect of this bombshell on the philosophical, spiritual, and moral climate of the time, save that it was obviously devastating. And then came Sigmund Freud who made no bones about turning the spotlight fully onto us, and brought out into the open the less noble but more natural aspects of our nature for all to see and think about. The re-evaluation of man that this occasioned is still going on, and our experiences in two world wars seem only to have confirmed many of his theories concerning the dark side of human nature. While Freud's psychological theories were coming home to roost, science, in the shape of Albert Einstein, was demonstrating the lack of any absolute certainty in our predictions about the physical world. His theory of relativity did as much in 1905 to shake the ideal positivistic science position as Darwin's theory of evolution had done earlier to shake the ideal positivistic humanities position. And even if the philosophical and moral implications of Rutherford's splitting of the atom in 1919 were not fully realized at the time, at least we can see that it was one more conclusive event in a chain of events which inevitably caused traditional values and attitudes to be questioned.

"What is beautiful? What is ugly? What is great, strong, weak? . . . What is 'I'?" Georges Ribemont-Dessaignes queried. He replied, "Don't know! Don't know, don't know, don't know!"[9] I doubt if such an uncertain and negative response to

---

[9] Georges Lemaitre, *From Cubism to Surrealism in French Literature,* p. 169.

such straightforward questions could have been given a hundred years earlier.

Most philosophical systems are ultimately concerned with providing possible answers to one major question, namely, "What concepts of 'reality' do we extract from consciousness and life?" And I think that one means by which we differentiate between cultures and societies is by recognizing the particular reality they found in life and to which they gave some tangible shape through philosophy, myth, ritual, or art. My argument, which is by no means new or original, is that the twentieth century is a period adrift when it comes to living a reality, or determining a reality principle which supports man in all of his physical and psychological insecurity. We live in a period of transition and suffer the comings and goings of fads and fashions in our philosophy and our ritual on a day to day or year to year basis. It is not my business here to inquire into the nature or significance of twentieth-century Existentialism — the one major philosophical and empirical system of our time — except to say that it is a philosophy based on the transitory nature of our living which tells us that reality lies in the qualitative value consciousness discovers in the moment of time *as it is lived*. In the course of our transition from the old Medieval-Renaissance world, with its overriding Christian and humanist philosophy, to whatever lies ahead, we necessarily entertain doubts about man and his purpose and tend to get on with the living on a day to day basis, rather than see a shape to the flow of time and thus feel part of a process in which we can believe.

World War I occurred at the time when the sequence of events I have briefly described were having their first telling effect on the European consciousness. As a result, it made a particularly strong impression on the minds of many artists and other thinkers — minds which by their nature attempt to live and shape reality. Further, it was a war unlike any that had gone before. It employed hundreds of thousands of men in a relatively static, piecemeal attrition of territory from fixed positions of unimaginable squalor and hardship. It was trench warfare on a vast scale prolonged for four unbelievably long years. The slaughter was immense and amidst such carnage it is difficult to support the view that man is a rational, sensible, and sensitive creature.[10] The announcement of 50,000 dead on the Somme in a single engagement could only support the celebrated Marquis de Sade's contention that, on the whole, human beings have a propensity for evil rather than good, depravity rather than virtue, and idiocy rather than intelligence. As the war progressed, the incompetence and insensitivity of more than one general and politician helped to destroy faith in the leaders and undermined the traditional respect for, and belief in, the idea that those in positions of authority are wiser and more able than the man in the street. It must have been a big disappointment to those who had witnessed the rise of middle-class economic and political power during the nineteenth century to discover that bourgeois leadership was as insensitive to the loss of human life as the aristocratic leadership of absolute monarchs. With the sufferings of the Franco-Prussian War of 1870 still alive in the

---

[10] There is no more vivid account of the World War I than Erich Maria Remarque's *All Quiet on the Western Front*.

memory, this new and far greater conflagration was a bitter reminder that man seemed incapable of learning from history; that there was little evidence to suggest a growth in human intelligence or dignity. Incompetence rather than efficiency, short-term expediency rather than long-term vision, personal gain rather than altruistic idealism, ignorance rather than knowledge, and stupidity rather than intelligence . . . it was the same story all over again. The only philosophy left seemed that of despair or ironic detachment and cynical comment.

AN ART OF NEGATIVE CAPABILITY

The spiritual and moral chaos caused by the war of 1914–18 is difficult to assess, and certainly the European consciousness was by no means healed when World War II erupted in 1939. However, in the year 1915, the neutral city of Zurich provided a refuge for a number of artists. Among them were Tristan Tzara, Hans Arp, Hugo Ball, Hans Richter, and Richard Huelsenbeck. They met casually in cafés and hit upon the idea of organizing an international cabaret entertainment. The programs were varied and included songs from France and Holland, Russian and Negro music, readings of poetry, and exhibitions of art. The story of how the name "Dada" came to be adopted by the group is well-known. The singer who performed for them from time to time was a certain Madame le Roy — a name which obviously did not suit the anti-establishment activities of the group — and searching a German-French dictionary for a more suitable one, Hugo Ball came across the word "Dada." It was adopted with great enthusiasm as the authoritative name of the movement. The fact that it was discovered by chance, and that its two syllables provide an odd "baby language" alliteration, made it a most suitable choice. For the appeal to chance was to become a major characteristic of the Dada method, and the naive and somewhat unintelligible character of the word provided the right note of irony. They called their literary, musical, and art entertainments the Cabaret Voltaire, another clear indication of the group's sarcastic and critical intentions. Their activities were designed to undermine the traditional bases of culture and social order in every possible way, and scholarly lectures on Paul Klee alternated with mystifying and often scandalizing entertainments. It is interesting to see the wide range of avant-garde artists who were exhibited in the Dada gallery in 1917. There were works by Arp, de Chirico, Max Ernst, Feininger, Kandinsky, Klee, Frans Marc, Kokoschka, Picasso, and Modigliani. The artists of the Zurich group themselves, of whom Arp was perhaps the most typical, borrowed freely from Cubism and adopted a very free use of collage and assemblage techniques to create their arbitrary, abstract, and "non-meaningful" designs. Huelsenbeck published a history of Dada in Hanover in the year 1920 which reveals the basic anti-establishment, anti-tradition sentiments of the movement. He writes:

> The Cabaret Voltaire group were all artists in the sense that
> they were keenly sensitive to newly developed artistic
> possibilities. Ball and I had been extremely active in helping

to spread expressionism in Germany; Ball was an intimate friend of Kandinsky in collaboration with whom he had attempted to found an expressionist theater in Munich. Arp in Paris had been in close contact with Picasso and Braque, the leaders of the Cubist movement, and was thoroughly convinced of the necessity of combatting naturalist conception in any form. Tristan Tzara, the romantic internationalist, whose propagandist zeal we have to thank for the enormous growth of Dada, brought with him from Rumania an unlimited literary facility. In that period, as we danced, sang, recited night after night in the Cabaret Voltaire, abstract art was for us tantamount to absolute honor. Naturalism was a psychological penetration of the motives of the bourgeois, in whom we saw our mortal enemy, and psychological penetration, despite all efforts at resistance, brings an identification with the various precepts of bourgeois morality. Archipenko, whom we honored as an unequalled model in the field of plastic art, maintained that art must be neither realistic nor idealistic, it must be true; and by this he meant above all that any imitation of nature, however concealed, is a lie. In this sense, Dada was to give the truth a new impetus. Dada was to be a rallying point for abstract energies and a lasting slingshot for the great international artistic movements.[11]

But Huelsenbeck was to be disappointed. After provocative Dada activity in New York, Paris, Berlin, and Cologne, which effectively scandalized the public and on at least two occasions invoked action by the police, Dada as a group movement was dead — dead of its internal dissensions and of its own polemic, for as a cry of negation it carried within itself the seeds of its own destruction. The Surrealists took over the Dada characteristics of the surprise effect, the chance discovery, the naive subject, and the irrational and free association of forms, but the satirical *spirit* of Dada lived on. It reflected too well the ethos of those years to disappear completely, and as the doubt and uncertainty persist into our own time, so Dada shock tactics reappear. Strange objects continued to be presented as art, and the self-conscious attempts to be "different" or unconventionally original which have characterized the art scene since the end of World War II reveal a strong element of Dada. In the beginning, Dada reflected an intellectual revolt born of the anguish of the 1914–18 war, and it is possible to discern a similar attitude underlying the emergence of Pop art in America in the 1960s. But we will discuss this later.

Marcel Duchamp, who settled in New York in 1915, sacrificed a career as an artist (in the conventional sense) to work to destroy the traditional values of art by "debunking" aestheticism and the concept of creative revelation. He, more than anyone else, epitomized the negative and destructive philosophy of Dada. His famous "readymades," of which the *Fountain* is a good example, were simply mass-produced objects which he willfully and arbitrarily elevated to the level of a

---

[11] Herbert Read, *A Concise History of Modern Painting,* p. 116.

work of art; and, as might be expected, they created a sensation. The question as to why a serious artist of our time should turn so single-mindedly against any profound truth of art is the major concern of this chapter; for this reason we have examined the growth of artistic or creative freedom and suggested the nature of the artist's psychological response to the period. Our conclusion is that when faith in man and his institutions is lacking, and when events themselves have produced a world in which established philosophies and beliefs have little relevance, then the one way to draw attention to the dearth of values is to ridicule those values. That is precisely what Duchamp set out to do. The method of his attack produces what I have called "an art of negative capability." For to place the *Fountain* as a sculptural object alongside a sculpture such as the *Aphrodite of Knidos* (Figure 2–3) is to do more than question the assumption that art has meaning; it renders art absurd and therefore man in his imaginative life absurd. Faced with the *Fountain* it is difficult not to ponder the possibility, and not to be disturbed by the thought that it might be so. The irony of a urinal as art is inescapable. Art becomes a gigantic hoax, a device that has very effectively "led us up the garden path" to believe in creativity as a sign of man's moral, intellectual, and spiritual superiority! *Fountain* gives us some uneasy moments; it makes non-sense as art, yet paradoxically forces us to honestly question the values of art. This negative capability is a characteristic of Dada activity in any art form. One could say that the Marquis de Sade's infamous *Justine* is literary Dada, although it was written a good hundred years before the formation of the art movement in 1915. For the scarcely credible practices de Sade describes are so consistently a-human, absurdly so in some cases, that the reader is forced to question what he believes to be the truth about good and evil. The hypocrisy and intellectual dishonesty of his time affected de Sade no less than that of this century affected Duchamp.

Of course there are ways to justify the *Fountain* as art; but, in my view, the act of finding a "readymade" and the imaginative leap that sees its negative significance are not enough to convey the status of art on any object. I am old-fashioned enough to believe that the artist must be physically involved in shaping or transforming the object. However, we must grant that once chosen by Duchamp, we are forced to look at this utilitarian object of his choice with critical eyes and perhaps even to appreciate the flow of its curvilinear surface and its overall proportions on purely sculptural terms. And certainly the Pop artists of more recent date have discovered that there are many ordinary things we use in everyday life which are strangely attractive, exotic, repulsive, erotic, or bizarre in their form. When such things are used as the subject for a painting, or have models made of them, they become surreal; for such is the nature of their shape that to become isolated as an image renders them unbelievable as "popular" objects of the environment. Therefore, those Pop artists who exploit the formal possibilities of such objects in this way have one leg on the traditional side of the fence, inasmuch as they shape their image. There are others, however, who stay closer to the "readymade" philosophy of Duchamp and either simply present the original object or reproduce a facsimile as faithfully as possible. I think that both groups have inherited the Dada spirit, although those who follow the "readymade" way, choosing the most mundane of objects and thus offending our sensibilities the most, are the new Dadaists par excellence. For when Oldenburg raises the sandwich to the level of art by making a vinyl model, and Warhol silk-screens faithful replicas of Campbell soup cans, I see the same desire to pull art down from the pedestal it has traditionally occupied that lies behind Duchamp's presentation of his fountain. In addition, the same ironic humor which accompanies the mere selection of a sandwich or a soup can is present in the selection of a urinal — a humor which mocks both our culture and ourselves. For if the sandwich and the urinal have become our ritual objects — our important "idols" so to speak — then we certainly cannot regard ourselves as either very spiritual or very profound.

I suppose it is stating the obvious to draw a parallel between our situation today and that of Europe in 1915. Yet the prevalence and appeal of Pop does indicate that the optimistic hopes for "a brave new world" which were so strong at the end of World War II have given way to a "don't know, don't know" uncertainty and disillusionment. We are still adrift in the continued absence of any viable faith as our society struggles with its conscience in the face of injustice and corruption in high places, expedient games of international power politics that treat men as pawns, and the considerable economic discrepancies between the haves and the have-nots throughout the world. A meaningful reality and purpose still eludes us, and we believe we can fill the vacuum by looking to technological progress and by experiencing new material standards for living. Unfortunately, it is difficult to experience, much less trust, the subjectivity of a true poetic awareness in the face of a collective cynicism which prefers sensational novelty — the happening — to a disclosure of more lasting values. Only a few of the greater artists today are visited by the Muse and know a private vision. And it is my opinion that Pop, like Dada, represents at best a cry of protest at the shallowness of modern life and at worst provides an artistic "cop-out." That it provides an ideal refuge for pseudo artists goes, I think, without saying.

At this point it is necessary to state that a concern for the ordinary things of life, the popular objects, does not in itself prevent the artist from exercising those transforming feats of the imagination — conscious and unconscious — which we have stressed go to make a powerful work of art. In Chapter 10, talking briefly about the eighteenth-century French painter Chardin, I wrote that he (Chardin) "created images in which the most ordinary household utensils are fashioned with loving care. Pewter mugs, stoneware pitchers, and copper kettles are invested with grace. They possess what the poet Robert Graves calls *báraka* — the quality of blessedness." Now nobody would suggest that Chardin's paintings of household objects are Pop, precisely for the reasons stated above. Even a casual glance at his *Kitchen Utensils* (Figure 12-2) will show that Chardin uses these ordinary objects of their day as vehicles to carry human feelings and sensibilities. As such, they symbolize man's sense of graciousness in life and convey his sensuous delight as well as spiritual satisfaction in the domestic environment. I am not trying to be facetious by comparing this work with Warhol's *Campbell Soup Cans* (Figure 12-3), but

FIG. 12–2 Jean-Baptiste Chardin (1699–1779). *Kitchen Utensils.* **Oil painting.** The Louvre, Paris

merely attempting to illustrate the negative aspects of twentieth-century Pop art. The very neutrality of this image denies any significance to the soup cans themselves (of course they are disposable) and tells us nothing about the man. (Anonymity is, in itself, a particularly bland form of irony which was cultivated at times by the early Dada movement.) Like all Dada-Pop images, Figure 12–3 arouses a response, if it arouses a response, by negative means. Its negative neutrality is reinforced when

FIG. 12–3 Andy Warhol (b. 1930–   ). *Campbell Soup Can.* **Silkscreen Photograph.** Courtesy Museum of Modern Art, New York

seen against the Chardin, and I for one can only feel that the modern creative consciousness is pathetically without passion and commitment when irony and cynicism can reduce its artistic statements to such an insipid dullness.

I have chosen to write this last chapter on the images of Dada and its up-to-date relation, Pop, for two reasons. First, they stand in such complete contrast to the psychological and philosophical position I have taken throughout — namely, that good art adds positive new dimensions and value to our awareness of living or being — that this position may be seen in a stronger light as a result of the comparison. And second, there is such a lot of Pop art about that many people may want to know what it signifies in terms of art and the creative consciousness. Writing with both of these reasons in mind also presented an opportunity to provide some background to explain the emancipation of the twentieth-century artist — to account for the artistic freedom he enjoys to be negative, frivolous, superficial, witty, or ironical in Pop or "camp" terms. For I have tried to show that such a complete and anarchic freedom evolved from the various aesthetic experiments initiated early in the century. But it was also necessary to suggest that the apparent frivolity and non-sense of Dada and its relation, Pop, are rooted like all images in the human attitudes that give them birth. I believe that it is important to understand these manifestations of twentieth-century consciousness as the result of a chain of events long spaced in time and brought to a head by two world wars. For all along this book has stressed that images are the embodiment of conscious and unconscious attitudes.

Yet, as I finish, I am forced to the conclusion that every person must come to terms with a work of art in his or her own way. It may be that the negative capability of the *Campbell Soup Cans* supports some people's belief in creative sensibility as effectively as the Chardin does for others. For myself, I can think of no better way to re-affirm my belief in the spiritual, or inspirational, nature of great art than by bringing this book to a close with the statement by Robert Graves which appeared in Chapter 5.

> "This is a critical, not a poetic age," I am told. "Inspiration is out. Contemporary poems must reflect the prevailing analytic spirit." But I am old-fashioned enough to demand *báraka*, an inspirational gift not yet extinct, which defies critical analysis.

INDEX

Note: Bold type indicates titles and page numbers for illustrations

207

211

212